THE *EROS* OF THE HUMAN SPIRIT

THE *EROS*
of the
HUMAN SPIRIT

The Writings of Bernard Lonergan, SJ

ELIZABETH J. SNEDDEN

Paulist Press
New York / Mahwah, NJ

Cover image by tovovan/Shutterstock.com
Cover design by Tamian Wood
Book design by Lynn Else

Library of Congress Cataloging-in-Publication Data
Names: Snedden, Elizabeth J., author.
Title: The eros of the human spirit : the writings of Bernard Lonergan, SJ / Elizabeth J. Snedden.
Description: New York : Paulist Press, 2017. | Includes bibliographical references.
Identifiers: LCCN 2017021097 (print) | LCCN 2017038889 (ebook) | ISBN 9781587687105 (ebook) | ISBN 9780809153428 (pbk. : alk. paper)
Subjects: LCSH: Lonergan, Bernard J. F. | God (Christianity)—Worship and love. | Catholic Church—Doctrines—History—20th century.
Classification: LCC BX4705.L7133 (ebook) | LCC BX4705.L7133 S64 2017 (print) | DDC 230/.2092—dc23
LC record available at https://lccn.loc.gov/2017021097

ISBN 978-0-8091-5342-8 (paperback)
ISBN 978-1-58768-710-5 (e-book)

Published by Paulist Press
997 Macarthur Boulevard
Mahwah, New Jersey 07430

www.paulistpress.com

Printed and bound in the
United States of America

To all students with questions

CONTENTS

Foreword ix

Introduction xv

1. To Know Oneself as Desirer and Knower 1

2. Self-Affirmation as a Knower in *Insight* 29

3. The Appropriation of Desire 48

4. The Appropriation of Desire in *Method in Theology* 71

5. Development in Religious Interiority 112

6. The *Eros* of the Spirit as Our Desire 143

Afterword 155

Notes 157

Bibliography 193

FOREWORD

The Eros *of the Human Spirit* communicates in a unique way the author's own appropriation of "the highest in us and in God the most like us" by taking up the immense challenge of tracing Bernard Lonergan's lifetime of appropriating his desire. By following the natural and inevitable spontaneities of his nature, his trail of asking and answering questions gradually enabled that natural desire to recognize itself as having been transformed and elevated by the gift of God's grace "poured into our hearts through the Holy Spirit that has been given to us" (Rom 5:5).

The originality, comprehensiveness, and delicacy of Snedden's writing is astonishing; it is hard to imagine what a challenging task it would have been to read this work had it not been expressed in such a vivid and beautifully composed manner. This qualification includes the ordering of the primary and secondary materials she employs, the examples provided, and her detailed and focused account of Lonergan's writings, all creating an aura that strikes one as emblematic of what Ezra Pound meant when he exclaimed, "Ripeness is all!"

Elizabeth Snedden's extraordinary career of questing and questioning that had begun at a surprisingly early age was, of course, the manifestation of the "natural and inevitable spontaneities" of what she learned to recognize as her work progressed as the dynamic desire built into her conscious intentionality. This young mind and heart was blessed to come from a loving family into the love-filled and nurturing atmosphere of her religious order's school, and then into membership in the order itself. She was extremely fortunate to have her desire to understand become increasingly focused in such a way that she was prepared to grasp the questions and appreciate the answers expressed in the works of Sebastian Moore, OSB, so that when she was ready to appropriate the range of desire not only of what Lonergan called a "sufficiently cultured consciousness" but also of "the unity of differentiated consciousness" under the tutelage of Kathleen Williams at Yarra, she could undertake with confidence and a certain degree of serenity the grand spiritual exercises of which this work is the outcome.

Snedden sets the stage by making imaginative use of *Babette's Feast*—a story about the pressure of love upon the intelligence of a woman who became a center of benevolence and beneficence. This typifies the genius of this work manifest throughout, inasmuch as when, as she tells us, Lonergan came to realize the unique fertility of understanding as "insight into phantasm" (i.e., you can only understand in relation to images that reveal what you are inquiring about), she writes in a way that the imaginal factor is constantly present; so she is able to convey not just the outcome of her appropriation but also provide the reader with clues to how she reached that understanding herself.

Again, *Babette's Feast* allows the reader to realize that Snedden is not simply out to retell all that Lonergan taught her in a well-organized and lucid manner—although she certainly does do that! But she is intent on embodying in prose the classic Dominican motto of *contemplata aliis tradere* (to pass on to others whatever she has carefully studied). *The* Eros *of the Human Spirit* succeeds in making accessible a potentially helpful procedure to any general reader genuinely interested in the workings of the mind, heart, and soul.

Moreover—and this is most significant—what Snedden transmits are the ways and means proper to the desire that, gradually over time, discloses that which is "the highest in us and in God the most like us." In accomplishing this, she manages to communicate how gradually learning the twists and turns and the ins and outs of Lonergan's ongoing appropriation of his own desires helped her, step by step, to appropriate (i.e., to identify in her own experience, to name, and decisively, to own) the range and depth of her own search for ultimate meaning and value in the desire that she is. It is not only a work of scholarship, but an *itinerarium mentis ad Deum* (the mind's journey to God).

In the first chapter, Snedden reenacts her personal moving

viewpoint that structures her telling the story of both Lonergan's evolving appropriation of desire and her own. She begins by tracing the life and thought of Lonergan from his early education in elementary and high school in Canada, his entry into the Jesuit seminary system and novitiate, his sojourn in England at Heythrop for philosophy and at the University of London for a general degree, followed by his three-year teaching stint (regency) as a Scholastic at Loyola in Montreal, to his being sent to Rome to study theology in preparation for ordination followed by a year in Amiens, France, for tertianship, before at last returning to do his doctorate in theology at the Gregorian University. Just as her account of Lonergan's doctoral dissertation on *gratia operans* is both accurate and original because it is concentrated on the aspects of it that are germane to the appropriation of desire, so also is this true of her more extensive treatment of the series of articles on St. Thomas's thought on the *Verbum*, which was produced after Lonergan returned to Montreal as a theology professor. Her selection of pre-*Insight* articles is astutely focused by her theme, and her thematization of salient points in "Finality, Love, Marriage" is both accurate and extraordinary on Lonergan's exposition of love within the perspective of evolutionary biology. Here her explication of the phylogenetic and ontogenetic unfolding of love within the processes of evolution will shape everything she treats in what follows.

Chapter 2 takes up *Insight*. Once she has elaborated the meaning and contents of the appropriation of one's own rational self-consciousness in a remarkably clear exposition of the *How* and *What* of the cognitional theory that issued from Lonergan's generalized empirical method, which grounds his methodically controlled epistemology and metaphysics, Snedden delineates sections of Lonergan's metaphysics of finality in order to show how desire fits into an evolutionary perspective from the perspective of modern science and history in a suggestive handling of the explanatory correlation between the human microcosm and the emergently probable intelligibility of the cosmos. This chapter makes evident (if it had not already been clear to readers before) that a profound interest in the field of what has come to be called "spirituality" not only need not shirk the study of classical, statistical, genetic, and dialectical methods on the level of the modern age, but can and ought to integrate them into a comprehensive viewpoint for treating humanity as desiring and desired by God.

Chapter 3 turns to a careful treatment of the way Lonergan's gradually deepening appropriation of desire in its rich cognitional dimensions could help penetrate the existential realm. Snedden offers a strikingly original account of how human responsibility makes more complete sense in terms of Lonergan's hard-won breakthrough (achieved with the help of phenomenologists Max Scheler and Dietrich von Hildebrand) to the transcendental notion of value. Here, we see the fruit of Snedden's earlier introduction of the desire-based meaning of the transcendental concepts of being, truth, goodness, and beauty. A key to this presentation is her marvelous explicitation of Lonergan's pithy essay, "Openness and Religious Experience," which brings out the contrast between the fact and the achievements of conscious intentionality, and explains how, whether in a condition of achievement or of derailment, that human dynamism remains open to grace as both saving and elevating.

In the following chapter, Snedden gives an utterly original interpretation of Lonergan's *Method in Theology* as an entry into the appropriation of existential desire. Here, her choice to focus on the functional specialties of dialectics and foundations allows her to thematize horizonal differences as genetically or dialectically rooted, as well as to elaborate further the concrete possibility of a foundational "total and basic horizon" both as open to an *Aufhebung* by the gift of God's love and as actually having undergone religious conversion by falling in love with God and being-in-love with God. She explains in detail how Lonergan's transcendental doctrine of methods could understand *Insight*'s "appropriation of rational self-consciousness" more adequately as an intellectual conversion *ex umbris et imaginibus in veritatem* (from shadows and images into truth), that is, for the most part made possible by a moral conversion, which in turn needs religious conversion to become effectual. Consequently, Snedden elucidates how Lonergan was then able to realize that what, therefore, takes precedence in the development of what she calls the "dynamism of open-ended consciousness" is no longer knowing but loving. And that's what heightens the probability that desire be concretely guided by the transcendental precepts: be attentive, be intelligent, be reasonable, be responsible. She provides remarkable concrete interpretations of these precepts by using suggestively interpreted illustrations from Rosemary Haughton's *The Transformation of Man*.

In chapter 5, following the trail of Lonergan's further developments in the post-*Method* writings, Snedden explores the disproportionate transcendence of the supernatural order opened by the ever more complete acknowledgment by Lonergan of the priority of love. Her intricate retrieval of the passionateness of being, which involves the interplay of feelings with symbols and myths vis-à-vis what Lonergan named the "external quasi-operator," affords her the opportunity to display how the work of Robert Doran, SJ, and Sebastian Moore contextualizes what the later Lonergan outlined in terms of psychic or affective conversion. Perhaps the highlight of this section is the way Moore's discussion of desire as intrinsically intersubjective and interpersonal, and as shadowed by guilt, helps us to apprehend the role the outer word in Christ Jesus plays in the liberation of the desire that we are. This discussion is culminated by a poignant return to Snedden's own biographical realization of the dynamics of experiencing, understanding, discerning, and committing to the reality of being drawn by God's love and responding to that love through the concrete interplay in her own life of the two vectors of human development.

Elizabeth Snedden's conclusions in the last chapter, together with a moving afterword, close a significant and unique contribution to Lonergan scholarship, while expressing gratitude to Sebastian Moore, Robert Doran, and his student Ravi Michael Louis for the aid they had given her.

The Eros *of the Human Spirit* is a truly interpersonal rendition of the appropriation of the desire to know and love God into which readers are invited to discover what happens to them. Elizabeth Snedden conveys to her readers the reality of *cor ad cor loquitur* (heart speaks to heart) in her conversation with Lonergan in the literary mode of *cor ad cor loquitur*.

Frederick G. Lawrence
Boston College, Massachusetts

INTRODUCTION

Sometimes human attraction to the divine presents a very unattractive face. We shrink from doctrinaire fanaticism, fear our own fascination with the spooky numinous, and can be buffeted by the enthusiasm of those who claim to know exactly what we need in matters religious. Investigation of the God thing can intensify feelings of inadequacy, yet it keeps drawing us. Are we seekers or are we the sought? And how can the Wholly Other take any cognizance of us? Is our preoccupation with another dimension of reality healthy? Does it, in fact, dehumanize us to the extent that atheistic humanists who ridicule "God botherers" are actually onto something? Does organized religion exploit this preoccupation with an afterlife to reinforce infantile dependency and self-abasement in the interests of control?

Conversely, some churchly voices down through the years have assured us that our desires are suspect, unruly at best, disordered and diabolic at their root; resulting from original sin, the flesh and the devil, and clear signs of their ongoing influence in human lives. Desire is better called concupiscence, they say, and our safest course will be to repress desires in general and endeavor to fix our yearning on a well-being focused strictly on the next life, with fear of failure and preemptive self-condemnation as protective allies in this one. Is this God's plan for godly living here on earth?

These seemingly bleak questions appear to presage little hope of a positive response. Still, we might begin to address them in the context of a reflection on the classic film *Babette's Feast*.[1] It introduces us to a barren, windswept coastal community in Jutland in which religion plays a dominant role in the social order. An inspiring preacher, now dead, has founded a strict sect that is no longer attracting new adherents. A small group of aging disciples attempt to follow his teachings in the afterglow of his memory, but without too much warmth reaching their hearts. The preacher's daughters, also aging, live together in a celibacy imposed on them earlier by their father's rather selfish estimate of their indispensable role in his life's work, and continue to provide his little flock with a regular gathering place and kindnesses in the form of simple food and good counsel. The essence of his message, as they recollect it, is that self-denial and ascetic living in this world are necessary to prepare them for a joyful afterlife in the longed-for New Jerusalem. This seems to make sense of their drab and frugal existence, dependent as it is on naturally freeze-dried cod prepared with coarse bread and beer in certain unappetizing combinations. They sing of their hopes for eternity, but they also bicker and suspect each other and hold long rancorous grudges over past wrongs. Only two sisters, Martine and Philippa, are consistently gentle and forbearing.

They have each glimpsed something of human love. In their youth, their widower father derided marriage and had turned away many suitors for their hands. Two remained in their memory, however, and the circumstances are shown in flashbacks by the filmmaker. For Martine, it was Loren, a young Swedish cavalry officer sent to rusticate for a summer with an elderly aunt because of his youthful misconduct. Watching Martine made him envisage for himself "a higher and purer life without creditors' letters or parental lectures and with a gentle angel at his side."[2] He attended several meetings, tongue-tied in the father's presence, and then judged himself unworthy of her. In the case of Philippa, it was the famous French baritone Achille Papin who heard her sing in church and dreamed of making her a star. He courted her during singing lessons until she was discomfited and asked to discontinue them. Both suitors left Jutland disappointed, but Papin never forgot Philippa.

Thirty-five years later, when he wished to help Babette Hersant escape counterrevolutionary bloodshed in Paris, he sent her to the sisters as a penniless widow with a letter explaining that she would be a good housekeeper. They took her in and she worked for them for the next fourteen years in exchange for her board, gradually easing their circumstances and, with shrewd bargaining and skillful use of local herbs, making slight improvements in the taste and appearance of the food she prepared for them and the needy of the village. Babette was a puzzle to them:

> And it happened when Martine or Philippa spoke to Babette that they would get no answers, and would wonder if she had even heard what they said. Or she would sit immovable on the three-legged kitchen chair, her strong hands in her lap and her dark eyes wide open, as enigmatical and fatal as a Pythia upon her tripod. At such moments, they realised that Babette was deep, and that in the soundings of her being there were passions, there were memories and longings of which they knew nothing at all.[3]

Yet, over time, hers became an unassuming and welcome presence. Her only connection to her former life was a lottery ticket renewed for her annually by a friend.

When Babette learns that she has won ten thousand francs in this lottery, everyone sadly assumes that she will return to Paris. She does not. Instead, she asks permission of the two sisters to plan and cook a "real French dinner" for the one hundredth anniversary of the founding pastor's birth and pay for it herself. It is, as she insists, the only time she has ever made any request of them. Martine and Philippa acquiesce reluctantly and hesitantly give their housekeeper a week's leave to visit Paris and make the necessary arrangements. As the ingredients that she has ordered begin to arrive in multiple packages—a turtle, poussins, bottles— Martine and Philippa become very fearful. Surely such luxurious things will lead to serious sin, expose the flock to devilish influence, and undo all the founder's good work. They gather the congregation and confess what they have unleashed. It is agreed between them that they will eat the dinner, but by keeping their thoughts on memories of their founder they will protect themselves against taking any pleasure in it, and certainly will never speak of what they are eating.

The whole film begins to fill with color as Babette uses her gifts as a creative culinary artist and re-creates for a little group of twelve the marvels of a feast she once used to prepare for wealthy patrons of the Café Anglais in Paris. Prodigal in her generosity,

Babette has purchased appropriately fine table linens, place settings, crystal glasses, and candles and wines to match each course. Now an important general, Martine's Loren has returned to visit his aunt and is invited with her to the feast. He had frequented the Café Anglais in its heyday, and all during the meal he reminisces about its legendary chef as he admires and wonders at each bite, each drop. His uncertainty about the lasting impact his memories of this group had had in his career is resolved in amazement and delight. The other guests maintain their promised silence about food, but their faces soften and express a growing wonder and joy. The setting is beautiful, the surprising food a work of art; Babette's loving provision is the grace note. There happens a real transformation in attitudes, a spiritual change in which each member of the stern preacher's flock lets drop old resentments and remembers early loves. They confess and forgive each other, and in their song about the New Jerusalem this night, there is evidence of its new, anticipated reality in their midst.

Martine is really distressed when she discovers that nothing remains of Babette's windfall, and that in "giving the whole substance of her house for love" (cf. Song 8:7), she has, in fact, lost her last chance of escaping poverty. In reply, Babette speaks of an artist never being poor, and in truth there has been joy and gift for herself as an artist in the preparation and service of this extraordinary meal. As Achille Papin had once explained to Philippa,

> It is terrible and unbearable to an artist…to be encouraged to do, to be applauded for doing his second best. Through all the world there goes one long cry from the heart of the artist: Give me leave to do my utmost.[4]

Her feast, in this lonely backwater, is a tribute to the goodness of creation, an expression of gratitude and love to these timid sisters who have been generous to Babette according to their lights, and at last a worthy expression of who Babette really is. In love and generosity, she has participated in God's plan for human flourishing, and her loving and self-aware offering of her creative best is the occasion of life-giving grace in her adoptive world.

Undoubtedly, Babette's puzzling silence reflected grief and memories of loved ones lost, but Martine and Philippa were not wrong in sensing her depth of longings, of which they had previously understood nothing at all. If they had, their formation may have made them shrink from them as dangerous papist aberrations. For these two, their father still spoke more loudly than their own desires, and even where their desire was life affirming—Martine let Loren know before he departed the second time that their earlier encounter had been very significant for her too, and Philippa still daydreamed of the training that would have developed and supported her voice, and the musical world it might have opened to her—both had assented not unwillingly to its suppression. It was God's will, and for their good, they believed.

What has this story to say to us in the light of our opening questions? It is not counseling the unbridled pursuit of sensuous pleasure as preferable to the faithful following of any religious tradition, nor is it proposing that one form of religious practice, for example, Babette's Catholicism, be substituted for the evangelical practice of this little sect. It is celebrating human goodness as such. It is a parable challenging narrow and fearful views of religion. It speaks of delight in beauty and the goodness of creation and skillful human achievement. It tells of creative gifts and generous love as expressions of the human spirit, as openings for the work of the Divine Spirit in human community. Self-restraint for love's sake can help to bring about God's plan for human flourishing in a way self-denial for its own sake cannot, and Babette's self-transcendence is at its most loving and most liberating when it enables her, as an artist, to "do her utmost." God is the utmost in love, a prodigal giver, and has chosen to create images of these traits in us. God's desire for us is life more abundant (cf. John 10:10).

The writer's own lived response to the challenge of religion was to stake everything on one identified thirst for God and to mistrust the rest. To the extent that I entered an enclosed religious order and submitted to an ascetic life within the restrictions of a rule of life and the dictates of obedience, poverty, and chastity, I rather protected myself against my desiring self and came to disregard and devalue much that was human and creative in my makeup. Fortunately, grace steered me to a religious congregation where, over the years, through prayer and as a learner and teacher, the wider possibilities of Love's plan for my life were revealed. In studying theology, I encountered the Canadian Jesuit priest, philosopher, and theologian Bernard Joseph Francis Lonergan (1904–84), and, with him, astounding new horizons of understanding and acceptance. As a Jesuit, Lonergan may have had his own skirmishes with the eddies of human desiring, but he could recognize and name the more significant vector, the strong undertow in his own consciousness of loving desire drawing him to know and to love the God of his life. In so doing, he not only tempted me to do the same but showed me how.

This study proposes entering God's desire for us, as evidenced in the way human beings are created. It discovers desire as integral to human living, and human capacity to search for truth, beauty, goodness, and love as rooted in the desire that moves us toward self-transcendence both in knowing and in loving. Human consciousness is intentional, as we will see, and its innate direction is toward total truth and utter goodness, the value beyond questioning. Questioning is, however, the dynamism by which spirit moves within us toward the true and the good of value. Our mind works by way of a self-assembling pattern or sequence of operations, and its recurrent activity leads by inquiry to cumulative and progressive results. We are created with "method" built in.

The pattern of this method can be discovered. We can appropriate, make our own, the steps to real knowing and life-giving choices. Biases as blocks to significant questions can be unmasked. Rapid and erroneous assumptions can be avoided. Desire can be welcomed and embraced as the life-giving, joy-enhancing reality it is meant to be. The fulfillment of human potentiality and the growth of reasonable, responsible, caring human cooperation in a friendly universe advance in tandem. The contrasts in the parable of *Babette's Feast* speak so strongly of a journey into gladness that my own self-appropriation as desiring and desired has made possible—gradually, and with the help of the life and writings of Bernard Lonergan. My moving viewpoint has shown that insight into what self-transcendence really means is the "leave to do my utmost" for which my being too has cried out all my life.

The pages that follow, therefore, will consider desire and its appropriation throughout the experiences and writings of Lonergan so that the moving viewpoint of his understanding and explanation can furnish a clearer exposition of this contention. In the early years, we can follow his transition from faculty psychology to intentionality analysis, and the startling findings that became a teaching tool in his first major philosophical work. It is not possible to short-circuit the painstaking work of self-appropriation as a knower, but the "pure, detached, disinterested, unrestricted desire to know" of which he writes is a strong motivating factor, and the outcome well worth the effort. He holds out the possibility of an increasingly authentic intellectual integrity in the pursuit of truth, the significance of which we investigate in the first two chapters.

Then, we turn our attention in chapter 3, as he did in the period between *Insight* and *Method*, to the fourth level of conscious intentionality and reflective questions concerning practical and moral choices and decisions to which intelligence and reasonableness spontaneously lead us. This entails a consideration of the notions of value and effective freedom within horizons, the current limits of an individual's vision and aspiration. To change horizons in a vertical exercise of freedom is to be converted, and moral conversion involves a systematic choice of value over the satisfaction of fleeting desires or the avoidance of discomfort. The failure of human beings to be consistently attentive, intelligent, reasonable, and responsible according to the promise inherent in their being is the fact of sin in individuals and of decline in human society. In chapter 4, we will examine God's response to human impotence— the salvific gift of God's Love poured out in human hearts by the Spirit.

In religious experience, we may come to know the infinite love that affirms our being, and the responsive love with which we are gifted. The most life-enhancing of all the conversions is the horizon shift involved in religious conversion. In chapter 4, we see this experiential encounter with God as an invitation to appropriate fully the desire that has been operative in us since the beginning of our lives. Self-appropriation becomes foundational for the work of theology in the development of this book, as it is in Lonergan's methodological framework.

To know ourselves as truth seekers, capable of love and goodness and called by the deepest drives within us to ongoing self-transcendence, is a joyful discovery for many, even most of us. That some do not make this discovery or, having heard of it, discount the reality in favor of a more fearful and restrictive life-scripting, is the problematic most directly addressed in chapter 5. How can we understand and deal with difficulties encountered in appropriating the "love without restriction" that is received as gift in religious conversion? How do we find healing and effective freedom to live the demands of intellectual and moral conversion in a way commensurate with our desire for goodness and truth? For this reason, we investigate the "way down" of so much given to us in heritage and belief and made our own within the context of human affectivity and the saving gift of God's love. We will ask whether a fourth conversion may be required, and in the work of former students of Lonergan also writing in this period, look for their expansion of the notion of desire and its appropriation. We will then consider how the authenticity of the individual is involved in concern for the major authenticity of the tradition that nurtures communities, and note the need for commitment and ongoing development in natural and religious interiority.

In *Babette's Feast*, Martine and Philippa's preacher father used to say portentously, "God's paths run across the sea and the snowy mountains, where man's eye sees no track." The invitation of this book is to follow God's paths through the life of our chosen guide, and to discern some outlines of a track in our own comparable experience. The outlook is far from bleak.

TO KNOW ONESELF AS DESIRER AND KNOWER

Human beings are unique among the species on the earth because, in their capacity for reflective self-awareness, they are a lifelong problem to themselves. *Homo sapiens* is *homo interrogans*, puzzled from infancy by their own restless yearnings, moved by insistent questioning about meaning and destiny. Humankind is questioning, yes, but also desirous, wanting to be and have more, and consistently disappointed when attainment leaves them still dissatisfied, moving on to desire something further. It is not easy to distinguish the desires we have from the desire we are. Making this distinction requires us to identify urges to act in certain ways as related to but distinct from the deeper currents within, in comparison with which these transitory impulses are just eddies spinning off into backwaters.

This chapter is an exploration of desire and its appropriation by the human subject based on the experiences and writings of Bernard Lonergan, who learned to identify the pull of the golden cord[1] drawing him toward understanding and love. He is preeminently an explanatory clarifier and enabler. In the context of his life experiences and these discoveries, we will explore his ability to understand and appropriate the powerful desire that moves human beings to question, and examine his initial and developing insights into the mystery of our never completely satisfied yearnings for truth, for ultimate meaning.

LONERGAN'S JOURNEY

Here we are concerned with Lonergan's early experiences of desire and appropriation insofar as these throw light on his writings concerning both. We begin by tracing the outworking of the powerful desire to know in Lonergan's early experiences. As he read the philosophical and theological thinkers presented in his Jesuit formation, he sought to find an adequate account of knowledge, one that accorded with his own developing understanding of cognitional process and methodology. Newman's insight into judgment as assent, Plato's reaching for answers anticipated in questions, and Augustine's introspective acuity gave his inquiring mind encouragement and stimulus, but it was in "reaching up to the mind of Aquinas" during ten years of doctoral studies that Lonergan reached the certainties he expressed in his *Verbum* articles. He concurs with Aquinas that we are by nature oriented into mystery and the mystery of God is to be the end of all our searching.

In these early stages, Lonergan is focused on the dynamism of questioning, the longing to understand correctly all that can be understood: the wonder of inquiry and the critical wonder leading to real assent. However, in his vocation to the Society of Jesus, there is an experience of the drawing power of the attraction of love that he will objectify only later. The question of his own motivation was to remain obscured until he could reach an adequate understanding of grace. For Lonergan, the "highest in us and in God the most like us" is initially the light of intellect leading to wisdom. He develops this idea in his philosophical/theological paper "The Natural Desire to See God."

It is in "Finality, Love, and Marriage" that Lonergan offers his first extended treatment of the centrality of love in the God-given direction of human life. The entire process of the world is moved by the desire for ultimate good: God attracts all things to respond to love by who or what they are.

Initially, Lonergan was in touch with his strong, compelling desire to know, and following it led him to the philosophical breakthroughs of *Insight*.[2] Later, he was to recognize the importance of appropriating also the movement of his heart toward ultimate goodness and unrestricted love.

Though reticent about his spiritual life, Lonergan agreed in 1980 to be interviewed by a team of editors at the Thomas More Institute in Montreal about the patterns of meaning he discerned in his intellectual life; in the interviews, he relaxed gradually into a welcome openness about himself as a person. These conversations, published after the final one was completed in 1982,[3] reveal something of the mind and heart of the thinker and the mystic, Bernard Lonergan.

More explicitly, biographical studies of his early development have been made by Richard Liddy and William Mathews, SJ. Liddy has made a thorough study of the influences preparing Lonergan for the "startling strangeness" of his intellectual conversion in 1936 and its expression in writings over the next twenty years.[4] William Mathews has published an intellectual biography of Lonergan titled *Lonergan's Quest: A Study of Desire in the Authoring of Insight*.[5] Papers and articles he has produced while working on it have been available for study over a number of years. Both have drawn on Lonergan's own recollections in *Caring About Meaning*, and this introduction is informed by all three resources.

Early Years

Born in 1904 to English-speaking parents in Québec, Bernard was sufficiently gifted to value the rigor of the elementary school education he received: "In the ungraded school you kept working."[6] He remembers hearing the work being done in the higher grades and growing in understanding, having his own insights in advance of level-appropriate instruction. He says he was "always learning." English composition was problematic until he felt he had something to say, but

> I liked math because you knew what you were doing
> and could get an answer....I remember in algebra doing
> a problem and getting a minus answer. I was sure I was
> wrong and I asked, but I was told, "Oh no, that's right."
> It was the revelation of negative numbers.[7]

In elementary religious education, the brothers impressed upon him that he was not going to understand the Trinity. "It was explained to us how Augustine, walking by the sea-shore, saw a little boy trying to pour the sea into a hole he had dug, and that trying to understand the Trinity is like that."[8] Rather than an excuse not to try to understand, this was for Lonergan a hint about the superabundance of what is to be understood: "As Vatican I says, *aliqua intelligentia eaque fructuosissima.* Most fruitful, provided you get there."[9]

His ability, along with the thorough grounding he had received, enabled him to complete a four-year high school course in under three, even with time out for serious illness. The curriculum at Loyola offered a sound foundation in the Latin and Greek classics, English and French literature, history and mathematics, as well as religion. He found "the Jesuits...the best-educated people I had met,"[10] and his insight into understanding deepened: "I acquired a great respect for intelligence."[11] He came early to expectations that the universe was intelligible, and was attracted to the mystery of the divine.

His decision to become a Jesuit was a clear sign of the drawing power of the desire for ultimate truth and goodness, a recognition of the pearl for which one would sell everything (cf. Matt 13:46). Lonergan, however, was not explicitly aware of this drawing power. He reports having been "troubled" by a sense of calling to religious life as an adolescent, and the only interesting thing about his vocation, he told his interviewers in 1980, was the fact that he persevered. Initially, it presented as a choice between the men's congregations he had known. Invited by one of the brothers, Bernard seems to have been deterred from entering with them by his father; later asked to consider the Jesuits, he offered as an excuse his ill health, which, in his mind, eliminated him as a candidate. Assured that there was nothing medically wrong with him, he found the question raised again, and the trepidation returned. On leaving Loyola in 1922, he recalls responding to the question without drama or any strong sense of affect, without waiting to work through the structured discernment process the Society of Jesus would have recommended:

> That I went to the Jesuits—there was really nothing exciting about that. I went out to the Sault to make a

retreat, an election, and I decided in the street-car on the way out. (It was a two-hour trip on the tram.)[12]

While possibly an offhand statement made by someone reticent about his interior life, there was an acknowledgment later in his life that he had been powerfully drawn, that grace was operative in attraction, decision, and follow-through.[13] At the time, however, the experience of love and awe does not seem to have been objectified for Lonergan; though in consciousness, the experience was not adverted to, understood, named, and verified. "It remain[ed] within subjectivity as a vector, an undertow, a fateful call to a dreaded holiness."[14] In a paper he presented to confreres and students of Regis College in 1965, he concluded that he had been in love with God without awareness of being-in-love.[15] We will return to this recognition in exploring the question of self-appropriation.

His four years in the novitiate at Guelph in Ontario were designed to form mind and character: a training in prayer and the *Spiritual Exercises of St. Ignatius*, and an ordered way of life involving asceticism, work, and study. The spiritual life was the focus of these "monastic" years. Formal studies in philosophy and theology were still to come. Later, he was critical of the interpretation of Ignatian spirituality made current in the Society at that time by the Superior General, Father Roothaan:

It was applying the three powers of the soul: the memory, the intellect and the will, the intellect being the faculty of reasoning. It was a rather big block in the spiritual life. It was the reduction of St. Ignatius to decadent conceptualist scholasticism.[16]

He referred to this emphasis as the stone he was offered when he asked for bread, but notes, "Not that I thought of it that way."[17] As a novice, he spent much time in structured prayer following the directive, "Try to find out what your motives are," an effort he came to consider as futile. Spiritual maturity was not to be anticipated before the age of thirty, he suggested, and the introspection asked of novices had yielded mostly puzzlement:

I'm saying that the fundamental thing in the spiritual life is God's grace and until you get an adequate account of that, which is entirely concerned with motives, talk about motives is mistaken. You just don't know what the fundamental motivations in you are.[18]

When he wrote in 1965 of the action of God in the life of a Jesuit, the "adequate account" of grace he had come to is nuanced, in touch with the desire that moves him, shot through with love:

Without any experience of just how and why, one is in a state of grace or one recovers it, one leaves all things to follow Christ, one binds oneself by vows of poverty, chastity, and obedience, one gets through one's daily heavy dose of prayer, one longs for the priesthood and later lives by it. Quietly, imperceptibly, there goes forward the transformation operated by the *Kurios*, but the delicacy, the gentleness, the deftness, of his continual operation in us hides the operation from us.[19]

His jocular way of talking about it in 1980 was simply, "When you learn about divine grace you stop worrying about your motives; somebody else is running the ship. You don't look for reasons why you are doing thus and so."[20]

Jesuit students were encouraged to do an external degree at the University of London concurrently with the philosophy and tutorials taught at Heythrop, and Lonergan was drawn to a course on methodology, because he felt there was absolutely no method to the philosophy he was being taught: "It wasn't going anywhere,"[21] despite the intellectual honesty and competence of his professors. The Suarezian Thomism they were required to present was not satisfying to the young Lonergan, who "shared the common view that held the manuals in little esteem."[22] Liddy believes that, even then, the source of his disillusionment with Suarezian Thomism lay in a theory of knowledge that did not cohere with his own self-knowledge.[23] He experienced the same lack of methodology in subsequent theological courses, but ultimately did not regret being denied the chance to study methodology in London, because he felt, with reason, that his own work on the subject was better than anything on offer in the late 1920s.

In the third year of philosophy, Lonergan read Newman's *Grammar of Assent*. It was a breakthrough. The young independent thinker had found an interlocutor:

> I was looking for someone who had some common sense and knew what he was talking about. And what was Newman talking about? About judgment as assent; about real apprehension and notional apprehension, notional assent and real assent. He was answering the liberal view that all judgments are more or less probable but nothing is certain. And he could give examples.[24]

Newman was addressing the same issue that preoccupied Lonergan, the nature of the human mind, and he found that Newman's method resonated with the way he himself knew things. Though there is no sign at this stage of his later interest in Aquinas, Lonergan's interest in philosophy was by now strongly marked, and it was particularly the theory of knowledge that piqued his curiosity, his drive to understand correctly. Newman directs attention to "the concrete, the interior, the facts of consciousness, as of primary importance, as distinct from what philosophers or scientists 'say' about knowledge."[25] So does Lonergan, and he guides his readers to do the same.

This path of inquiry was not abandoned by Lonergan during his formation between 1930 and 1933, a period of teaching, known as regency, at Loyola in Montreal. Two classic writers took him further in his quest for understanding. First, he read *Plato's Doctrine of Ideas* by John Alexander Stewart,[26] which he had already encountered in England. Stewart focuses attention on the psychological experience of arriving at the Ideas that underlies Plato's theory. Later, Lonergan explains why this brought such a sense of release:

> I believed in intelligence and I thought concepts were overrated. When I found…that an idea, for Plato, was like Descartes' equation for the circle, I was home. You get the equation of the circle just by understanding.[27]

Lonergan delighted in the early dialogues, discovering Plato as a questioner, a methodologist, a philosopher reaching toward answers anticipated in questions. "My idea of Plato is that he is the perfect introduction to philosophy. I don't think he has the answers but certainly he can build up interest and start one into serious questions."[28] Lonergan was teaching adolescents by day and following his own serious questioning as best he could in his own time.

The second influence was Augustine, again mainly through his earlier works. Lonergan read the *Cassiciacum Dialogues* in the summer of 1933, encountering Augustine's Neoplatonist ideas and his religious conversion experience expressed in *Confessions* in August of 386 CE. Valuing his liberal education, as did Lonergan, honestly seeking truth in his exploration of the philosophical schools of his day, and allowing all relevant questions to arise in a mind healed and enlightened by religious experience, Augustine had discovered that he was trying to "picture" imaginatively realities that cannot be so imagined; spirits were not another kind of body. He wrote in the *Dialogues* of his insight into the incorporeal nature of God and the human soul.[29]

Augustine's method was to reach for understanding through question and answer, and in so doing he demonstrated a considerable introspective acuity that Lonergan appreciated. "Augustine was not a technical theologian, a theoretical theologian," but "a person who knew the human soul in an extraordinary way. He knows more about consciousness than Thomas does."[30] Augustine sought to understand, *intelligere*, and the heartfelt commitment to truth and wisdom arising out of his religious conversion resonated deeply with Lonergan. "Augustine was so concerned with understanding, so unmindful of universal concepts, that I began a long period of trying to write an intelligible account of my convictions."[31] Only fragments remain of a twenty-five-thousand-word paper on the nature of faith Lonergan wrote in the summer of 1933, before his departure for theological studies in Rome, and sent to his friend Henry Smeaton, SJ, but in his obituary for Lonergan, Father Crowe remembers that summer:

> The area was marshy, the mosquitos bad, so lights did
> not go on in the evening. But Bernie could be heard

night after night typing through the twilight and into the dark—a trivial little fact that acquires enormous interest in the light of later information.[32]

This glimpse of Lonergan as a student on holiday shows the capacity for total absorption in the intellectual quest that he would later describe in *Insight* as the outworking of the desire to know:

The fact of inquiry is beyond all doubt. It can absorb a man. It can keep him for hours, day after day, year after year in the narrow prison of his study or his laboratory. It can send him on dangerous voyages of exploration. It can withdraw him from other interests, other pursuits, other pleasures, other achievements. It can fill his waking thoughts, hide from him the world of ordinary affairs, invade the very fabric of his dreams. It can demand endless sacrifices that are made without regret though there is only the hope, never a certain promise, of success.[33]

The quest continued during the next four years in Rome. Crowe notes that Lonergan interpreted his call there as a mark of confidence from his religious superiors after a troubled regency period: "His hope of an academic career [had] been clarified and given substance, and so he mapped out in considerable detail his ideas for the integral renewal of Catholic thought."[34]

It was during a course in Christology given by Bernard Leeming, SJ, in 1935–36 that Lonergan had what he was to describe as the key moment in his own intellectual conversion. He was engaged in a painstaking search for an understanding of faith statements about Christ that he could also affirm as true. His experience of the tension of inquiry is well described in a passage from *Insight*:

In the theorist, intent upon a problem, even the subconscious goes to work to yield at unexpected moments the suggestive images of clues and missing links, of patterns and perspectives, that evoke the desiderated insight and the delighted cry, "Eureka!" In reflection, there arises a passionless calm. Memory ferrets out instances that would run counter to the prospective judgment. Imagination anticipates the shape of possibilities that would prove the judgment wrong. So deep is the penetration, so firm the dominance, so strange the transformation of sensitive spontaneity, that memories and anticipations rise above the threshold of consciousness only if they possess at least a plausible relevance to the decision to be made.[35]

It is significant that this breakthrough occurred while he was intent upon a problem, and came as a release of the tension of inquiry.[36] Lonergan maintained that faith is often a catalyst in intellectual conversion, and for him, the disciplined and rigorous thought of these years had been sustained by the judgments of faith:

> So there was considerable room for development after Aristotle and you get it in St. Thomas when he distinguishes existence from essence...and to make them distinct really you have to have something equivalent to an intellectual conversion, even if you don't know what is meant by an intellectual conversion. I had the intellectual conversion myself when in doing theology I saw that you can't have one person in two natures in Christ unless there is a real distinction between the natures and something else that is one. But that is the long way round.[37]

Lonergan had been moving nearer to this moment of coalescing insights for ten years or more.[38] When he was convinced that there could not be a hypostatic union without a real distinction between essence and existence, it was a rounding out of all the intellectual influences of his life to date: "This, of course, was all the more acceptable, since Aquinas' *esse* corresponded to Augustine's *veritas* and both harmonized with Maréchal's view of judgment."[39] It was thus the final clarification of one important element in the appropriation of his own knowing: essence and existence as really distinct were the objective correlatives of understanding and judgment in his heuristic framework. Lonergan now knew that he knew, and this certainty instilled in him a joyful confidence that he had found here a significant gift to offer the community of scholars and the world.[40]

This offering was not to happen immediately, however. After his ordination in Rome, Lonergan had a year of tertianship—a final year of formation—of ascetical training and reflection in Amiens before returning to the Gregorian University to do a doctorate, not in philosophy as he might have expected, but in theology, as decided by his superiors. With his abiding interests in epistemology, sociology, and economics placed on hold, he pursued now his equally keen interest in historical consciousness, following a suggestion from his chosen director that he might "shed some light" on a difficult article in the *Summa*[41] by studying the *loca parallela* and the historical sources: his dissertation topic was approved as "A History of St. Thomas's Thought on Operative Grace."[42] Historical scholarship for Lonergan was

> a long journey through variant readings, shifts in vocabulary, enriching perspectives—all duly documented— that establish as definitively as can be expected what the great man thought on some minor topic within the horizon of his time and place and with no great relevance to other times and places. Only from a long series of such dissertations can the full picture be constructed—a picture as accurate as it is intricate, broad indeed but with endless detail, rich in implications for other times if only one has the time to sort them out, discern the precise import of each, and infer exactly what does and does not follow.[43]

Bringing to the task what Liddy sees as the key expression of Lonergan's intellectual conversion, his ongoing reflections on methodology, namely intellectually creative ways of asking and answering questions,[44] Lonergan retrieved Thomas's actual position on grace by tracing his intellectual development on the subject. He had come late to the appreciation of Thomas, but this doctoral research marked the beginning of an apprenticeship that changed him profoundly, eleven years "reaching up to the mind of Aquinas."[45] He recognized,

> It is only through a personal appropriation of one's own rational self-consciousness that one can hope to reach

the mind of Aquinas and, once that mind is reached, then it is difficult not to import his compelling genius to the problems of this later day.[46]

His apprenticeship to this compelling genius, begun in 1938, continued through to 1949. Having discovered and appreciated, as Crowe testifies,[47] the way Aquinas worked and questioned and thought, and understood and thought again, and judged and wrote, even so, for Lonergan, the greatest single benefit of his doctoral research was the reinforcement of his sense of God as mystery. "Lonergan never lost what Thomas above all theologians could teach, that theology can be done, must be done, that when it is done, we are confronted with mystery and bow our heads in adoration."[48] He knew from experience, as did Thomas, that the scope of human questioning far exceeds our capacity for finding correct answers, and that every small answer provokes further questioning. The field of mystery may be contracted by the advance of knowledge, but it cannot be eliminated from human living. Lonergan knew well that we are by nature oriented into mystery and the mystery of God is to be the end of all our searching.

EARLY WRITINGS—PRE-*INSIGHT*

For the rest of his life, Lonergan would devote himself to the Leonine purpose, *vetera novis augere et perficere*:[49] to enlarge and complete the old by addition of the new. But during the 1940s, his main concern was to establish exactly what the *vetera* were. He is very clearly doing this in two writings of this period: the *Verbum* articles (1946–49); and "The Natural Desire to See God" (1949). An opening to the *nova*, "problems of this later day," is made in "Finality, Love, Marriage" (1943). We will now explore the development of Lonergan's insights into desire and his practice and theory of self-appropriation in each of these articles.

Verbum: Word and Idea in Aquinas (1946–49)

Verbum: Word and Idea in Aquinas[50] comprises five articles that appeared in *Theological Studies* between 1946 and 1949 and were gathered together and published as a book in 1967 with a new introduction by Lonergan. For three years, he had been collecting materials for an account of Aquinas's views on understanding and the inner word,[51] and in *Verbum*, he begins with the core of psychological fact. The first article was a whole year in production because Lonergan had to come to terms with the change that he had effected in his thinking from faculty psychology to intentionality analysis.[52] He would later recast metaphysics explicitly in accord with his own intentionality analysis; even at this stage, he can no longer work in the Scholastic categories:

> I have begun, not from the metaphysical framework, but from the psychological content of Thomist theory of intellect: logic might favor the opposite procedure but, after attempting it in a variety of ways, I found it unmanageable.[53]

However, Lonergan is writing more than a study of cognitional theory; he is interested, as was Aquinas, in an exploration of the analogies used in trinitarian theology for the procession of Word and Spirit, and in these articles, he takes Thomist scholarship into a rediscovery of the beautiful clarity of Aquinas:

> [Thomas's] thought on *verbum* was, in the main, a statement for his technically minded age of the psychological analogy of the trinitarian processions. Its simplicity, its profundity, and its brilliance have long been obscured by interpreters unaware of the relevant psychological facts and unequal to the task of handling merely linguistic problems.[54]

Lonergan recognized in Aquinas what he describes as "an experimental knowledge of his own soul,"[55] and the highly nuanced, deeply penetrating, firmly outlined theory of the nature of human knowledge he had reached. Once the intellect perceives the intelligibility in the data presented in phantasm—an insight occurs—there is an *emanatio intelligibilis*, what Augustine refers to as a verbum *intus prolatum*,[56] a word proceeding interiorly. This is a procession from the act of insight, by way of the elements of the phantasm relevant to the act of understanding, to the act expressing in concept, language, or image what has been understood. In this procession, purely of spirit, act from act, Aquinas saw the most appropriate analogy available to the human mind for the infinite mystery of the procession of the Word within the Trinity. Then Lonergan makes clear that, for Aquinas, the second procession grounding a real relation of origin in the Trinity is not the procession of the act of love from the will...but the procession in the will, as rational appetite, of the act of love from the inner word in the intellect.[57]

The most suitable place to look for an analogical knowledge of the mystery of God is in humankind, the image of God, and specifically in rational consciousness, illuminated by the light that is "a certain participated likeness of the uncreated light of God."[58]

> Theologically, the [*Verbum*] articles are a study of the life of God in its internal dynamism and movement. But philosophically, they are a study of human life in its internal dynamism and movement on the level of spirit, that is, in the twofold procession of inner word and love, and so...in the image of God.[59]

Lonergan appreciates "the light that naturally is within us" as a participation in uncreated light, and "constitutive of our very power of understanding. It is the principle of inquiry and discourse."[60] So integral is the search for understanding and truth in human consciousness to our being as willed by God, that the action of God in human life is always, for Lonergan, to be recognized in the full enabling of this dynamism.

In the *Verbum* articles, Lonergan refers to *desire* most frequently as wonder and inquiry, or the wonder of inquiry. We have shown *inquiry* to have been the main activity of his life thus far; *wonder* renders its affective nuance. The activity of inquiry is tinged with awe and love, and is a response to an attraction. Though faith makes the search especially loving and worshipful for Lonergan, not only philosophers and theologians exhibit this response:

> Let active intelligence intervene: there is a care for the why and the wherefore; there is wonder and inquiry;

there is the alertness of the scientist or technician, the mathematician or philosopher, for whom the imagined object no longer is merely given but also a something-to-be-understood.[61]

The desired understanding may be reached in the inner word, and expressed, but human desire is not content with just any explanation. Wonder and inquiry are only satisfied when further reflection reaches some certainty that the explanation accords with truth. This is the act of judgment-assent.

> Insight is the goal to which the wonder of inquiry tends. The inner word of judgment is the expression of a reflective act of understanding and that reflective act is the goal toward which critical wonder tends.[62]

Both the *verbum* of insight/understanding and the *verbum* of truth proceed within us and are within the scope of our introspective attentiveness.

The wonder of inquiry can be called "critical" because it needs to reach what really is, what Aquinas and Lonergan call "actual contingent being." Thomistic thought stresses the native infinity of intellect: he also showed that, because of its infinite range, "the object of intellect must be *ens* (being); that this object cannot be unknown; it is known per se and naturally."[63] We have a notion of being and not being; we instinctively recognize that contradictory statements about the same aspect of the same thing cannot both be true, and that the whole is greater than its parts, but our knowledge of the real develops. Lonergan indicates that we learn to discriminate, differentiate, and categorize the details of a scheme that we possessed somehow from the start. All our learning is predominantly heuristic: we desire to know the unknown we are already stretching toward.

The whole of each thing is real, and by reality Lonergan means, at first, "nothing less than the universe in the multiplicity of its members, in the totality and individuality of each, in the interrelations of all."[64] This is the being that our minds can compass with some adequacy. However, we sense, through the range of our questioning, that there is more to reality than the material universe in which we are at home. In *Verbum*, Lonergan affirms the Thomist dictum that there are different modes of knowing being: "Since understanding is by identity and *ens* includes all reality, only infinite understanding can be the direct and immediate apprehension of the proper object of intellect, *ens intelligibile*."[65] Only God is the infinite act of understanding. Though our desire for understanding is unlimited, the achievement of this desire is not proper to us as finite. What we desire so intensely can come only as gift:

> The specific drive of our nature is to understand, and indeed to understand everything, neither confusing the trees with the forest nor content to contemplate the forest without seeing all the trees. For the spirit of inquiry within us never calls a halt, never can be satisfied, until our intellects, united to God as body to soul, know *ipsum intelligere* and through that vision, though then knowing aught else is a trifle, contemplate the universe as well.[66]

For Augustine, Aquinas, and Lonergan, this drive is a God-given attraction, a desire that is a sign of divine intention to grant the gift.

In *Verbum*, there is, therefore, an advance in Lonergan's explanation of what he will come to call *self-appropriation*, and precisely in relation to the desire that moves us. For him, "the native infinity of intellect as intellect is a datum of rational consciousness. It appears in that restless spirit of inquiry, that endless search for causes which, as Aquinas argued, can rest and end only in a supernatural vision of God."[67] He offers evidence for the belief that the Thomist theory of intellect had an empirical and introspective basis,[68] and shows that we can and must explore this doubling back on itself[69] of awareness if we are to understand the image of God that we are, an image that alone grounds an adequate analogical insight into the mystery of the triune God. "To follow Aquinas here, one must practice introspective rational psychology; without that, one can no more know the created image of the Blessed Trinity, as Aquinas conceived it, than a blind man can know colors."[70] Lonergan quoted Augustine's exhortation for readers to look within themselves:

Naturally enough, as Augustine's discovery was part and parcel of his own mind's knowledge of itself, so he begged his readers to look within themselves and there to discover the speech of spirit within spirit, an inner *verbum* prior to any use of language, yet distinct from the mind itself and from its memory or its present apprehension of objects.[71]

Augustine's practice of psychological introspection and the uncannily accurate introspective skill of Aquinas were commended by Lonergan in the introduction to *Verbum*. However, neither thematizes its use. Lonergan provides an explanatory account of the intellectual operations of understanding and definition in chapter 1, and of reflection and judgment in chapter 2. Through a careful study of these chapters, a person well versed in Thomist metaphysics might better understand human knowing than generations of Scholastic philosophers. However, *Verbum* is not yet a step-by-step process inviting the reader to such self-appropriation. For this we must wait for *Insight*.

In the *Verbum* articles, Lonergan is clearly evaluating his sources and their writings in terms of their self-knowledge and his own insight into cognitional processes. He recommends "introspective rational psychology" as the key to understanding them. "The wonder of inquiry" is, at this stage, his best description of the desire, the powerful attraction that is drawing him to seek ultimate truth. God's uncreated Light, after which we grope and strain, is ontologically first, but what is first, *quoad nos*, is our own immanent intellectual light that we can access, since it grounds all intelligibility in our knowing.

Known with this qualified immediacy, it justifies itself as the potentially boundless base whence we can posit, and through our positing know, the universe: and as the principle of our knowledge of reality, it also is the most convincing sample in us of the stuff of which the author of the universe and of our minds consists. Between these poles, the highest in us and in God the most like us, our wisdom moves to knowledge of itself and of its source… and is acquired gradually.[72]

After noting with relish the vivid but uncharacteristic use here of the word *stuff* by Lonergan, he who had recorded with compassion Augustine's struggle to reach the insight that God was not any sort of stuff[73]—even "infinite white light" is an imaginable "body"—we are left wondering whether this strongly intellectualist position would still be wholeheartedly endorsed by the later Lonergan. It could well be that loving came to replace knowing as the "highest in us and in God the most like us."

"The Natural Desire to See God" (1949)

In *Verbum*, Lonergan commented that Aquinas knew perfectly well what Aristotle meant by the wonder that is the source of all science and philosophy, and by insight into phantasm: "He can take these positions, fuse and transform them, and come forth with a natural desire for the beatific vision; a position which is notoriously unintelligible to people who do not grasp just what understanding is."[74] Lonergan had traced the historical development of Aquinas's proposal that it is human to desire knowledge of God by his essence, even though such knowledge is beyond on our natural capacity. In a paper presented to the Jesuit Philosophical Association in 1949,[75] Lonergan uses his grasp of what understanding is to assert the intelligibility of this desire. Here, he delineates the proper roles of philosophy and theology in the quest for clarification.

Lonergan begins with the thesis that the *desires* of the human intellect are manifested in questions, and that all questions can be reduced to two, *quid sit*, "What is it?" (what it is) and *an sit*, "Is it?" (whether it is): "There exists then a desire that is natural to intellect, that arises from the mere fact that we possess intellects, that is defined by the questions, *an sit* and *quid sit*."[76] We seek understanding of what we experience and then assurance that what we understand really is so. To ask why light refracts is to ask for an explanation of refraction. When we obtain an adequate explanation, "then and only then are we able to state what refraction is. Until then, we can do no more than assign a nominal definition which tells, not what refraction is, but what we mean by the term, refraction.[77]

The need for explanatory rather than nominal definition characterized Lonergan's desire for understanding and will receive further attention in *Insight*. Both forms of definition require an insight, but a nominal definition requires no more than an insight into the proper use of language, while an explanatory one supposes an insight into the objects to which language refers.[78]

Lonergan is careful to distinguish two kinds of natural fulfillment for the desire to know: proper and analogical. Proper fulfillment of the desire involves the appropriate knowledge of created reality only.[79] Beyond that, we can only seek a resemblance in an imaginable, created reality that may yield some understanding of mystery, and use the traditional methods of the *via affirmationis*, the *via negationis*, and the *via eminentiae* to reach toward a glimpse of its meaning.[80] A limited understanding of the revealed mysteries of faith is to be reached through analogy with nature and through the connection of the mysteries one with another. However, Lonergan reminds his readers that the analogy of the mysteries with nature is not fully natural—nor is the desire it fulfills either simply natural or really satisfied.[81]

> Analogical fulfilment is fulfilment only in an improper sense. It does not satisfy our intellects. It goes part of the way but not the whole way. It answers some questions but raises others. Fulfilment by analogy is a matter of decreasing returns, for the further one pushes the issue, the clearer it becomes that there is much we do not know.[82]

What *is*, in the material order, is the proportionate object of human knowing, but the adequate object of intellect is being itself, the transcendental *ens*. We may distinguish proportionate (imaginable) and adequate (transcendental—*ens*) objects of the human intellect, but our desire is for both: "We keep on asking why, and we desist ultimately not because we do not desire but because we recognize our impotence to satisfy our desire."[83] That we should be moved so powerfully by the desire of our intellects, natural in origin but transcendental in its object, is a paradox.

Lonergan is clear. The question *quid sit Deus*, asking what God is, occurs naturally as soon as we hear of God's existence. This question is expressive of the desire to see God, to know what God is, and what Aquinas calls *videre Deum per essentiam*, to see

19

God by his essence.[84] The desire to understand God is both natural and transcendental, but, for Lonergan, as for Aquinas, the fulfillment of this desire is strictly supernatural, the immediate vision of God in heaven. Lonergan's conclusion is not philosophical but theological.

> Such, then, is the thesis. There exists a natural desire to understand. Its range is set by the adequate object of intellect. Its proper fulfilment is obtained by the reception of a form proportionate to the object understood. This natural desire extends to understanding God. In that case its fulfilment is the beatific vision. Still, only the theologian can affirm a natural desire to see God; a philosopher has to be content with paradox.[85]

In this paper, Lonergan goes on to refute static essentialist and closed conceptualist ideas[86] about the natural desire to see God: his presuppositions are dynamic and existential intellectualist ones, according to which "the world-order is an intelligible unity mirroring forth the glory of God." This intelligible unity is knowable imperfectly by philosophy, less imperfectly by theology, but satisfactorily only because of the beatific vision.[87]

It is interesting to note that while Lonergan refers, at this stage, to the thought of Thomas on the question of whether full human happiness consists in seeing the divine essence, and whether there is a natural desire to know what God is, he does so without citing the principal passage treating this question, *Summa theologiae*, 1-2, q. 3, a. 8, which was to become a leitmotiv in his work through the 1950s. In "The Natural Desire to See God," Lonergan states his own theoretical position on the question with the cogency of a man of faith in touch with his own desire and possessing the philosophical and theological clarity called for by the debate of that time.[88]

Lonergan elaborates in this article his certainty that the desire manifested in questioning is integral to being human, but that its scope transcends created realities to seek the total intelligibility of Being Itself. He invites us to understand our questioning, its natural origins and its transcendental object, in the light of faith.

"Finality, Love, Marriage" (1943)

The sense of an intelligible world order expressed in "The Natural Desire to See God," in which lower orders are intrinsically subordinated to higher ones, Lonergan had earlier developed in a more nuanced way in an article titled "Finality, Love, Marriage" (*Theological Studies* 4, 1943).[89] We treat this paper here, out of sequence, because it moves beyond the *vetera*—Lonergan's reaching up to the mind of Aquinas in the preceding articles—and represents an early attempt to address the *nova* in theology.[90] Significantly for our investigation into Lonergan's appropriation of desire, it also gives an insight into his understanding, at the age of thirty-nine, of the centrality of love in the God-given direction of human life, and foreshadows his more developed extension, in later years, of the dynamism of intellect into the responsible and affective spheres.[91]

In "Finality, Love, Marriage," Lonergan was addressing a question concerning the ends of marriage, which he was lecturing on in Montreal at the time, and doing so in terms of different levels of the person (physical, chemical, biological, sensitive psychological, and intellectual), and ascending orders of human love (sexual attraction, friendship, human and divine love). In the ends of marriage, he identifies a horizontal or essential priority of lower levels, but also a vertical finality of lower levels toward higher realizations to which he accords a priority of excellence.

Integral to Lonergan's understanding of *desire*, at this stage of our inquiry, is the concept of final causality.[92] Finality is commonly described as the response of appetite to motive,[93] and the orientation of processes to terms. The human sex drive is a capacity to respond to the attractiveness of another person, and coupling is the way in which the continuation of our species is assured. However, Lonergan invites the reader to move beyond obvious instances and conceive things generally. The mere fact of response or orientation does not constitute finality. "If appetite responds because motive moves, if process is oriented because an intelligent agent envisages and intends a term, there is causality indeed; but it is efficient and not final."[94]

> Rigorously one must maintain that there is final causality if, and only if, appetite responds because the motive

is good; if, and only if, process is oriented because the term is good.[95]

Our capacity for response can be derailed by the apparently desirable, such as power to coerce and dominate, but we are made for the goodness to be realized in inclusive relationships. Eating and drinking, delightful in themselves and necessary for the sustaining of healthy life, become destructive when overindulgence makes them ends in themselves. "Final causality has to do with relationship to the end, that is, relationship to the good that matters utterly."[96]

The final cause is the good as cause, because finality is *cuius gratia*, the end for which something is, that for which it is made. For Thomas, the whole created universe is in love with God: *omnia appetunt Deum,*[97] *omnia intendunt assimilari Deo.*[98] In the existing universe, all reality responds to God as absolute motive and tends to God as absolute term; but on each level, it does so differently, according to the mode of response, of orientation. Lonergan distinguishes, in terms of a hierarchy of horizontal strata of being, the different modes of appetition and process: "It is essence that limits, that ties things down to a given grade of being, that makes them respond to motives of a given type, that assigns them their proper and proportionate ends."[99] If the Psalms invite the trees of the forest to exult before the Lord, there is an understanding that they do so by processes natural to their species: in growth, in photosynthesis, in seed production, in the beauty of their proper form. Human eyes are wondrously formed to respond to light, are oriented to seeing the material world, but uncreated light is beyond their sight, although the human mind is made also for that. There are, therefore, "two distinct types of finality: the absolute finality of all things to God in his intrinsic goodness; the horizontal finality of limiting essence to limited mode of appetition and process."[100] Accordingly, in the context of the question of the ends of marriage, Lonergan can say that human fecundity, the procreation and education of children, that is, horizontal finality, is the more essential end of the institution of marriage.

However, Lonergan recognizes a third type of finality, within the absolute finality of all things to the goodness of God, "the finality of any lower level of appetition and process to any higher level."[101]

This concept, recognized but scarcely attended to before Lonergan, is vertical finality. Chemical elements such as hydrogen and oxygen have their own horizontal finality, but they enter into compounds, are taken into the higher systems of living organisms, and contribute to animal flourishing. In many ways, "vertical finality is of the very idea of a hierarchical universe, of the ordination of things devised and exploited by the divine Artisan."[102] Whereas horizontal finality holds even for isolated objects, vertical finality results from "the fertility of concrete plurality": great variation in species, large numbers, long times and multiple opportunities for interaction, change, and development. Later, Lonergan will more directly address the huge implications of creation reaching self-consciousness in humanity, with its possibility of communal response to ultimate desire.[103] Already here he signals a multifaceted interdependence, with an upward thrust, evident in the whole of creation.

> On finality is affirmed, besides the absolute reference of all things to God and the horizontal reference of each thing to its commensurate motives and ends, a vertical dynamism and tendency, an upthrust from lower to higher levels of appetition and process.[104]

Lonergan will also move away from the hierarchical, spatial concept of levels in theological discourse, but even here we note a significant anticipation of his mature use of the concept of sublation that will nuance it:[105]

> For the cosmos is not an aggregate of isolated objects hierarchically arranged on isolated levels, but a dynamic whole in which instrumentally, dispositively, materially, obedientially, one level of being or activity subserves another. The interconnections are endless and manifest.[106]

It is within this understanding of vertical finality that Lonergan sees the integration of human sexuality with the processes of reason and grace to yield the incorporation of lower-level activities within the higher: a dynamic upthrust from sexual attraction to the love of friendship, to divine charity, to an advance together in

Christian perfection, ultimately to the beatific vision. In this way, while the more essential end of marriage is the procreation and education of children, he concludes that the more excellent end of marriage is to be found in the expansion of the love of the couple into "a common consciousness and conscience in the pursuit of life, the good life, and eternal life."[107] The vertical end of marriage is more excellent only relatively, however: all finality is to the absolute good. For Lonergan, vertical and horizontal finalities are not alternatives and "the vertical emerges all the more strongly as the horizontal is realized the more fully."[108] The more generous and sensitively expressive sex is for a couple, the stronger the chance of a true friendship developing out of initial romantic love; the better the committed companionship, the greater the opening to unselfish sharing in God-given charity, which in turn is preparation for the longed-for consummation of human love in the beatific vision.

Having established this, he goes on to analyze the concept of love, giving with concision the most extensive treatment of love anywhere in his collected works.[109]

Lonergan treats of love both in terms of the human will as rational appetite, and of the human subject who loves. Love is firstly the basic form of willing, seen under two aspects. One is active: essentially a matter of desire, movement, striving for the good; the other is more passive: a matter of completion, delight, resting in the good. As the pure response of appetite to the good, love delights in the sheer goodness of the beloved for his or her own sake, *nihil aliud...quam complacentia boni*,[110] "while active desire, hope, joy, hatred, aversion, fear, sadness are consequents of the basic response and reflect objective modifications in the circumstances of the motive good."[111] Desire is for the beloved as not fully attained; hope is desire confident of reaching union; sadness responds to absence or estrangement from the one desired. Besides being the basic form of appetition, love "is the first principle of process to the end loved, and the whole of the process is thus but the self-expression of the love that is its first principle."[112]

From the point of view of the loving human subject, Lonergan sees love as the principle of union between different subjects; love unites them in pursuit of a common goal or as the ground of their exultation together in the attainment of the good that is love's end. The love that is friendship is key in this paper: true friendship has its basis neither in pleasure nor in advantage, according to Aristotle's thought in the *Nichomachean Ethics*,[113] but only in the objective lovableness of the virtuous person. Becoming knowledgeable and virtuous is to be a true friend to oneself and only thus can one be a true friend to another. The excellence recognized in the friend, or the potential for it that leads one friend to desire it for the other, and the individual's own lovableness in pursuit of such excellence are all examples of finality toward the ultimate goodness of God, whose love draws all into cooperation in the divine plan for a friendly universe. Lonergan is here following Aquinas's refinement[114] of Aristotle's treatment of friendship as paradigmatic for the consideration of love:

> For it is only in a tendency to an absolute that one can transcend both egoism and altruism; and such transcendence is implicit in the Aristotelian notion of true friendship with its basis not in pleasure nor in advantage but in the objective lovableness of the virtuous man.[115]

God is absolute motive and absolute term, the one who activates our capacity to respond to the good, and so draws us on beyond any limited desire we currently have for ourselves or others.

Lonergan does not ignore the tensions that are generated in the human person by the multiplicity of specialized appetites tending toward their appropriate end and spontaneous loves for a variety of goods. "In this tension the rational part of man is at a disadvantage, for natural spontaneity takes care of itself while knowledge and virtue have to be acquired."[116] However, his treatment of the dialectical and social obstacles to the ascent of love, and the possibility of their progressive overcoming through redemption and "the divine solidarity in grace which is the mystical body of Christ,"[117] go beyond our present purpose.

These obstacles and their overcoming are, however, the setting for his model of the ascent of love toward its true good: "One has to set the complex nature of love in the empty category of vertical finality; one has to study the ascent of love from the level of nature to the level of the beatific vision."[118] On every level, love has a passive aspect insofar as it is a response to motive good, an immanent aspect inasmuch as it is a perfection of the lover, and an active aspect inasmuch as it is productive of further instances of the good. The whole is interpenetrated in fully human living by rational love examining and selecting its motives, deliberately willing its own perfection, and freely proceeding to effect further instances of the good. The lower level of natural spontaneity is obviously the work of God, "who implants in nature its proper mode of response and orientation."[119] At the level of reason, there is already an antecedent spontaneity to truth and goodness, and on the highest level of grace, there is an elevating transformation of this antecedent spontaneity, "so that the truth through which God rules man's autonomy is the truth God reveals beyond reason's reach, and the good that is motive is the divine goodness that is motive of infused charity."[120] As the higher levels perfect the lower, so the lower predispose toward the higher, since all come from and return to God, and it is precisely in this predisposition that Lonergan finds the ascent of love that gives marriage its finality to Christian charity and perfection:

> Now towards this high goal of charity it is no small beginning in the weak and imperfect heart of fallen man to be startled by a beauty that shifts the center of appetition out of self; and such a shift is effected on the level of sensitive spontaneity by *erôs* leaping in through delighted eyes and establishing itself as unrest in absence and an imperious demand for company. Next, company may reveal deeper qualities of mind and character to shift again the center from the merely organistic tendencies of nature to the rational level of friendship with its enduring basis in the excellence of a good person. Finally grace inserts into charity the love that nature gives and reason approves.[121]

In this beautiful description of development within a loving relationship, Lonergan demonstrates for the passive aspect of love, a dispositive upward tendency from *eros* to friendship, and from friendship to a special order of charity.

He is able to do the same with love as immanent perfection in the lover. By loving in accord with a right order (first God absolutely, then creatures "according to the measure of their excellence, which also is measure of their proximity to God by assimilation"[122]), human persons make themselves good, and thence lovable. When love is habitual and reciprocated, it unites lovers in a larger unit, "with each to the other as another self, a *dimidium animae suae.*"[123] Not only on the levels of spontaneity and reason, but also on the level of grace, he argues, marriage is "the real apprehension, the intense appetition, the full expression of union with another self,"[124] and the bringing together of a couple extends to children and the community in which they are raised. The ascending finalistic drive of the sacrament is to "the very summit of Christian perfection, in which…all members of the mystical body are known and loved as other selves."[125]

The third and active aspect of love is one of activity and production. The person who loves will try to grow in love by focusing on the desired good; will seek to express love in ways that resemble the desired goodness; separated from the desired good, the lover will seek to possess it; and if the motive good is merely a project, love will use every endeavor to produce it.

> For just as habitual and reciprocated love has the formal effect of constituting a union, of setting up mutual other selves, so a common end, defined by a common motive and sought in the common effort of friends sharing a common life, actuates the common consciousness of mutual other selves.[126]

In Lonergan's vision of the ascent of love, it is this aspect that most clearly leads to development, in the individual and the group. He makes it clear that this ascent is an integrative influence:

> Granted several levels of activity and love, then there is an intensification of the higher by the lower, a stability resulting not from mere absence of tension but from positive harmony between different levels, and, most dynamic, the integration by which the lower in its expansion involves a development in the higher.[127]

Attractive as this perspective is, Lonergan is not unaware of how "the reason and rational appetite of fallen man limp in the disequilibrium of high aspiration and poor performance."[128] Human ignorance and frailty can too readily tend to center an infinite craving, St. Augustine's *Fecisti nos ad te, Domine, et inquietum est cor nostrum donec requiescat in te*,[129] on a finite object or release. Subsequent rationalization leads to the deforming of knowledge into harmony with disorderly loves. Lonergan's hope, and ours, is in the gratuitous action of God.

> To pierce the darkness of such ideology the divine Logos came into the world; to sap its root in weak human will he sent his Spirit of Love into our hearts; and in this redemption we are justified, rectified, renewed, yet never in this life to the point that further justification, rectification, renewal ceases to be possible.[130]

In a world where God is absolute motive and absolute term of all things, it is God who activates our appetite, our capacity to respond to the good. The redeeming action of God in Christ continues in human history through the Spirit's healing of the selfishness that blocks the ascent of love.

In "Finality, Love, Marriage," we have seen Lonergan's early insight into the desire for ultimate good that moves all of world process as the way in which God attracts all things to respond to love through who or what they are. In the second part of his life, he will give further clarification of the fulfillment of desire involved in "what we are doing when we are loving."[131] In the *Verbum* articles and "The Natural Desire to See God," Lonergan has made clear the significance he places on our recognition of the desire to know what moves us in our questioning. For myself, Lonergan became my interlocutor in a search for self-appropriation, self-acceptance, and encounter with Mystery in the fullness of human authenticity in a way that parallels his early years of dialogue with himself and the great thinkers of the past.

In the next chapter, we will examine Lonergan's first masterpiece, his explanatory and pedagogical account in *Insight: A Study of Human Understanding*, of response to the desire to know, namely what we are doing when we are knowing and what it is we know when we do so. This will yield a fuller account of both the desire to know and the possibility of its appropriation.

2

SELF-AFFIRMATION AS A KNOWER IN *INSIGHT*

To appropriate our desire for the fullness of truth and discover our capacity to attain objective knowledge, we need to consider how the human mind works. In this chapter, we are looking for a method of coming to know our own knowing, which is accessible to ordinary human attentiveness and understanding, offers insight into an invariant pattern that is valid across cultures and epochs, and can be affirmed as true by anyone willing and able to make the effort. Such a method, we maintain, is given in Lonergan's intentionality analysis in his major philosophical work *Insight*. The intention, therefore, is to show the relationship of this pattern to our deepest desires and to optimal human functioning, and suggest how, in a faith perspective, we recognize it to be significant in the divine plan and desire for human living. It is presented as a key to the personal appropriation of desire, a particularly effective one, open to all who have the questions.

After Lonergan finished writing the *Verbum* articles, which we considered in the previous chapter, he began working on *Insight: A Study of Human Understanding*,[1] which he wrote from 1949 to 1953. During the first three years, his intention was "an exploration of methods generally in preparation for a study of the method of theology,"[2] a desire that had been growing through his years of study. Before returning to Rome to teach in 1953, he rounded off what he had done to that point and published it. Significantly, *Insight* does show all method as based in the invariant pattern of cognitional operations and systematizes the personal discovery of oneself as a knower. It further represents a development of his thinking about the desire to know as the *eros* of the human mind, and anticipates a future exploration of the good as a universal sublating in human authenticity of the intelligible, the true, the one.[3]

REALLY KNOWING WHAT IT IS TO KNOW

With the publication of *Insight: A Study of Human Understanding* in 1957, Lonergan thematizes and systematizes cognitional and moral self-appropriation and presents it pedagogically. The startling change that he experienced in 1935–36 and that he later came to refer to as "intellectual conversion" was foundational for all his subsequent work. Though this term was frequently used in Lonergan's notes on "Intelligence and Reality," he never uses it in *Insight*. Richard M. Liddy, a student of Lonergan's, suggests that Lonergan was concerned to avoid what might be perceived as its "religious overtones" in a work written not just for believers but for "any sufficiently cultured consciousness."[4] Most notably, it is in *Insight* that he sets out to mediate self-appropriation as a knower to his readers: "So it is that my detailed investigations of the thought of Aquinas on *gratia operans*[5] and on *verbum* have been followed by the present essay in aid of a personal appropriation of one's own rational self-consciousness."[6] Readers are invited to follow the step-by-step pedagogy of the book and so reach an understanding of the pattern of their own ways of coming to know:

> The aim is not to set forth a list of the abstract properties of human knowledge but to assist the reader in effecting a personal appropriation of the concrete dynamic structure immanent and recurrently operative in his own cognitional activities.[7]

As will be shown, Lonergan's invitation to self-appropriation is a call to do more than heighten the consciousness that is already present in all the cognitional activities of a person awake: it is to reach a self-understanding that can be verified by attention to inner experience.

> The first eight chapters of *Insight* are a series of five-finger exercises inviting the reader to discover in himself and for himself just what happens when he understands. My aim is to help people experience themselves understanding, advert to the experience, distinguish it from other experiences, name and identify it, and recognize it when it recurs.[8]

Though Lonergan can state it so simply, he recognizes that this learning will take time and considerable effort, even with the help of the methodological process he provides: "the process of self-appropriation occurs only slowly, and usually, only through a struggle with some such book as *Insight*."[9] It involves clearly identifying in one's own consciousness the central act of understanding, and then distinguishing it from all the cognitive activities that precede and follow from it.

The central act of understanding, the insight that gives the book its name, differs from the operation of the senses in its instantaneous nature. We can be conscious of ourselves as hearing for the duration of a sound that captures our attention. Seeing is an operation we are aware of whenever our eyes are open, and we can alternate seeing and not seeing. This is so vivid an experience that for many it comes to represent the quintessence of knowing.[10] Hearing and seeing with eyes open are continuous operations. However, the flash of understanding whereby we discern a pattern, an explanation, a solution in the data our mind is playing with, comes as a sudden discovery that is both surprising and unimaginable. Insight into intelligibility replaces puzzlement, and we can neither compel nor predict it. "It is insight that makes the difference between the tantalizing problem and the evident solution."[11] To attend to understanding, we can only confront real problems and puzzle over them until insight comes and we catch it breaking through.

To this end, Lonergan turns to scientific method to find "the fields of intellectual endeavor in which the greatest care is devoted to exactitude and, in fact, the greatest exactitude is attained."[12] In the first chapter, it was mathematics; the second to fifth chapters draw on physics for illustrations. The clarity and exactitude of modern scientific thinking is a key advantage for Lonergan; the criterion of the real implicit in scientific questions is another. "It has taken modern science four centuries to make the discovery that the objects of its inquiry need not be imaginable entities moving through imaginable processes in an imaginable space-time."[13] He systematizes for the reader the distinction between imagination and insight, between "taking a look" inwardly or outwardly, and knowing as the result of experiencing, understanding, and judging correctly. Asked by his publisher, who was preparing a blurb for a reprint in 1977, "What might the reader experience in pursuing this book?" he wrote,

> Examples of insight are drawn from mathematics, physics, common sense and philosophy. The temptation will be to think of such objects and neglect his own operations with respect to the objects. This is missing the whole point. The various objects are mentioned only to invite the reader to heighten his consciousness of the operations he is performing in dealing with the objects. Once this pitfall is avoided, and the avoidance is not easy, there can emerge a growing illumination that leads the reader no longer to need Lonergan because he has found out for himself and can work on his own.[14]

The wide field of examples provided is designed to ensure that those not at home in either mathematics or science, and in fact more baffled by the examples given than by anything in Lonergan's concise explanatory text, will still be able to find a context in which the illuminating experience of meaning breaking through the fog may occur, and be noticed. Lonergan shows parallels between common-sense and empirical science—both are developments of intelligence and involve observation, the self-correcting processes of trial and error, and coalescing insights yielding further answers and yet more questions.[15] Both employ the same inbuilt method of human intentional consciousness, though whereas common sense is mainly concerned with making and doing, the relationships and transformation of human beings and their environment, pure science aims to come closer to the natural world and relationships within it, as it is in itself. Chapters 6, "Common Sense and Its Subject," and 7, "Common Sense as Object," are rich in practical insights. For some readers, it may even be the appreciation of a good joke that is an instance of what they are seeking—why is everyone laughing? The breakthrough into understanding is pleasurable whenever is happens, though the sooner the better in the case of a joke.

It was the mark of Lonergan's pedagogical purpose that he wrote *Insight* from a moving viewpoint.[16] The whole vision is not revealed at once: he begins with the simplest elements, then extends, building step by step on what has been learned in a series of higher viewpoints. The book's structure shows a two-part division: chapters 1 to 10, "Insight as Activity," in which he explains the structure of knowing, and justifies his insistence on the need for reflective insight and the act of judgment;[17] and chapters 11 to 20, "Insight as Knowledge," with the pivotal chapter 11 being the first time the reader is called to make a significant judgment, to affirm his or her own knowing.[18] This self-affirmation goes well beyond any assumption we may have made hitherto about our own and others' ability to know. Successful negotiation of this step means the breaking of the duality of our knowing. Along with the rest of the animal kingdom, we share an extroverted consciousness oriented toward biological ends that recognizes and responds to "the already out there now real." It is our ability to question and reach a correct understanding that is the form of knowing that is fully human. The discovery of the difference—and Lonergan holds that "one has not made it yet if one has no clear memory of its startling strangeness"[19]—is integral to self-knowledge and so to self-appropriation as a knower and becomes for the reader a criterion of the real. Lonergan the teacher is firm: "To say it all with the greatest brevity: one has not only to read *Insight* but also to discover oneself in oneself."[20]

The work is demanding, but it establishes a foundation for a growth in authentic response to the desire to know:

> The labor of self-appropriation cannot occur at a single leap. Essentially it is a development of the subject and in the subject and, like all development; it can be solid and fruitful only by being painstaking and slow.[21]

Though Lonergan is not making it explicit, this development presents an opening to advances in self-understanding, beyond the cognitional and moral levels, to the fully existential level where the self-constituting subject seeks the values revealed in intentional feelings.[22] He admits that his promise "has the ring of a slogan" but sums up as follows the positive content of this work:

> Thoroughly understand what it is to understand, and not only will you understand the broad line of all that there is to be understood, but also you will possess a fixed base, an invariant pattern, opening upon all further developments of understanding.[23]

To do this requires identifying the operations by which we come to know, and then showing how they are dynamically structured, each operation presupposing and completing the activity that precedes it. In cognitional consciousness, experience forms the first level, that of the data of sense and the data of inner experience or our own awareness of ourselves as seeing, hearing, touching, tasting, and imagining. Questioning what we experience (questions for intelligence—where, what, how, why, when, who, what for?—rising in us spontaneously) promotes us to the next level. Insight or direct understanding is this second level that grasps the unity presented in data, the *Aha-erlebnis* or eureka moment. However, not every bright idea is the right idea. We want to understand correctly, so questions arise for reflection (Is that really so? Could there be any other explanation to account for the data? Does this explanation account for all the data?). The third and final level of this cognitional structure is that of judgment or reflective understanding, by which we affirm or deny the understanding achieved at the second level, or defer so doing until further evidence can be obtained. As his readers, we are invited to apply this transcendental method that is the dynamic structure of our consciousness to our own conscious, cognitive activity,[24] and thus to come to know ourselves as knowers. Chapter 11 confronts the reader with the realization that self-affirmation as a knower is recognition of a fact. Only by use of these disputed operations could one argue against the fact, "but the fact of the asking and the possibility of the answering are themselves the sufficient reason for the answer."[25] We then recognize in our insistent questioning the desire for truth—the God-given action of spirit within us. We can then confirm as fact the openness that constitutes us as human.

THE PURE, DETACHED, DISINTERESTED, UNRESTRICTED DESIRE TO KNOW

We are integrally desirous creatures. In the purely biological pattern of experience, there are drives that operate intermittently, "sequences which converge upon terminal activities of intussusception or reproduction, or, when negative in scope, self-preservation."[26] We desire safety, food, warmth, freedom of movement, companionship, and positive stroking almost as much as the social animals that are our domestic pets, because of the animal life we share with them. But over and above "the biological account books of pleasure and pain," human life knows the "spontaneous, self-justifying joy" of liberation from biological purposiveness in play and creativity, in artistic expression of the "deep-set wonder in which all questions have their source and ground."[27] This is the aesthetic pattern of experience, and the desire moving in it goes beyond survival and reproduction: it is desire for the beautiful as much as for the true, the good.

The third pattern of experience treated in *Insight* is the intellectual pattern, and here Lonergan is completely at home. Because of his painstaking self-appropriation, Lonergan can describe and explain the desire and the response that have brought him to this stage of his intellectual journey. He identifies at the core of human cognitional structure "the pure desire to know" as the dynamism orienting it to the universe of being, to what is real, to the true. This desire is the spirit of inquiry to be recognized in questions for understanding; it is a drive to seek an adequate understanding and then to identify what it is to act in accordance with the realm of fact. Whether appropriated or not, it operates spontaneously in consciousness:

> We are committed, not by knowing what it is and that it is worthwhile, but by an inability to avoid experience, by the subtle conquest in us of the *eros* that would

understand, by the inevitable aftermath of that sweet adventure when a rationality identical with us demands the absolute, refuses unreserved assent to less than the unconditioned, and when that is attained, imposes upon us a commitment in which we bow to an immanent *Anankê*.[28]

The dynamic orientation operative deep within ourselves, which Lonergan invites his readers to discover, the "drive to understand" that emerges "when the noise of other appetites are stilled," which has the power to withdraw humans from "other interests, other pleasures, other achievements," send us on "dangerous voyages of exploration," and "demand endless sacrifices."[29] This is what he calls the *pure, detached, disinterested, unrestricted desire to know*.

Lonergan characterizes it as *pure*, because of its integrity, not because it is disconnected from all that makes us "a little lower than God" (Ps 8:5). It is essentially human, an *eros* of the mind that human beings can no more divest themselves of than they can their sensuality. "To inquire and understand, to reflect and judge, to deliberate and choose are as much an exigence of human nature as waking and sleeping, eating and drinking, talking and loving."[30] The primordial drive of the human being is the pure question. We might call it alertness of mind, intellectual curiosity, the spirit of inquiry, the drive to wonder about experiences and images. "It is prior to any insights, any concepts, any words; for insights, concepts, words have to do with answers, and before we look for answers we want them; such wanting is the pure question."[31] It makes us open to experience, raises relevant questions about it, requires us to affirm any insight that meets the conditions for reality but prevents us from giving too ready an assent to those that do not fulfill the conditions, and so keeps us engaged in the ongoing search for solutions. The pure desire to know is

the absorption of investigation, the joy of discovery, the assurance of judgment, the modesty of limited knowledge. It is the relentless serenity, the unhurried determination, the imperturbable drive of question following appositely on question in the genesis of truth.[32]

36

There is a pure desire to know that follows up questions with further questions, involving us in a self-correcting process of learning and leaving us unsatisfied until we know all that remains to be known about what engages us.

This pure desire to know is *disinterested*. Insights are pleasurable and we desire the satisfaction to be had in acts of understanding, understanding fully, and understanding correctly. However, mistaken understanding is equally pleasurable if we fail to recognize it as such, and yet the pure desire despises it. The disinterested desire to know is not desire for satisfaction, but for the correctness of the content. It will not settle for mistakes or half-truths but "heads beyond one's own joy in one's own insight to the further question [of] whether one's own insight is correct."[33]

It is also *detached*: it will not countenance the inhibitions of cognitional process that arise from other human desires and drives, nor the twisting of processes in favor of one or other outcome particularly sought,[34] "the attached and interested desires of man's sensitivity and intersubjectivity."[35] When the flow of our dynamic conscious intentionality is impeded by conscious or unconscious blocking of the questions that would generate unwanted answers, our judgements and decisions based on them are biased and unreliable. Lonergan gives a precise meaning in *Insight* for the term *bias*, which is best summarized as an aberration of human understanding that excludes and represses insights, along with the further relevant questions they would have engendered. Bias can be operative in us as individuals and in the social groups to which we belong.

As individuals, we may be affected by a preconscious aberrant censorship, blind spots, repression, and inhibitions arising from the psychological depths and commonly marked by sexual overtones.[36] The bias of unconscious motivation distorts the dramatic, active pattern of our living. We may not appreciate, without professional help, the extent to which we are avoiding the light in order to avoid pain, though even in these cases of dramatic or neurotic bias, we are left suspicious and disquieted.

In individual bias, elementary passions such as fear or desire can block the insights that would give us a rounded and balanced view of our situation, and thus skew our understanding of both personal and group matters. Egoistically, we can seek our own advantage and deny the inner dynamism that urges us to extend to others in responsible benevolence the satisfying solution we have come to for ourselves. Further questions that might lead to unwanted insights are ignored or repressed, and the development of our practical intelligence is hindered. However, we do not thus disregard our inner, God-seeking truth without damage to our inner integrity, damage of which we cannot but be aware. Our disjointed consciousness becomes bad conscience:

> The egoist's uneasy conscience is his awareness of his sin against the light. Operative within him, there is the *eros* of the mind, the desire and the drive to understand; he knows its value, for he gives it free rein where his own interests are concerned; yet he also repudiates its mastery, for he will not grant serious consideration to its further relevant questions.[37]

Egoistic or individual bias, as refusal to understand and hence to choose the world of value because of a prior choice for self-interest and personal satisfaction, leads to an isolation of oneself from others, a hindrance to achievement of the openness to which human beings are called.

Group bias is equally a refusal of the further questions that might lead to unwanted insights, but in this case, it is supported by others, at least those of our own group, and it leads us to choose the group's interest when it conflicts with the good of society. "The group is prone to have a blind spot for the insights which reveal its well-being to be excessive or its usefulness at an end."[38] Groups, just as truly as individuals, are open to knowing what really is the case, and open to change for the better. They achieve this only when they follow the transcendental precepts, defined by Lonergan at this stage as the following: Be attentive. Be intelligent. Be reasonable. Be responsible. This is the inbuilt method of human consciousness that needs to be given free rein in each member of each group. When a few members or even one individual holds out against the truth to which the majority has assented, there cannot be full collaboration or the best outcomes in achieving concrete instances of the human good. Progress in society, the general good, requires that groups work together, attentively, intelligently, reasonably, and responsibly. Groups that work against one another to keep from themselves and from everyone else whatever might call into question their own status, are contributing to social decline, and the results are all too obvious in group egoisms of wealth, race, or ethnic origin. Our culture is "marred and distorted by sin."[39]

The irrational bias that arises from individual and group egoism restricts the whole domain of truth and value to the confines of our need for self-gratification and self-promotion. Truth is sacrificed to rationalization. This bias opens a gap between the essential freedom of human persons and the effective freedom that they exercise.[40] Though human beings can make choices, their choice can be constrained by factors such as narrow group-think or fear suppressing questions leading to insight:

> Effective freedom itself has to be won. The key point is to reach a willingness to persuade oneself and to submit to the persuasion of others. For then one can be persuaded to a universal willingness; so one becomes antecedently willing to learn all there is to be learnt about... the enlargement of one's freedom from external constraints and psychoneural interferences.[41]

Concrete situations resulting from human sin, "infected with the social surd," seem to provide evidence in their apparent intractability "that only in an increasingly limited fashion can intelligence and reasonableness and good will have any real bearing on the conduct of human affairs."[42] Individuals rationalize, societies create ideologies, and the whole process of decline becomes entrenched.

At the root of all these forms of bias,[43] there is a tendency to choose the immediacy of the tangibly satisfying over what is the truly valuable. In lieu of the slow acquiring of understanding and willingness to live rightly, and then the adaptation that makes right living habitual, there is self-surrender to the human plight,[44] choosing the easy way out when avoiding sin by adequate reflection becomes burdensome. This is a shortsighted[45] gratification of our desire to avoid pain or to achieve pleasure, power, or dramatic effect[46] on others.

Disoriented self-seeking runs counter to our true self-interest, the finality of our being, that love that is in us drawing us to absolute goodness and the knowledge of all truth, and it cannot but leave us with the taste of ashes in our mouth—at least initially. It is unfortunately true that persistent denial of the call to transcend self-will ultimately leads to a dulling of this disquiet. Then it will perhaps take the shattering of our "peace at any price" by some crisis, to allow the underlying longing for the true and the good to resurface and be again welcomed as our guide to a fully human way of living. In subsequent writings, Lonergan treats of the redemptive action of grace in this experience of shattering.[47] Bias affects the free operation of transcendental consciousness by determining not only which questions will be allowed to surface but what we are inclined to notice, how we will reach conclusions, and where we will seek support within a narrowed horizon.

To give free rein to the pure, detached, disinterested desire to know is to admit all its questions for intelligence and reflection because the pure, detached, disinterested desire to know is *unrestricted*. Human capacity to understand is not unrestricted, but the desire is prior to understanding and simply as desire it is orientation to the totality of being. We want to understand completely, to know everything about everything. When one question is answered, the answer may well give rise to a whole new set of questions. Not all questions are equally significant, and just as the pure desire is the intelligent and rational basis from which we can discern between correct and incorrect answers, so it helps distinguish between valid and mistaken questions.[48] None are to be rejected unintelligently, uncritically. However, the existence of this unrestricted desire as the wellspring of our questioning is beyond doubt. "Neither centuries of inquiry nor enormous libraries of answers have revealed any tendency for the stream of further questions to diminish."[49]

The pure desire to know is unrestricted in that it reaches out insistently even to the mystery of God to which our human capacity for understanding is not proportionate in and of itself.[50] The pure desire moves us to question, heads us toward an objective that becomes known only through its own unfolding in understanding and judgment. The dynamism of consciousness is directed toward all that can be known, but "man's unrestricted desire to know is mated to a limited capacity to attain knowledge."[51] There is a clear possibility of the human community eventually coming to understand the workings of the natural universe, and to this end, we are told but have no way of confirming, there are more scientists doing research now than the total number who have ever done so in history. This is horizontal finality within the universe of proportionate knowledge, human intelligence directed to its natural goals.

However, we are also capable of asking questions that transcend this universe and can conceive of possibilities beyond it. The questions arise and we seem to be instinctively aware of vertical finality. We are oriented by unquenchable desire for more, for a destiny properly speaking supernatural and meaning that fully satisfies. "Being" is whatever can be grasped intelligently and affirmed reasonably, and the possibility of transcendent knowledge is the possibility of grasping intelligently and affirming reasonably the existence of a transcendent being, being itself.[52] It is toward this that the pure desire is drawing us. The proof of the possibility, Lonergan claims,[53] is the fact that such intelligent grasp and reasonable affirmation do happen and to a remarkable degree, we suggest, throughout human history and the great majority of cultures. As the notion of being, the pure desire is all-pervasive and underpins and penetrates all cognitional contents, constituting them as such:

> Self-affirmation is the affirmation of the knower, conscious empirically, intelligently, rationally. The pure desire to know is a constituent element both of the affirming and of the self that is affirmed. But the pure desire to know is the notion of being as it is spontaneously operative in cognitional process, and being itself is the to-be-known towards which the process heads.[54]

Desire will lead us toward the totality to be known through all correct answers, and, as the moving viewpoint brings us toward the end of *Insight*'s pedagogical presentation, we recognize that such a totality would utterly transcend human achievement. It can be encompassed only by an unrestricted act of understanding. Our desire is drawing us toward Being Itself, the mysterious source of all that is, God as "the transcendent idea of being and the transcendent reality of being."[55]

In *Insight*, Lonergan further clarifies what he means by vertical finality: initially he shows that in this concrete universe, "besides the tendencies and desires confined to any given level, there are the tendencies and desires that go beyond any given level; they are the reality of finality conceived as an upwardly but indeterminately directed dynamism."[56] Subsequently, the moving viewpoint goes beyond this position in the final chapter of *Insight* to see how "every tendency and force, every movement and change, every desire and striving is designed to bring about the order of the universe in the manner in which they contribute to it" and that order to the perfection and excellence that is its primary source and ground.[57]

At this stage, Lonergan sees the pure desire to know as the chief operator in all human development, but he makes it clear that it does not operate consistently in all human endeavors. At any stage of our development, each of us is an individual existing unity, differentiated by physical, chemical, organic, psychic, and intellectual conjugates.[58] Development that is initiated at one level by the dynamism of finality operative at that level needs to be integrated at others; there is tension between the development achieved and the scheme of recurrence that threatens again to disrupt the inertia. It is difficult enough for us, even in knowing, to be dominated simply by the detached and disinterested desire. It is far more difficult to permit that detachment and disinterestedness to dominate our whole lives in a fully moral, fully relational personal integrity.

Lonergan is aware of the further desires that may appear to impede the functioning of the pure, detached, disinterested, and unrestricted desire to know. His remedy, at least in part, is self-appropriation:

> The point here, as elsewhere, is appropriation: the point is to discover, to identify, to become familiar with the activities of one's own intelligence; the point is to become able to discriminate with ease and from personal conviction between one's purely intellectual activities and the manifold of other, 'existential' concerns that invade and mix and blend with the operations of intellect to render it ambivalent and its pronunciations ambiguous.[59]

Our deepest, God-given desire, proportionate to us as human beings, is for truth and the rational good. Therefore, normative objectivity is opposed to the false subjectivity of wishful thinking, of rash or excessively cautious judgments, of allowing joy or sadness, hope or fear, love or detestation, to interfere with the proper march of cognitional process.[60] *Insight* aims to show that

> [theology]…is relevant to the scientist as a scientist inasmuch as the untrammeled unfolding of his detached, disinterested and unrestricted desire to understand his own field correctly is open to a variety of interferences that ultimately can be surmounted only by accepting the ultimate implications of the unrestricted desire.[61]

If one turns from outward behavior to inner experience, Lonergan maintains, one finds that consciousness shifts into quite different patterns as one engages in different types of activity: absorption in intellectual issues tends to eliminate sensitive emotions and conations, and inversely, mystical absorption tends to eliminate the flow of sensitive presentations and imaginative representations.[62] But persons of common sense must also learn to discriminate: the core of habitual practical understanding, built up and adjusted by further learning in new situations, is not adequate to all domains, and

> above all they know that they must master their own hearts, that the pull of desire, the push of fear, the deeper currents of passion are poor counselors, for they rob a man of that full, untroubled, unhurried view demanded by sure and balanced judgment.[63]

The range of our desire to know is inclusive, encompassing the whole universe of being to which our minds are proportionate, its practical possibilities as well as its facts. The self-conscious subject is not only a knower, but also a doer, and one for whom there is a dynamic exigence for self-consistency in knowing and doing:[64] "the penetrating, honest, complete consistency that alone meets the requirements of the detached, disinterested, unrestricted desire to know."[65] That desire reaches beyond our knowing to seek intelligent transformations of the environment in which we live and our own spontaneous ways of living: for it invites us to guide our actions by referring them, not as an animal to a habitat, but as intelligent beings "to the intelligible context of some universal order that is or is to be."[66]

DESIRE IN AN *EVOLUTIONARY* PERSPECTIVE

In *Insight*, Lonergan demonstrates his understanding of this order of the universe as an intelligible one, but not because all natural processes invariably follow classical laws—more often events and developments occur in keeping with statistical laws of probability, and continue according to probabilities of survival.[67] The heuristic anticipations of classical and statistical procedures are complementary, for they involve both systematically and non-systematically related data—witness the often-heard proviso, "other things being equal." Classical laws, Lonergan notes, tell what would happen if conditions were fulfilled; statistical laws tell how often conditions are fulfilled. He appeals to our experience of schemes of recurrence operating in the world[68] and sees that it is possible to attribute a probability to the emergence and to the survival of a scheme of recurrence. Scientists may well operate in this way to account for the frequency and variety of marsupial species[69] surviving on the Australian continent. A universe in which both classical and statistical laws are verified will be characterized by a process of emergent probability:

> Emergent probability is the successive realization of the possibilities of concrete situations in accord with their probabilities…concrete extensions and concrete durations are the field or matter or potency in which emergent probability is the immanent form or intelligibility.[70]

Thus, Lonergan espouses an evolutionary process of development as part of a world order. Because it is the actual world order, originating from God conceived as infinite act of understanding and total goodness, it is also inherently good and immanently intelligible in itself, though not effortlessly so for us, as generations of scientists, researchers, and philosophers will attest. This conviction grounds an acceptance of slow progress. It calls out compassion and patience with human failures in attentiveness, adequate understanding, and consistently reasonable decision-making, in ourselves and in others, because we believe that God is patient and omniscient in these matters too and that God has a solution for the problem of evil. This solution Lonergan demonstrates to be a rationally suitable one,[71] both wise and good, and though it requires the eyes of faith to discern its actuality, he leaves until later works its theological elaboration. At this stage the moving viewpoint is clear: our desire for total truth and goodness is within and for the universe as it is:

> Again, the order of the universe is its intelligibility to be grasped by following the appropriate classical or statistical or genetic or dialectical method.[72] Hence, to will the order of the universe is not to will the clockwork perfection of mechanistic thought but the emergent probability of the universe that exists. It is not to demand that all things be perfect in their inception but to expect and will that they grow and develop. It is not to exclude from man's world the social surd,[73] nor to ignore it (for it is a fact), nor to mistake it for an intelligibility and so systematize and perpetuate it, but to acknowledge it as a problem and to embrace its solution.[74]

Human progress and development is also subject to emergent probability, though not in the same way as chemical, physical, and biological realities are. God's solution for the problem of evil involves admitting the reality of this problem—an appropriation task—and accepting the grace that works with human and divine love to promote the better functioning of our human consciousness in accord with the pure desire.

> Still, if human affairs fall under the dominion of emergent probability, they do so in their own way.…There are human schemes that emerge and function automatically once there occurs an appropriate conjunction of abstract laws and concrete circumstances. But as human intelligence develops, there is a significant change of roles. Less and less importance attaches to the probabilities

of appropriate constellations of circumstances. More and more importance attaches to the probabilities of the occurrence of insight, communication, persuasion, agreement, decision. Man does not have to wait for his environment to make him.[75]

Human beings are essentially free[76] and they are self-constituting, but "the difference between essential and effective freedom is the difference between a dynamic structure and its operational range."[77] Existential human freedom—its extent and limitations—are further explored in Lonergan's later writings and will be examined in the following chapter.

In *Insight*, Lonergan invites us to recognize and affirm in our own conscious experience the pure, detached, disinterested, and unrestricted desire to know. It not only desires, he tells us, it desires intelligently and reasonably; it desires to understand because it is intelligent, and it desires to grasp the understood as unconditioned because it desires to be reasonable. As humans, we are conscious empirically, intelligently, rationally, and the pure desire to know is a constituent element both of our affirming and of the self that is affirmed.

In conclusion, the desire to know, which is central to Lonergan's life and study, is shown to be integral to the authentic functioning of human consciousness, the empirical method in which the action of the Spirit moves in accord with the dynamism of our questioning to enable human flourishing, both for individuals and the groups they form. This *eros* of the human spirit, our God-given desire to understand, to reflect further, and assent to truth in the measure that it is attained, Lonergan demonstrates is essentially pure, detached, disinterested, and unrestricted.

This does not mean that its optimal functioning will be the case in every person, every social group, at all times. When the flow of our dynamic conscious intentionality is impeded by conscious or unconscious blocking of the questions that would generate unwanted answers, our judgments and decisions based on them are biased and unreliable. However, in the pedagogical presentation of *Insight*, we are offered a way to understand and affirm our own knowing and appropriate at this level the desire we are, step by step according to the moving viewpoint favored by Lonergan the teacher.

For a person of faith, to grasp the intelligibility of the universe is to see in it an evolutionary order willed by the Creator, where natural processes, events, and developments occur in keeping not only with classical laws but more frequently with statistical laws of probability and survival. This conviction grounds an acceptance of slow progress: our desire for total truth and goodness is within and for the universe as it is and for each human person as they are—as elements within emergent probability. This enables us to touch into the patience and benevolent purposes of God.

To know ourselves as a knower is not an easy task. But learning to recognize and affirm in our own conscious experience the outworking of the desire to know is perhaps the first and best way to learn how to appropriate desire, and come to learn how all other yearnings and attractions fit within the broader vertical finality of our orientation into Divine Mystery—though it is not the only way, as we will consider in subsequent chapters.

As Lonergan turned to the completion of his self-chosen task, which, as we have seen, was to develop a method for theology, his self-appropriation was to take him more deeply into the existential level where our decisions and choices make us who we are to become, and where he identifies love and Love itself as the most significant end of all our desiring. In the following chapter, we will turn to this realization and to the period between the publication of *Insight* and that of *Method in Theology*.

3

THE APPROPRIATION
OF DESIRE

Beyond the all-embracing desire to know things by their essence, but continuous with it, we are moved to desire by the attraction of the good and the beautiful and, above all, by love. We turn now to the loving desire impelling us to self-transcendence, desire moving in the operations of evaluation, choice, and decision-making and revealed in feelings and values.

In this chapter, the focus moves to the fourth level of conscious intentionality and, as our viewpoint shifts, we note Lonergan's growing interest in the existential concerns of human living and development. *Method in Theology* is taking shape in his mind.[1] We will examine the concept of the authentic subject, progressively constituting her- or himself by existential choices, and in effect establishing the worldview or horizon within which freedom will be exercised. Our God-given conscious intentionality interacts with the human formation available to us in our efforts to live authentically as responsible, moral beings. Most significant is the life-changing discovery of God's love poured out in our hearts by the Holy Spirit. God's love can so establish itself at the fourth and highest level of our conscious intentionality that it gradually frees us to follow our desire for goodness and the fullness of love—and to make it our own in some way appropriate to the nature of this wondrous, ongoing gift.

THE DESIRING SUBJECT

Lonergan continues to write of the desire to know things by their essence in articles of the immediate post-*Insight* period: the desire that can be known, for "the pure, detached, disinterested and unrestricted desire to know, when it is functioning, is no less immediate than the levels of consciousness when they are functioning."[2]

However, in 1964, when he offered a clear and succinct overview of his cognitional structure in response to some daunted by the demands of *Insight*, there are clear signs that he was deepening his attention to the interpersonal, the existential, the world of values. Knowing reality is subsumed by choosing the good:

> Though being and the good are coextensive, the subject moves to a further dimension of consciousness as his concern shifts from knowing being to realizing the good.[3]

In the context of *Insight*, the subject was "any object, say A, where it is true that A affirms himself as a knower,"[4] as one conscious empirically, intelligently, and rationally. Ten years later, in the Aquinas Lecture titled "The Subject," he is still asking for self-appropriation as a knower: the study of the subject is "the study of oneself inasmuch as one is conscious."[5] He invites close attention to the data of one's own consciousness, to discern the different levels of consciousness: from the dreaming to the waking subject, to oneself as intelligently inquiring subject, rationally reflecting subject, and now particularly as responsibly deliberating subject. For the subject is a knower, but also a doer, "one that deliberates, evaluates, chooses, acts."[6] According to the measure of his or her freedom and responsibility in the choices made and acts performed, the subject develops personality or fails to, builds or destroys character, constituting him- or herself as the person she or he is to be. "Then the existential subject exists and his character, his personal essence is at stake."[7] This is human consciousness at its fullest, the existential subject, the human person as self-completing.

To read correctly the metaphor of *levels* of consciousness, where Lonergan has the existential subject standing, as it were, on the top level, it is helpful to look at these levels as our becoming subjects by degrees, as successive instances of sublation and as "the unfolding of a single transcendental intending of plural, interchangeable objectives, (approximately the Scholastic transcendentals, *ens, unum, verum, bonum*)."[8]

First, we are, as it were, subjects by degrees. Comatose or in deep, dreamless sleep, the human being is only potentially a subject. "Next, we have a minimal degree of consciousness and subjectivity when we are the helpless subjects of our dreams."[9] Awake, even if only just, we are already *experiential subjects*, operating on the empirical level, aware of dawn light or darkness, warmth or chill, perhaps even the smell of coffee. Lucid perceptions and imaginative anticipations of the day's activities may rouse in us feelings of delight or dread.

Second, the levels of consciousness are to be understood as successive instances of sublation. Lonergan chooses to use Karl Rahner's understanding of this category rather than Hegel's:

> What sublates goes beyond what is sublated, introduces something new and distinct, puts everything on a new basis, yet so far from interfering with the sublated or destroying it, on the contrary needs it, includes it, preserves all its proper features and properties, and carries them forward to a fuller realization within a richer context.[10]

The *intelligent subject*, operating on the intellectual level, sublates the experiential; that is, it retains, preserves, completes, and goes beyond the experiential when we ask questions about our experience. We investigate, for example, who is making the coffee and how much of it, grow in understanding, interrogate those spontaneous feelings, and express the insights and answers we come to. As *rational subjects*, we go beyond the experiential and the intelligent, sublating their contributions as we "question our own understanding, check our formulations and expressions, ask whether we have got things right, marshal the evidence *pro* and *con*, judge this to be so and that not to be so."[11] The yes or no reached, rational consciousness, is, in turn, sublated in the *existential* or *responsible subject*, when we deliberate and evaluate our options, reaching a decision about action based on what we have determined to be true and worthwhile, and carrying it out (or failing to do so). The levels of consciousness are thus distinct but related.

> Human intelligence goes beyond human sensitivity, yet it cannot get along without sensitivity. Human judgment goes beyond sensitivity and intelligence yet cannot function except in conjunction with them. Human action finally, must in similar fashion both presuppose and complete human sensitivity, intelligence and judgment.[12]

On all four levels, we are operating in a conscious and intentional manner, and so can be aware of ourselves operating as subjects. However, "as we mount from level to level, it is a fuller self of which we are aware and the awareness itself is different."[13] Just as we can appropriate ourselves as capable of intelligent and responsible activity in our world, so too can we own the desire that moves us to do good in the situations we attend to. Knowing ourselves at this level is not merely an interesting fact but a calling.

Third, as we have noted, we can look at the human subject as called by the innate pattern of human consciousness to be self-transcendent. Questioning the data of sense, asking what, why, how, and what for, we are moved by the desire to understand— "we intend the idea or form, the intelligible unity or relatedness that organizes data into intelligible wholes."[14] We transcend ourselves as merely experiential by this inquiry, by seeking insight, accumulating insights, intending intelligibility. Self-transcendence is at work when we are reflective and critical in the face of even our brightest insights, questioning whether the understanding we have reached is reality, and so transcend ourselves as intelligent in intending truth.

Responsibility goes beyond fact and desire and possibility to discern what is truly worthwhile (and not just apparently so) and thus we transcend ourselves as rational by intending the good:

In the measure that one's living, one's aims, one's achievements are a response to values, in that measure self-transcendence is effected in the field of action. One has got beyond mere selfishness. One has become a principle of benevolence and beneficence. One has become capable of genuine collaboration and true love.[15]

Human authenticity results from following the built-in law of the human spirit. Being totally open to all questioning is our capacity for self-transcendence, and this self-transcendence achieved is the sign of authentic subjectivity; but now Lonergan is recognizing, more explicitly than he did in *Insight*, "the relations between the dynamic structure of objective knowing and the larger dynamic structure that is human living."[16] In each case, the dynamism is desire, but here love is key.

Human authenticity is never a once-and-for-all achievement. Lonergan constantly reminds us that it is "always precarious, always a withdrawal from unauthenticity, always in danger of slipping back into unauthenticity."[17] Human beings manage to transcend themselves with any consistency only when they fall in love. Many are astonished to find themselves more generous in their judgments and responses, less self-centered, and more alive than they can ever remember being before, when all their thoughts and feelings are moved to respond to the "love object," the beloved person they have miraculously encountered—or given birth to. The true well-being of the other is sought, and one's best is spontaneously on offer. "Then their being becomes being-in-love."[18] Being-in-love is the proper fulfillment of the human capacity for self-transcendence.

Lonergan noted in a later commentary on *Insight* that the high aspirations but poor performance of human beings made the realization of the authenticity to which they are called problematic, and saw the answer in God's redemptive action:

In my rather theological analysis of human history, my first approximation was the assumption that men always do what is intelligent and reasonable, and its implication was an ever-increasing progress. The second approximation was the radical inverse insight that men can be biased, and so unintelligent and unreasonable in their choices and decisions. The third approximation was the redemptive process resulting from God's gift of his grace to individuals and from the manifestation of his love in Christ Jesus.[19]

He explains this encounter with grace, specifically religious experience, in terms of the human being as called to authentic self-transcendence by the dynamic operations of consciousness and as intrinsic openness to God seeking to be in communion with humankind. This outline is given succinctly in a brief paper called "Openness and Religious Experience"[20] that Lonergan wrote for a congress of philosophers in 1960.

OPENNESS AS FACT, ACHIEVEMENT, AND GIFT

We can consider the openness that is an intrinsic component in the makeup of human beings as *fact, achievement, and gift*. Lonergan is concerned to show that the openness of human intentional consciousness is openness to everything, up to and including the yet unknown divine, and that God's action in human lives addresses this openness. The essential impulse of the inquiring, searching human being that moves us to wonder and question, and leaves us dissatisfied until we truly know, and then act accordingly, is the first dimension of openness. It has been shown to be the way we are made. Lonergan calls it *openness as fact*: recall, in the previous chapter, the invitation to confirm as fact the openness that constitutes us as human.

As fact, openness is the inner self, the self as ground of all aspiration. Obviously, however, "as fact it does not consistently and completely dominate human consciousness."[21] When we have adverted to this call in our being, acknowledged and accepted it, its implications for all our thinking and acting have still to be worked out and successfully applied to actual thinking and actual acting. Lonergan spells out the call to live the self-transcendence of authenticity:

> To be authentically human is to follow the built-in law of the human spirit. Because we can experience, we should

attend. Because we can understand, we should inquire. Because we can reach the truth, we should reflect and check. Because we can realize values in ourselves and others, we should deliberate. In the measure that we follow these precepts, in the measure that we fulfill these conditions of being human persons, we also *achieve* self-transcendence both in the field of knowledge and in the field of action.[22]

Openness as achievement is reached only when we follow the pure desire that moves in our conscious intentionality, and to be an authentic human subject is to be intelligently aware, rationally aware, responsibly and morally aware, and self-transcending with some consistency. However, human authenticity is never a once-and-for-all achievement. Lonergan constantly reminds us that it is "always precarious, always a withdrawal from unauthenticity, always in danger of slipping back into unauthenticity."[23] Furthermore, as well as authenticity, there can be unauthenticity. "Do you realize," asks Fred Lawrence, "that people's inability *consistently* to be intelligent, reasonable and responsible in history is what is meant by sin?"[24] The actual orientation of consciousness does not always coincide with the exigencies of the pure, detached, disinterested, unrestricted desire to know. The primordial fact of openness and orientation to the divine "is no more than a principle of possible achievement, a definition of the ultimate horizon that is to be reached only through successive enlargements of the actual horizon."[25] Lonergan remarks wryly that such successive enlargements only too clearly lie under some law of diminishing returns.[26]

The human being is essentially a creature of time; at birth, our higher powers are "the spiritual counterpart of *materia prima*, and their indeterminate potentiality points at once in all directions."[27] As children, we need to be "persuaded, cajoled, ordered, compelled to do what is right,"[28] and our first, undeveloped moral sense emerges only between the ages of three and seven. We begin as a self that is the center of the universe and only gradually do we come to perceive another self that we could, and know we should, become.[29] When we are said "to reach the age of reason" at about seven, the reason we attain is still far from maturity. There is an intellectual lag; we are physically developed beyond our intellectual development, so that in the turmoil of puberty, our desire to do, decide, and discover more and more for ourselves quickly outruns our ability for reasonable judgment and thus responsible deciding. This fact is responsible for a good measure of the tragic quality of human existence, for, as Lonergan puts it in *Insight*,

> Man develops biologically to develop psychically, and he develops psychically to develop intellectually and rationally. The higher integrations suffer the disadvantage of emerging later. They are the demands of finality upon us before they are realities in us. They are manifested more commonly in aspiration and in dissatisfaction with oneself than in the rounded achievement of complete genuineness, perfect openness, universal willingness.[30]

In this period, well before the existential moment of moral conversion, when we discover that we are self-constituting, that it is up to us to choose who and what we will become as a person, our youthful judgments and choices are already beginning to shape us. "Indiscretions on Facebook will impact on your future," people are telling children today, but other early experiments in the dramatic pattern of experience can have more serious consequences. For as well as functioning biologically, aesthetically, and intellectually, "one man in his life plays many parts,"[31] and the way in which we take our place on the various stages as well as in the stages of our life has to do with this pattern of experience. In the direction of our life stories, there is a dramatic component:

> Not only, then, is man capable of aesthetic liberation and artistic creation, but his first work of art is his own living. The fair, the beautiful, the admirable is embodied by man in his own body and actions before it is given a still freer realization in painting and sculpture, in music and poetry. Style is the man before it appears in the artistic product.[32]

We live in the presence of others, and the desire to dignify our living and present ourselves well is innate. It is thus a concern to win approval for good performance, to avoid ridicule, embarrassment, and shame. Early experiences and interactions have influence, and so does the powerful peer group in childhood and adolescence; the results are a pattern that "penetrates below the surface of consciousness to exercise its own domination and control, and to effect, prior to conscious discrimination, its own selections and arrangements."[33] We may well ask ourselves, "Why on earth did I do/say that?"

With time, our knowledge of human reality does increase, educative processes and human relationships strengthen and refine our responses to human values, and mentors increasingly step back, leaving us to ourselves "so that our freedom may exercise its ever-advancing thrust towards authenticity."[34] We experience an inner need to be true to our deepest selves and to achieve integrity. Though this drives us to understand based on the data, judge from the evidence, and then choose, decide, and act in accordance with what we have determined to be the right and reasonable course of conduct, sometimes a given way of acting is so far outside the mindset of our culture or environment, our personal tastes and experience, as to be beyond the range of our "antecedent willingness,"[35] and we are simply not ready for it. As the human person grows, "one has to live and make decisions in the light of one's undeveloped intelligence and under the guidance of one's incomplete willingness."[36] Thus, we find that our attention too often remains on illicit proposals:

> The incompleteness of their intelligibility and the incoherence of their apparent reasonableness are disregarded; and in this contraction of consciousness, which is the basic sin, there occurs wrong action, which is more conspicuous but really derivative.[37]

In fact, "since the good is ever unique and evil manifold, the odds always are that man will do what is wrong."[38] Furthermore, "the law of psychological continuity" means that we are inclined to act as we have acted before. An act of sinning begets a spontaneous inclination to do so again, and this can harden over time into an entrenched orientation to evil, a bad habit or a "contraction of consciousness" that we may be able to resist, with great effort, but which statistically we probably will not—if left to ourselves!

Openness as achievement would appear to be beyond us, whatever we may say about our desire for total goodness and total love. How, then, are we to understand "the redemptive process resulting from God's gift of his grace to individuals"?

Lonergan writes in "Openness and Religious Experience" that openness as achievement rises from openness as fact but that it conditions, and is conditioned by, openness as gift. He distinguishes a third facet of human openness, *openness as gift*:

> Openness as fact is the pure desire to know....[Openness as] achievement itself arises when the actual orientation of consciousness coincides with the exigencies of the pure, detached, disinterested, unrestricted desire to know....But there is also openness as gift, as an effect of divine grace. Man's natural openness is complete. The pure desire is unrestricted.[39]

Openness as gift, he says simply, is the self-entering into personal relationship with God. It is an effect of grace. If we are to grasp this mystery, we need to see in grace both continuity and a radical discontinuity. On the one hand, grace comes to heal and perfect our wounded humanity, completing and actualizing our capacity for self-transcendence, open as it is by nature to an infinite intelligibility, all truth, absolute goodness. On the other hand, "it is not the gift of something created, but the self-bestowal of God himself."[40] It introduces into our story a new relationship with the Holy, the mystery of love and awe,[41] which fascinates and possesses us, in which we know ourselves as accepted and loved.

There is a way of coming to understand something about religious experience, and therefore grace, Lonergan suggests, by looking at the experience of human love and friendship. This is where continuity is most apparent and where often God comes to find us. Our redeeming God is the same Infinite Act of Understanding Love[42] that set the universe on its evolutionary path and created in us the pure desire to know and to love. God has so ordained human existence that we are transformed through our experience of being-in-love into a dynamic state in which self-transcending feelings prevail and orient us to the good of the beloved other:

There also is development from above downwards. There is the transformation of falling in love: the domestic love of the family; the human love of one's tribe, one's city, one's country, mankind; the divine love that orientates man in his cosmos and expresses itself in his worship.[43]

Far from love making us blind, Lonergan writes, "Where hatred sees only evil, love reveals values. At once it commands commitment and joyfully carries it out, no matter what the sacrifice involved."[44] It has the power to dissolve bias, of whatever kind. "Where hatred plods around in ever narrower vicious circles, love breaks the bonds of psychological and social determinisms."[45] Charles Hefling writes of the love that Dante encountered, the sort of love that goes beyond the gratification of a need:

> …a love that transforms, releases new energy, frees those who experience it by pulling them out of their self-enclosed desires and fears and launches them in a new direction….Beatrice was the occasion of Dante's love, and therefore the *Comedy* portrays her as the guide and the way to abundant life. Yet in the poem as in the experience that inspired it, she is incidental….Dante was truly in love *with* Beatrice, but he was even more truly in love *through* Beatrice.[46]

When our being becomes being-in-love, this becomes the foundation and first principle of our living, and all our desires and fears, our joys and sorrows, our discernment of values, our decisions and deeds are under its sway. While it lasts, the isolation of the individual is broken and we function spontaneously not just for ourselves but for others as well. The enlargement of our horizon that occurs when we are in love *with* our Beatrice is the gateway to a new and more loving and lovable way of being in the world, so we are also in love *through* her: our being has become being-in-love. This is not to say that no setbacks or lack of generosity, no muddled thinking or failure of willingness will ever occur, for Lonergan makes it clear that human self-transcendence is always dialectical, that is it must always contend with its opposite. Even where affective self-transcendence is enabling an individual to grow in responsibility and generosity, there remains "tension between the self as transcending and the self as transcended."[47] But human love is an initial and significant shift in the probabilities.

The concept of being-in-love with God is a key contribution of *Method in Theology*, and is examined more fully in the next chapter. Here we note that the gift of grace comes to heal and perfect the loving desire for God, for goodness and for human authenticity, implanted in our humanness and experienced in all our loving, and focuses it in the operations of consciousness. Its fulfillment is in the beatific vision of God:

> There is also an ultimate enlargement, beyond the resources of every finite consciousness, where there enters into clear view God as unknown, when the subject knows God face to face, knows as he is known. This ultimate enlargement alone approximates to the possibility of openness defined by the pure desire; as well, it is an openness as gift, as an effect of grace and indeed, of grace not as merely *sanans* but as *elevans*, as *lumen gloriae*.[48]

Lonergan takes this recognition further in "*Existenz* and *Aggiornamento*" (1965), where he sees implicit in all human choice of values the absolute good that is God,[49] and invites the reader to a faith-based *Besinnung*, a becoming aware of ourselves as part of a community in Christ oriented to the Father:

> In Christ Jesus we are not only referred to God, as to some omega point, but we are on our way to God. The fount of our living is not *erôs* but *agapê*, not desire of an end that uses means but love of an end that overflows. As God did not create the world to obtain something for himself but rather overflowed from love of the infinite to loving even the finite…as Christ in his humanity did not will means to reach an end, but possessed the end, the vision of God, and overflowed in love to loving us, so too those in Christ participate in the charity of Christ: they love God *super omnia* and so can love their neighbours as themselves.[50]

Operative in us by grace there is a dynamism that Lonergan refers to here for the first time as "being in love with God." We may be in love with God without being aware of it, which Lonergan calls the being in Christ of substance rather than of subject. This was perhaps the case at the time of his early response to vocation, where he moved rather bleakly toward the life of total dedication to which he sensed he was being drawn. However, this love can also surface in awareness, be adverted to, understood, and known, which is the being in Christ of subject:

> Inasmuch as being in Christ is the being of subject, the hand of the Lord ceases to be hidden. In ways you all have experienced, in ways some have experienced more frequently or more intensely than others, in ways you have still to experience, and in ways none of us in this life will ever experience, the substance in Christ Jesus becomes the subject in Christ Jesus. The love of God, being in love with God, can be as full and as dominant, as overwhelming and as lasting an experience as human love.[51]

Lonergan is to recognize the centrality of this "being in love" increasingly in his subsequent theological work and will later add "Be in love" to the transcendental imperatives he lists for the first time in this paper as the following: Be intelligent, Be reasonable, Be responsible.[52]

Being-in-love with God is religious conversion. Lonergan writes in "Theology in its New Context" (1968) of its effects in changing the horizon of individuals and orienting their relationships:

> Conversion occurs in the lives of individuals. It is not merely a change or even a development; rather, it is a radical transformation on which follows, on all levels of living, an interlocked series of changes and developments. What hitherto was unnoticed becomes vivid and present. What had been of no concern becomes a matter of high import. So great a change in one's apprehensions and one's values accompanies no less a change in

60

oneself, in one's relations to other persons, and in one's relations to God.[53]

When we fall in love, the love into which we fall is not some single act or series of acts, "but a dynamic state that prompts and molds all our thoughts and feelings, all our judgments and decisions."[54]

We are moved, by desire, to transcend ourselves in the dynamism of our intentionality, from experiencing through questioning and insight to understanding, from understanding through questions of reflection to verification, from correct judgment to right action. In "The Future of Christianity" (1969), Lonergan writes that God's gift of his love to us is the crowning point of our self-transcendence:

> St. Augustine wrote: "Thou hast made us for thyself, O Lord, and our hearts are restless till they rest in thee." But that resting in God is something, not that we achieve, but that we receive, accept, ratify. It comes quietly, secretly, unobtrusively. We know about it when we notice its fruits in our lives. It is the profoundest fulfilment of the human spirit. Because it is fulfilment, it gives us peace, the peace that the world cannot give. Because it is fulfilment, it gives us joy, a joy that can endure despite the sorrows of failure, humiliation, privation, pain, betrayal, desertion. Because it is fulfilment, its absence is revealed, now in the trivialization of human life in debauchery, now in the fanaticism with which limited goals are pursued violently and recklessly, now in the despair that condemns man and his world as absurd.[55]

He speaks of desire now as "our massive thrust to self-transcendence." We transcend ourselves by seeking the intelligible, the true, the real, the good, love. What fulfills that seeking, the God in whom we rest, must be the summit of intelligibility, truth, reality, goodness, and love.[56]

Where before knowledge preceded, founded, and justified loving, now falling-in-love and being-in-love culminate and complete the process of self-transcendence, which begins with knowledge but goes beyond it, as Blaise Pascal saw when he remarked that the heart has reasons which reason does not know.[57]

We have noted the predilection[58] of Lonergan, in the period before the writing of *Insight*, for the passage in St. Thomas that treats the desire of intellect for understanding of what God is. In the eighteen years between *Insight* and *Method in Theology* (1954–72), there is a significant shift from the appropriation of cognitional operations to existential questions of value on the fourth level of consciousness. These years are marked by a similar predilection: the passage in question is from St. Paul and speaks of the love of God that floods our hearts through the Holy Spirit who is given to us (see Rom 5:5).

In 1970, Lonergan shared with an in-house audience[59] the developed understanding of the way "the gift of God's love takes over the ground and root of the fourth and highest level of man's waking consciousness,"[60] which was to be foundational in *Method*. He distinguishes the being-in-love of human intimacy in the pair bond and family, and the love of one's fellows in society, and then refers to Romans 5:5 to speak of the love of God "with all your heart, and with all your soul, and with all your mind, and with all your strength" (Mark 12:30), which results from God's love flooding our hearts through the Holy Spirit given to us. Lonergan had described the pure desire to know as unrestricted. He chooses the same word to describe this powerful attraction that is at the same time an overflowing of benevolence: "Being in love with God, as experienced, is being in love in an unrestricted fashion. All love is self-surrender, but being in love with God is being in love without limits or qualifications or conditions or reservations."[61] This love establishes a new horizon, that of a complete self-transcendence grounded "in the divine lover whose love makes those he loves in love with him, and so with one another."[62] Those whose desire finds its spring in such immense love find that their hearts grow toward the concerns—and the dimensions—of God's own.

SELF-APPROPRIATION

It is possible to identify a threefold focus in the appropriation of desire discerned in Lonergan's practice and recommended in his published writings of this period between *Insight* and *Method*: first, self-knowledge mediated by introspection, here extended to include the fourth level of conscious intentionality; second, self-knowledge mediated by our interactions in the human community; and third, a self-knowledge mediated by prayer and religious experience.

Lonergan deepened his insight into existentialist and phenomenological philosophy during a period of theological teaching at the Gregorian in Rome, 1953–65.[63] Here, he sought to bring second- and third-year students to the "limited but most fruitful understanding of the mysteries through analogy with nature and the inner coherence of the mysteries among themselves," which is possible for human intelligence,[64] in courses on the Trinity and the incarnation. With doctoral students, he could pursue his interest in methodology,[65] and, in published articles of that period, we can see elements of his thought reaching clarity.

The operations of consciousness, which Lonergan taught us to discern in our knowing, include those of evaluation, deliberation, and choice; they are similarly available to observation. In the years following the publication of *Insight*, Lonergan explored further the idea of horizon: each person's horizon represents the current limits of their view, the interests and concerns, the scope of matters experienced and understood or deemed relevant for inquiry. "To each of us his own private world is very real indeed. Spontaneously, it lays claim to being the one real world, the standard, the criterion, the absolute, by which everything is judged, measured, evaluated." In *Insight*,[66] he was concerned that this private "real world" be open to the corrections to be made by true judgment so that it could be brought into conformity with the universe of being.[67] Through his work on *Insight*, Lonergan has achieved the "turn to the subject" at the cognitional level. Now he extends the horizons of self-appropriation to address more explicitly the affective, the existential fourth level of consciousness where the human subject is constituting him or herself.

63

If one deliberates and chooses, one has moved to the level of the rationally conscious, free responsible subject that by his choices makes himself what he is to be and his world what it is to be....There exist subjects that are empirically, intellectually, morally conscious. Not all know themselves as such, for consciousness is not human knowing but only a potential component in the structured whole that is human knowing. But all can know themselves as such, for they have only to attend to what they are already conscious of, and understand what they attend to, and pass judgment on the correctness of their understanding.[68]

This reduplication of the processes of knowing, which Lonergan is still referring to as introspection,[69] is not the only way of coming to self-knowledge, as we will see in this and the following chapter, but it remains a key one.

The drive of human desire moves us beyond the cognitional to seek true value, the good, without abandoning anything of the pure desire to know. Just as intelligence had been shown to sublate sense, and reasonableness sublates intelligence, "so deliberation sublates and thereby unifies knowing and feeling."[70] By self-appropriation, this desire can be known also in its operations at the fourth level, though Lonergan did not systematize the process in a comparable way.

By 1968, Lonergan pays more positive attention to the role of feelings in our conscious intentionality: "Such feeling gives our intentional consciousness its mass, momentum, drive, power. Without our feelings, our knowing and deciding would be paper thin."[71] He recognizes that it is by our feelings that "we are oriented massively and dynamically in a world mediated by meaning," and invites us to an Ignatian awareness that our feelings respond to values in accord with some scale of preference.[72] These feelings may be momentary or deep and lasting, but they are more than just revelatory of values: they "give us the power and momentum to rise above ourselves and accomplish what objectively is good." As we learn to know our feelings we can choose to follow the desire that we identify as the action of the Spirit in our hearts:

But there also are feelings so deep and strong, *especially when deliberately reinforced*, that they channel attention, shape one's horizon, direct one's life. Here the supreme illustration is loving. A man or woman that falls in love is engaged in loving not only when attending to the beloved but at all times. Besides particular acts of loving, there is a prior state of being in love, and that prior state is, as it were, the fount of all one's actions.[73]

This love is not the product of our own knowing and choosing, but it is not unconscious. Lonergan regards it as a conscious, dynamic state, "manifesting itself in the harvest of the Spirit: love, joy, peace, patience, kindness, generosity, faithfulness, gentleness, and self-control (see Gal. 5:22)."[74] Authentic human love has these effects in large measure, and we are aware of them in ourselves and others: divine love helps to make them habitual, anchors them in our living. Like Paul, we call them the fruits of the Spirit of Love.

The second dimension to be explored in the search for self-appropriation as a desirer is that of human community. The existential self is also known in reflection on choices made or actions taken and the response of others to our living:

To say what one knows presupposes the labor of coming to know. But to show what one is, it is enough to be it; showing will follow; every movement, every word, every deed reveal what the subject is. They reveal it to others, and the others, in the self-revelation that is their response, obliquely reveal to the intelligent subject what he is. In the main it is not by introspection but by reflecting on our living in common with others that we come to know ourselves.[75]

This is a further way of coming to appropriate our desiring selves, and some would say a safer and more reliable one, but its measure of success depends on the quality of interactions in the communities to which we belong and our receptivity to feedback. We can be confronted with ourselves more effectively by being confronted with others than by solitary introspection. As we are drawn to admire values incarnated in those we meet, we can recognize the power these values also have in ourselves. What the desire is that is effectively moving us may be a first revelation of the action of grace.

> It is one thing to be in love, and another to discover that what has happened to you is that you have fallen in love. Being oneself is prior to knowing oneself. St. Ignatius said that love shows itself more in deeds than in words; but being in love is neither deeds nor words; it is the prior conscious reality that words and, more securely, deeds reveal.[76]

Lonergan's own realization, in retrospect, of the depth of the love moving him as a young man to commit his life to the service of God, he had somewhat shyly communicated in the *Besinnungen* of this period to which we have referred earlier.[77] The meaning of his own response to vocation became clearer throughout his time in the Society of Jesus. In 1962, Lonergan is writing of self-appropriation, the aim of *Insight*, as a movement to the world of interiority.[78] Interiority is to be distinguished from the world of common sense (the world of community, of the visible world familiar to us) and the world of theory (of philosophy and science) in which our intelligence is concerned with an exact understanding of things as they are in themselves. Interiority is a third world, one that regards immediate internal experience:

> The questions raised by the existentialists are questions that regard interiority: Do you know what that means? Do you know what it means to have a mind of your own? Is that just a phrase? Do you know what it means to respect others? Or to be in love with them? Do you know what it is to suffer? Do you really know? Do you know what it is to pray? Do you know what it is to die? Do you know what it is to live in the presence of God? These are questions about interiority.[79]

These three worlds are distinct but related. Differentiations of consciousness enable us to move between them: in the world of theory, a scientist is absorbed in testing his hypothesis during working hours but still needs to be able to respond with common sense to the practical and relational needs of his family outside them; it is interiority that will enable him to distinguish these two worlds and make choices appropriately between them. Lonergan uses the word *mediation* to describe the interrelatedness of these worlds. "There is that much more meaning to one's speaking [in the world of common sense] in the measure that one's interiority has developed."[80] A familiarity with the things of the mind and heart gives depth to communication and makes a person more intuitively aware of what is really happening in interactions with others, more able to respond instead of just reacting.

Knowledge of God, Lonergan maintains, is never immediate in this life. It can be mediated by our knowledge of the created world; it is often mediated by the world of community in which a tradition of revelation is transmitted; it may be mediated by theory in a natural philosophy of religion; or it may be mediated by one's interiority:

> The outstanding example in that field is of course the life of the mystic, in which interiority develops and constitutes, as it were, a means through which God's presence ceases to be an unidentified undertow in one's living.[81]

Lonergan, in touch with his own interiority, is paying increasing attention to this undertow that is the action of God drawing human beings by a desire they often don't name, but could come to know. He had become aware, in himself, of a deep but obscure conviction that he could not get out of trying to be holy and knew that he had been nurturing this directedness in his life of prayer. In the immediacy of our experience of self, he writes in 1963,

> There are supernatural realities that do not pertain to our nature, that result from the communication to us of Christ's life....It is ours essentially by a gift. Still, in the concrete, it is part of our concrete reality, and in that sense it proceeds through the mediation of prayer from being a sort of vegetative living to a conscious living.[82]

This conscious living of the graced desire, which is our sharing in trinitarian love, can develop in us over time and become habitual in the sense that we revert to it easily:

> Just as we are immediate to ourselves by consciousness without any self-knowledge, and through our consciousness by philosophic study and self-appropriation we can come to a fuller knowledge of ourselves, so also what we are by the grace of God, by the gift of God, can have an objectification within us. What is immediate can be mediated by our acts, and gradually reveal to us in ever fuller fashion, in a more conscious and more pressing fashion, the fundamental fact about us: the great gift and grace that Jesus Christ brought to us.[83]

In this grace, Lonergan the theologian knew that he was becoming himself, "not just by experiences, insights, judgments, by choices, decisions, conversion, not just freely and deliberately, not just deeply and strongly, but as one who is carried along."[84]

He did not assume that his self-appropriation was complete or that human cooperation with grace would always be adequate, but he had come to a large measure of trust in the "someone else who was running the ship."[85]

> But I must not misrepresent. We do not know ourselves very well; we cannot chart the future; we cannot control our environment completely or the influences that work on us; we cannot explore our unconscious and preconscious mechanisms. Our course is in the night; our control is only rough and approximate; we have to believe and trust, to risk and dare....To speak of *Existenz*, on being oneself...is what the Germans call a *Besinnung*, a becoming aware, a growth in self-consciousness, a heightening of one's self-appropriation, that is possible because our separate, unrevealed, hidden cores have a common circle of reference, the human community, and an ultimate point of reference, which is God, who is all in all, (τα πάντα ἐν πάσιν θεός).[86]

In conclusion, we have considered three ways to appropriate our own desiring: first, by paying further attention to the inner movements of our minds and hearts, with particular reference to the fourth level of deliberation, choice and the pursuit of true value, where we are forming personality and character; second, by openness to learning about ourselves through interactions with others in the communities to which we belong—others whose responses can enlighten or give us feedback and whose generous living of incarnate values draws us powerfully to want to do likewise; and third, by perseverance in prayerful search for union with God and reflection on the received tradition that enshrines so much wisdom.

The desire we come to know and choose to live out of is the drive that moves us to follow wholeheartedly the God-given bent of our conscious intentionality. It is at depth the desire for utter goodness, for the fullness of love, and it most readily finds expression in thought and action when we fall in love. Love for another human being or one's country or the cosmos already increases the probabilities of making self-transcending choices in keeping with the desire that moves us. The openness to all truth, all goodness, even God, which is the fact of how we are made, becomes openness as achievement when we follow it and live accordingly. We see, however, that this could be more than problematic were it not for the self-giving of God that Lonergan calls openness as gift. Grace heals and completes the capacity for self-transcendence that constitutes fully human living. We come to see how being-in-love with God dismantles and abolishes the horizon within which our knowing and choosing take place, and sets up a new horizon within which the love of God transvalues our values and the eyes of that love transform our knowing.

In February 1965, Lonergan had a most significant personal breakthrough. His great desire for many years had been to write a methodology for theology, to which *Insight* was just the prologue, but clarity was proving elusive. Release from the tension of inquiry came suddenly and, as it often does, in a moment of complete relaxation.[87] Lonergan was coming out of a movie with a group of friends when the insight toward which he had been groping came in a flash. Theology should be done as a creative collaborative exercise in which functional specialties would follow the movement of

69

generalized empirical method given in transcendental consciousness, and conversion would have a foundational place. He affirmed and developed this insight in his second classic work, *Method in Theology* (1972), which gives us also his most developed thinking on meaning, the human good, and being-in-love with God in an unrestricted manner as experienced and known.

4

THE APPROPRIATION OF DESIRE IN
METHOD IN THEOLOGY

Published in 1972, Lonergan's classic work *Method in Theology* is the culmination and summary of over two decades of searching for an adequate methodology for theology based on the cognitional theory of his earlier masterpiece, *Insight*. During the gestation of this book, Lonergan had a series of original insights into the relation between the pattern of operations in human learning and the steps to be followed in any human science based on the past and oriented to the future, and, in this work, presents them as his generalized empirical method.

Method was to be a costly gift, the product of his mind and heart working together, and was finished under pressure. He had to endure painful surgery for lung cancer, which, in 1965, put an end to his theology teaching at the Gregorian in Rome. His recovery was slow, and, based on the trust he placed in his nurse, Sister Florian (Winifred Tattersell),[1] and the erroneous belief that she had assessed his life expectancy at a maximum of five years, he felt a great urgency about the completion of *Method*. This sense of urgency accounts for the summary nature of this work, "maddeningly dense, allusive and elliptical all at the same time";[2] but parts are lyrical and expressive too. For this, we may also have Sister Florian to thank; she seems to have helped him come to a deeper appreciation of the beauty and transforming power of human love during long months of skillful and nurturing care. Finished in some haste, therefore, *Method* nevertheless establishes theology on a new and life-giving pathway of creative collaboration and dialogue for the twenty-first century. It makes the appropriation of desire a key task for theologians. It asks them to know the nature of the love that is moving them forward in their search for God.

The procedures of the human mind, as we have already noted, are themselves a method in the sense that Lonergan uses the term: "a normative pattern of recurrent and related operations yielding cumulative and progressive results."[3] The pattern of our consciousness differs from a pavlova recipe, for example, where we may think we have the normative recipe,[4] but recurrent operations (adding ingredients, whisking, baking) are presumed to yield, in each case, the same perfect dessert, meringue-like on the outside, risen and marshmallowy on the inside. By contrast, the essence, both of our learning ability and of Lonergan's meaning of method, is that results build on what has gone before and keep developing toward a goal:

> There is a method, then, where there are distinct operations, where each operation is related to the others, where the set of relations forms a pattern, where the pattern is described as the right way of doing the job, where operations in accord with the pattern may be repeated indefinitely, and where the fruits of such repetition are, not repetitious, but cumulative and progressive.[5]

There needs to be ongoing discoveries, and each discovery needs to be integrated with the others before the conditions for that "cumulative and progressive" can claim to be achieved.

FUNCTIONAL SPECIALTIES

In this method of doing theology, Lonergan acknowledges the diversity of work being done by specialists in many areas, field specialists and subject specialists, but envisages a collaborative and interdependent system of eight functional specialties dividing and clarifying the process from data to results.

The eight functional specialties are intrinsically related to transcendental method:[6] the person performing each is a knower, preferably one who has appropriated the dynamic structure of his or her own consciousness; each of the functional specialties seeks the end proper to one of the operations; their sequence follows, in an ascending and descending order, the order of the operations; the method proper to each of the functional specialties itself follows the dynamic structure of human consciousness.

Theology is done by theologians, and they come to know what they know by following the steps Lonergan identifies as "the native spontaneities and inevitabilities of our consciousness which assembles its own constituent parts and unites them in a rounded whole."[7] His contention in *Method in Theology* is that, by "self-appropriation," theologians can reach an ever-expanding awareness of their own knowing, choosing, and loving, and of how they operate in and through the operations of conscious intentionality to achieve certain goals. This intellectual conversion is essential to the proper functioning of his method.

> In a sense everyone knows and observes transcendental method. Everyone does so, precisely in the measure that he is attentive, intelligent, reasonable, responsible. But in another sense it is quite difficult to be at home in transcendental method....It is a matter of heightening one's consciousness by objectifying it, and that is something that each one, ultimately, has to do in himself and for himself.[8]

"In the proceedings of the human mind we…discern a transcendental method, that is a basic pattern of operations employed in every cognitional enterprise."[9] This basic pattern gives Lonergan's theological method its unity and relatedness. Each of the functional specialties seeks the end proper to one of the operations of transcendental method. The first four, which form the mediated phase, by which theology appropriates what others have said and done in the past (*discens*),[10] follow the operations in ascending order. *Research* seeks the end proper to *experiencing*—the apprehension of data—by making available information relevant to theology in forms such as maps, dictionaries, critical editions of texts, and ancient languages. *Interpretation* seeks the end proper to *understanding*—insight into the meaning of the data—grasping "the meaning in its proper historical context, in accord with its proper mode and level of thought and expression."[11] *History* seeks the end proper to *judging*—acceptance or rejection of hypotheses or theories put forward to account for the past—seeking to grasp "what was going forward in particular groups at particular places and times."[12] *Dialectic* seeks the end proper to *deciding*—acknowledgment of value and selection of methods or means leading to their realization. It is concerned to explore conflicts arising in research, interpretation, and the history of religious thinking and community structures based on this, with a view to determining which are irreconcilables, and which are genetic, just different stages of development of the ideas in question.

In the second, or mediating phase (*docens*),[13] where theology addresses its own times and culture, transmitting the tradition into the future, the functional specialties follow in descending order. *Foundations* also relates to *deciding*. It presents the horizon within which the meaning of doctrines can or cannot be apprehended and thematizes conversion, out of which the theologian takes his or her stand in relationship to God and the issues treated in the other fourth level specialty, Dialectic. *Doctrines* relates to *judging*, expressing judgments of fact and judgments of value concerning the "negations and affirmations not only of dogmatic theology but also of moral, ascetical, mystical, pastoral and any similar branch."[14] *Systematics* relates to *understanding*. It attempts to meet questions raised in doctrines in a gradual process of reconciling all we hold to be true. Theologians working in this specialty are "concerned to work out appropriate systems of conceptualization, to remove apparent inconsistencies, to move towards some grasp of spiritual matters, both from their own inner coherence and from the analogies offered by more familiar human experience."[15] *Communications* relates to *experiencing*, making the work of the other seven functional specialties accessible to particular people in current times through various carriers of meaning, producing data for the present and the future.

The functional specialties are thus successive parts of one process from data to results, and their clarity and interrelatedness derive from their relationship to the levels of conscious intentionality. Each of the functional specialties, however, employs not just one but all four levels of conscious and intentional operations. For example, within the functional specialty Research,

> the textual critic will select the method (level of decision) that he feels will lead to the discovery (level of understanding) of what one may reasonably affirm (level of judgment) was written in the original text (level of experience). The textual critic, then, operates on all four levels, but his goal is the end proper to the first level, namely to ascertain the data.[16]

The same is true in each specialty according to its proper tasks. Lonergan's method thus makes specific for theology the transcendental precepts: Be attentive; Be intelligent; Be reasonable; Be responsible. "Transcendental method adds considerable light and precision to the performance of theological tasks."[17] Each specialty has its proper excellence, but none is isolated from the other seven—they are functionally related to each other in a cumulative process.

> Experience is open to further data. Understanding to a fuller and more penetrating grasp. Judgment to acknowledgment of new and more adequate perspectives, of more nuanced pronouncements, of more detailed information. Decision, finally, is reached only partially by dialectic, which tends to eliminate evidently foolish oppositions and so narrows down issues, but it is not to be expected to go to the roots of all conflict for, ultimately, conflicts have their ground in the heart of man.[18]

DIALECTICS AND FOUNDATIONS

This reference to the heart is significant. The two fourth-level specialties, Dialectics and Foundations, with which we are particularly concerned, are an original contribution, and indicative of the distinctly new emphasis Lonergan brings to theological method. They form a pivot or transition between the investigation of the cultural past and the committed stance of theology *in oratione recta*, during the second phase:

> What mediates between past and future is personal decision. One accepts what one has studied in order to make it part of one's own stand, position, message; or, alternatively, one rejects it and will make that rejection a more or less important part of one's message.[19]

Dialectic

In Dialectic, the theologian considers the significance of what the past has to offer and determines, when there are conflicting views of the significance of the past, which is the most accurate and valuable. This moves away from the pre–Vatican II emphasis within apologetics on proving certain doctrinal propositions, refuting others, and convincing the undecided.

> By dialectic, then, is understood a generalized apologetic conducted in an ecumenical spirit, aiming ultimately at a comprehensive viewpoint, and proceeding towards that goal by acknowledging differences, seeking their grounds, real and apparent, and eliminating superfluous oppositions.[20]

Dialectic follows the functional specialties of Research, Interpretation, and History, and completes the stage of indirect discourse—the process of appropriating what others have said and done in the past. The past does not present a unified picture: there are internal and external conflicts in the history of Christian movements, and many diverging viewpoints that give rise to them. So, Dialectic involves evaluation of differing orientations in research, differing interpretations, differing accounts of the past and the present, conflicting pronouncements of theologians and authorities, an evaluation of the relative worth of different viewpoints. Lutheran, Calvinist, Anabaptist, Anglican, Roman Catholic, and Orthodox theologians may offer divergent interpretations of the same New Testament data, and there is a whole history of past and present differing interpretations behind each, and an entire series of prophetic witnesses to the Christian fact.

> In such a context, the only way that the historically conscious contemporary theologian can remain faithful to the demands of his discipline is to operate within a genuinely dialectic context.[21]

To do so is to recognize that some differences will be resolved with consideration of fresh data, others are merely perspectival, due to the complexity of historical realities, and could be brought together into a larger whole. However, going to the roots of conflict may reveal more fundamental dialectical differences in religious outlook, ethical stance, or cognitional theory that profoundly modify one's mentality. These can be overcome only through a conversion, religious, moral, or intellectual. "The function of dialectic will be to bring such conflicts to light and to provide a technique that objectifies subjective differences and promotes conversion."[22]

Our field of vision, the scope of our knowledge, and the range of our interests are bounded according to when and where we live, our personal development, and the education we receive. The contexts, which result from past achievement and, in turn, condition future learning, are what Lonergan refers to as *horizons*. Differences in horizon may be complementary when people recognize their need for each other's motivation and knowledge for the functioning of a communal world; they may be genetic, related as successive stages in some process of development. Neither of these is a dialectic difference. For Lonergan, it is situations where what is intelligible, true, or good for one is unintelligible, false, or evil for another, and in which the horizon of the other is interpreted as wishful thinking, ignorance, fallacy, backwardness, or infidelity—in other words, real dialectical differences—which call for conversion.

Theologians doing dialectic and discovering the root causes of conflict are brought face to face with questions of authenticity—their own and others'—and become aware of their own need for conversion. Crowe warns readers of Kierkegaard:

If he (Kierkegaard) does not haunt your theology, then I would say quite bluntly that you are not yet ready for Lonergan's dialectic and foundations. Kierkegaard has an unparalleled talent for forcing us out of the neutral stance of, say, the student of religions, and challenging us to our own personal commitment—which is just where Lonergan's dialectic directs us, and what his second phase of the theological tasks would have us realize.[23]

Foundations

In Foundations, theologians reflect on the new horizons— intellectual, moral, and religious—arrived at and chosen through encounter with the truths and values discovered in Research, Interpretation, History, and Dialectic. "The evaluative decisions we make determine more than just the matter in hand. They establish our own character."[24] Whereas before Vatican II, fundamental or foundational theology was regarded as a series of basic propositions from which conclusions could be deduced, Lonergan finds theological foundations not in propositions but in persons, freely valuing and deciding within new horizons—which they experience as a gift from the Divine—what their personal stance will be:

> The threefold conversion (religious, moral, intellectual) is not a set of propositions that a theologian utters, but a fundamental and momentous change in the human reality that a theologian is.[25]

The term *conversion* refers to a vertical exercise of freedom, whereby one moves from one horizon to another, an about-turn, a significant change in which characteristic features of the old must be discarded in favor of a "new sequence which can keep revealing ever greater depth, breadth and wealth."[26] It marks a new beginning, a movement into the horizon of the transcendental notions. *Insight* invited the reader to a clarification and reflective self-appropriation of the self-transcendence proper to the human process of coming to know. By the time Lonergan wrote *Method*, he had come to see conversion as threefold: intellectual, moral, and religious.

Intellectual conversion is "the discovery of the significance of the pure desire to know...the principle which underpins, penetrates, and promotes forward all of our cognitional operations. It is the principle which awakes questioning."[27] One who is intellectually converted will not be inclined to mistake the process of "taking a look" for knowing. Observing the data or hearing the words is only the first stage in knowing. Then the intellectually converted recognize in their first insight into something, or even the clustering of insights, not what they intend to know, but the intelligibility that may be relevant to what they intend to know. They are alerted to the natural and active criteria of their own minds: "Why do you say that? Are you sure you have all the relevant data? What is the evidence for that assertion? What is the quality of that evidence? Is that in fact the case? Is that the only conclusion you can draw?" Knowing involves not just experiencing but also the capacity and willingness to understand and to try to affirm that understanding in judgment. It may be said that awareness and sensitivity to what is involved in knowing constitute intellectual conversion. "Intellectual conversion is a grasp of our potential to understand what an object means and to judge whether that understanding is correct."[28] Lonergan goes further by asserting that the only certain way of gaining that awareness and sensitivity is the slow and difficult process of self-appropriation whereby we discover in our own consciousness the dynamic relationships leading from one operation to another:

> To discover the self-transcendence proper to the human process of coming to know, is to break often long-ingrained habits of thought and speech. It is to acquire the mastery in one's own house that is to be had only when one knows precisely what one is doing when one is knowing. It is a conversion, a new beginning, a fresh start. It opens the way to ever further clarifications and developments.[29]

Habitual awareness of the elements of intellectual conversion is a key way in which the dialectician can evaluate various competing propositions. Many of the issues dividing Christianity need to be tackled at the cognitional level. The way in which dialecticians are recommended to work, however, is not by head-butting. The way is dialogue in a discernment that appreciates "all that has been intelligent, true and good in the past, even in the lives and thoughts of opponents."[30] It also recognizes deficiencies in one-self and those with whom one is allied, and then the action can become reciprocal.

> The theologian's strategy will be, not to prove his own position, not to refute counter-positions, but to exhibit diversity and to point to the evidence for its roots. In this manner he will be attractive to those that appreciate full human authenticity and he will convince those that attain it. Indeed, the basic idea of the method we are trying to develop takes its stand on discovering what human authenticity is and showing how to appeal to it.[31]

This is usually an effective way to operate because authenticity is truly our deepest need and most prized achievement—to this our desires are drawing us strongly. Moral conversion favors this openness in dialogue.

Moral conversion is also an exercise in vertical freedom, where one opts for the truly good, for value over satisfaction. It is the change from using the seeking of pleasure and avoiding of pain as the basis of choice, as children might want to do, to the preference for what is truly worthwhile, even if somewhat arduous, of the mature adult. Because human beings can ask questions about objective value, and answer them, and live by the answers,

> we can effect in our living a moral self-transcendence. That moral self-transcendence is the possibility of benevolence and beneficence, of honest collaboration and true love, of swinging completely out of the habitat of an animal and becoming a person in a human society.[32]

Yet, as Lonergan points out, "Such conversion, of course, falls far short of moral perfection. Deciding is one thing, doing is another."[33] There is a long process to be undertaken before anyone can claim to be a virtuous person: of tackling bias in all its forms, evaluating one's own intentional responses to values and their implied preferences, developing moral knowledge, and learning from the example and criticism of others. Authenticity is never a permanent acquisition in this sphere as in any other: "It is ever a withdrawal from unauthenticity, and every successful withdrawal brings to light the need for still further withdrawals."[34] Sin and repentance are realities in the life of a theologian too.

However, the criterion of moral conversion can also help to resolve the disputes confronting the theologian doing dialectic. It calls into question any theoretical view of human motivation that is exclusively materialist or exclusively value related. Human beings are not just "sophisticated stimulus-response mechanisms" as some behaviorists, economic materialists, and scientific determinists might allege, but neither are they likely to be totally free of individual and group bias and other weaknesses human flesh is heir to. "Sin is alienation from man's authentic being, which is self-transcendence, and sin justifies itself by ideology."[35] Moral conversion will bring to the task of dialectic insight competing theories offering solutions to the problems of society.

> There is a still further dimension to being human, and there we emerge as persons, meet one another in a common concern for values, seek to abolish the organization of human living on the basis of competing egoisms and to replace it by an organization on the basis of man's perceptiveness and intelligence, his reasonableness, and his responsible exercise of freedom.[36]

Equally significant, however, moral conversion as lived brings to the work of dialectic the possibility of the requisite humility and ecumenical openness in the theologian doing it. Crowe has written persuasively of his hope for this:

> We have daily experience…of how much in theology is the reflection, not to say rationalization, of one's life choices. We may have similar experiences of how blind other theologians often seem to be to this feature of their work. And, observing this, we may feel led on, by grace

or natural honesty, to ask: am I also blind? Is my own theology the reflection or the rationalization of my life choices? With such questions, we are at the heart of dialectic and foundations; we are questioning our personal authenticity and entertaining the possibility of the need for our own conversion.[37]

Crowe goes on to ask whether an Augustinian confession of what we have been—of the past that has made us what we are—may not be required as an integral part of theology when we enter upon the tasks of Dialectics and Foundations.

For Lonergan in *Method*,[38] the question of God emerges when we inquire about the possibility of fruitful inquiry, reflect on the nature of reflection, and deliberate on the worth of deliberation.[39]

> Man's transcendental subjectivity is mutilated or abolished, unless he is stretching forth towards the intelligible, the unconditioned, the good of value. The reach, not of his attainment, but of his intending is unrestricted. There lies within his horizon a region for the divine, a shrine for ultimate holiness. It cannot be ignored. The atheist may pronounce it empty. The agnostic may urge that he finds his investigation has been inconclusive. The contemporary humanist will refuse to allow the question to arise. But their negations presuppose the spark in our clod, our native orientation to the divine.[40]

God is part and parcel of human authenticity, because human authenticity requires constant self-transcendence and if "specific loves, such as friendship or the love of marriage, actualize important parts of our capacity for self-transcendence, the love of God actualizes its ultimate basis, the unlimited potential of our knowledge and love."[41] The prior word God speaks, by pouring out his love in our hearts, enables us to experience an otherworldly falling in love; being-in-love in an unrestricted manner. "Religious conversion is being grasped by ultimate concern."[42] In religious conversion, therefore, is the fulfillment of our fourth level of human consciousness, of the choosing and loving that complete what our prior experiencing, understanding, and judging have sought. It sets up a new horizon, resets our values and alters our knowing.

> It gives you the horizon in which questions about God are significant. There are people to whom you can talk about God and they listen eagerly. There are others who just react: "What on earth is he talking about? How on earth could I be interested in that?" Conversion is in Ezekiel: God plucking out the heart of stone. The heart of stone doesn't want to get rid of its stoniness. And that's the fundamental thing about religious conversion. I don't say there is nothing else happening, but I am saying that's what the key point is.[43]

For the theologian engaged in dialectic, religious conversion becomes a criterion for evaluation by enlarging his or her perspective beyond the finite realities of this world to matters of ultimate meaning and value. Religious viewpoints can be evaluated in terms of the attentiveness, understanding, judgment, and responsibility they encourage among their adherents, the way they foster more trust, more hope, and more love in action and attitude. Evil can be faced with courage and determination because it will not have the final word. Religious conversion enables the dialectician to recognize the action of the Spirit where this occurs, because it is coherent with his or her knowledge of it in experience.

Religious conversion is "the ultimate stage in a person's self-transcendence. It's God's free gift. It involves a transvaluation of value in your living, but it is not something produced by knowing. It's going beyond your present horizon; it's taking you beyond your present horizon."[44]

In *Method*, the three conversions are treated by Lonergan in the chapter on dialectic, although he maintains that conversion is a prerequisite only in the functional specialties of the second phase, where it constitutes "an explicit, established, universally recognized criterion of proper procedure."[45] Conversion operates implicitly in the confrontation of dialectic, and Crowe draws attention to Lonergan's complex position on this question by putting together two quotations. On the one hand, "anyone can do research, interpret, write history, line up opposed positions," but on the other, "though believers and agnostics follow the same methods, they will not obtain the same results."[46] The conversions are, in fact, operative in dialectic, and "the degree of their presence or absence both in ourselves as we evaluate and in the views which we evaluate is of immense significance. To the extent that we lack the attitude of openness which characterizes each of the conversions we cannot recognize their lack in the views and positions we are evaluating."[47]

Human authenticity, the result of intellectual, moral, and religious self-transcendence, does not guarantee freedom from oversights, misunderstandings, mistakes, and sin; but it does lead theologians to the uncovering of still more oversights, the acknowledgment of still further failures to understand, the correcting of still more mistakes, and to repentance for more and more deeply hidden sins. In the measure of their own growth in self-transcendence, theologians come to discern the ambivalence in others, the intelligent, the true, and the good as well as the mistakes, the misinformation and the evil in opponents and in their own tradition.

Foundations is the functional specialty that follows dialectic, the first in the committed, second phase of theology, "where the listening subject speaks"[48] and takes responsibility for speaking. Dialectic has prepared for this by bringing conflicts to light, eliminating evidently foolish oppositions, narrowing down issues, objectifying and revealing them in their fundamental options so that the choices to be made in foundations will be clear. But decision, finally, is reached only partially by dialectic. It does not take sides—the person does, and this stance becomes the foundational reality for the direct discourse of theology: "Foundations takes sides; it selects as its stand some coherent set out of the array of opposing positions, and in so far as it is guided by authentic conversion, its selection will be an implicit objectification of what conversion is."[49] Foundations begins "a new and creative phase of theology, with the self-involvement of the theologian and with a Spirit-guided process."[50] As a fourth-level specialty, it involves a decision that selects one horizon and rejects others. "It is a fully conscious decision about one's horizon, one's outlook, one's world view. It deliberately sets the framework, in which doctrines have their meaning, in which systematics reconciles, in which communications are effective."[51]

This will not be done arbitrarily. It will be done in keeping with the demands of the human spirit that we be attentive, intelligent, reasonable, and in love, otherwise it is without authenticity. Such an obvious choice about horizon is not self-evident in a world where many just drift—Lonergan calls it a high achievement—and though intensely personal it is not purely private. Conversion means more than a change of horizon, it means beginning to belong to a new social group, or at least belonging in a new way.

> Discovery of our interiority, of the Spirit who abides there, of our correspondence or lack of it with the Spirit, is not a solo flight. Laying the foundations for doctrines is not a solo task. It is the work of a community in the faith, a work in which I challenge others and invite them to self-scrutiny, but inexorably am myself challenged by them and invited to my own self-scrutiny. In each encounter, there is need of extreme openness and sincere efforts to break down the wall between private faith and the public enterprise of theology.[52]

It is clear that the theologian has a personal contribution to make in the second, committed phase of theology, and therefore a certain autonomy; authentic conversion provides the horizon within which doctrines are to be apprehended, and understanding of their content and appropriate ways to transmit these within given cultural mixes sought.[53] "Each theologian will judge the authenticity of the authors of views, and he will do so by the touchstone of his own authenticity."[54] This is to be the criterion of the autonomy of the theologian and hence the vital importance of self-appropriation, familiarity with his or her natural and religious interiority. We need to be able to discover what in ourselves is inauthentic to be able to turn away from it with the grace of God, to discover what the fullness of human authenticity might be and embrace it wholeheartedly.

As we have noted, Dialectic and Foundations are linked by their pivotal position in the ascending-descending order of the functional specialties, their sharing of the fourth-level mode of conscious intentionality, and their integral role in Lonergan's view of theology as a "dialogue of disciplines."[55] The fourth level—at which

Lonergan places religious experience—is the level of responsibility "on which we are concerned with ourselves, our own operations, our goals, and so deliberate about possible courses of action, evaluate them, decide and carry out our decisions."[56] At each level, there has been a fuller self to be aware of, and at this existential level, "the intention of the intelligible, the true, the real, becomes also the intention of the good, the question of value, of what is worthwhile, when the already acting subject confronts his world and adverts to his own acting in it."[57] The existential level involves the theologian in evaluation and deliberation, in responsible decision-making and the notion of value and the good; this is the level of personal, communal, and historical self-constitution. At this stage, the person is discovering him- or herself as a moral being, choosing between courses of action, and at the same time, making him- or herself an authentic human being or an inauthentic one. When the theologian has become convinced that something is true and good, he or she is faced with a personal decision. To be authentic as a theologian means the steady application of the inquiring mind in accord with the *eros* of the pure, unrestricted desire to know all truth; desire's loving search for complete union with the Beloved will be the sustaining impetus for this undertaking.

In *Method*, Lonergan treats of feelings, values, and conversions, and religious experience and the summit of human development as "being-in-love with God." Now the pure and unrestricted desire to know of *Insight* has been "swept up into…the passionateness of being."[58] He shows that the dynamism of consciousness leads, in a spontaneous, self-assembling pattern of operations, of sublation and transcendence, beyond the ongoing discovery and affirmation of truth to the pursuit of value and absolute goodness, and he invites the reader to verify this too in attention to the data of consciousness. Our being, all being, is oriented in vertical finality toward the One who is transcendent in lovableness,[59] and to this end "God's love has been poured into our hearts through the Holy Spirit that has been given to us" (Rom 5:5). This finality, in consciousness, is the desire examined in *Method*. Ways for the theologian—for anyone with a sufficiently cultured background—to appropriate the love without restriction or qualification or reserve that best expresses this desire will next be considered in the light of the wisdom embodied in *Method* and in terms of the categorical imperatives this work is based on: Be attentive; Be intelligent; Be reasonable; Be responsible; Be in love.[60]

If we want to know what is going on within us, if we want to learn to integrate religious experience with the rest of our living, Lonergan maintains, we have to inquire, investigate, take counsel, so that we come to understand, affirm, and live out of this gift.[61] As pure experience, religious experience is not something that we can know and understand quite as readily as we have come to work out the meanings and realities of what is encountered in sense data, by the self-correcting process of learning. However, the data of consciousness trigger an equally developmental process, involving, in this case, attention to inner experience, inquiry, insight into the intelligibility of the experience, reflection, and testing this understanding for indications of compatibility with truth as one knows it. Finally, our questioning can lead us to operate in the light of the meaning we have found in these inner events.

BE ATTENTIVE!

This developmental process will operate in us whether or not we have fully achieved the self-appropriation as a knower of which Lonergan writes in *Insight* and in *Method*.[62] However, interiorly differentiated consciousness[63] not only heightens awareness of these operations, but can achieve knowledge of them and so enable an individual to follow deliberately the norms immanent in the God-given pattern of intentional consciousness. The data of consciousness to which we are called to attend in religious experience are the effects of the powerful love that comes into our lives as the fourth-level fulfillment of all that our efforts to be attentive, intelligent, reasonable, responsible, and in love have been seeking.

Just as the operations of both intentional consciousness and theological method begin with data, so does the appropriation of desire. To understand the passionateness of our own being, we can, first, attend to what is going on in our own conscious awareness; second, notice patterns emerging in our actions and attitudes over time; third, be open to the experience and feedback of others in the human and especially the Christian community; and fourth, we should pay attention to knowledge born of religious love, assented to and deepened in a life of prayer.

The first of these sources of data is consciousness itself. As we have noted earlier, human beings have a direction before they know it. Being precedes knowing and our ceaseless questioning is the result of our "being a problem to ourselves"[64] as we strive to make sense of that inner directedness. Beyond attention to the processes involved in coming to know, Lonergan invites the reader of *Method* to advert to his or her feelings and the existential choices made at the level of evaluation, choice, and decision. Throughout a lifetime's practice of attentiveness to the quality and movement of his own feelings to discern the action of the Spirit moving him to choose the good,[65] Lonergan developed a familiarity with his own interiority at this level. In *Insight*, he had already recognized feelings and emotions as elements within experience, as data to be understood and even guarded against as potentially skewing the clear functioning of intellectual light. In 1972, he goes further, maintaining that it is by our feelings that we are "massively and dynamically oriented"[66] in the world mediated by meaning. Feelings give intentional consciousness "its mass, momentum, drive, power,"[67] and it is advisable to take full cognizance of them, whether we consider them to be admirable, deplorable, or indifferent, rather than to brush them aside, overrule them, ignore them.

Familiar as his own feelings were, Lonergan possibly felt he had not reached his own high standards for attaining explanatory theory on the subject of feelings, because in writing *Method*, he draws heavily on the work of two ethicists who studied the phenomenology of affectivity: Max Scheler and Dietrich von Hildebrand.[68] They did help to clarify his thinking and provided terms and relations he could use to develop seminal insights from his earlier work, but he developed their contributions in a way that is distinctively his own, particularly by correcting their differing misunderstandings of the nexus between feelings and cognition.[69] Without feelings, he maintains, "our knowing and deciding would be paper thin."[70]

From von Hildebrand, he took the distinction between, on the one hand, nonintentional states and trends,[71] and, on the other, intentional responses. Feelings that are intentional responses relate us to what is intended, apprehended, represented. They do this in two ways: relating us to objects either in terms of personal or group satisfaction and dissatisfaction (what is perceived as agreeable or disagreeable) or in terms of values:

> Whether the ontic value of persons or the qualitative value of beauty, understanding, truth, virtuous acts, noble deeds. In general, response to value both carries us towards self-transcendence and selects an object for the sake of whom or of which we transcend ourselves. In contrast, response to the agreeable or disagreeable is ambiguous.[72]

The attractive object of desire may be objectively good as well as personally satisfying, but the true good can equally be something difficult, even unpleasant, and then our choice of value over our own comfort is manifestly an act of self-transcendence.

It was from Scheler that Lonergan derived the concept of the *ordo amoris*, the individual scale of preferences according to which each person's feelings respond to values. Objectively, in Lonergan's view, there is an ascending order from vital values such as health and fitness, through social values such as systematized education or the organs of civil society, to the cultural values that give meaning to human lives. Personal value ranks higher again: "the person in his self-transcendence, as loving and being loved, as originator of values in himself and in his milieu, as an inspiration and invitation to others to do likewise."[73] Religious values stand highest in themselves, though some individuals may not acknowledge this in practice. The personal *ordo amoris* is linked to personal horizons, which may vary widely according to the quality of the formation received, the love and security within which they have developed, and the extent to which the person has dealt with the transformational conversion encounters of their lives,[74] but what we desire in practice is available to attentive scrutiny. We can experience ourselves comparing and choosing. We can grow in awareness that our existential decisions are constituting the person we are becoming and that this person is increasingly in love with God.

It is worth noting the efforts of William James (1842–1910), the American philosopher and academic psychologist, and Rudolph Otto (1869–1937), the German professor of comparative religions, in being attentive to religious experience and conveying its essential character. They each produced a taxonomy of the varieties of religious experience. Where they differ is on the question of whether or not there is a single and distinctively religious moment of consciousness. For James, the religious feelings and conduct of saintly Christians, Stoics, and Buddhists are remarkably similar, though their thoughts might differ widely. He identifies a "faith state" that he regarded as a biological as well as a psychological condition, marking religious experiences across cultures:

> An excitement of the cheerful, expansive, "dynamogenic" order which, like any tonic, freshens our vital powers...this emotion overcomes temperamental melancholy and imparts endurance to the Subject, or a zest, or a meaning, or an enchantment and glory to the common objects of life.[75]

"This readiness for great things and this sense that the world by its importance, wonderfulness, etc., is apt for their production," which James sees as "the undifferentiated germ of all the higher faiths,"[76] is clearly related to the openness as gift of which Lonergan spoke. There is joy and energy in the experience of the unrestricted love of God transvaluing our values, broadening our horizon to encompass God's beneficent plan for the universe, and working within fourth-level consciousness to make human authenticity realizable. Whom it is we love is neither given nor as yet understood, but we sense the lack of restriction in this loving, and our capacity for moral self-transcendence finds a fulfillment that brings deep joy and profound peace.[77]

In James's study, the initial occurrence of this religious experience is most frequently the "being born again" experience of his own New England Protestant culture. It comes suddenly, unexpectedly, and will subsequently provide a memorable point from which to "date" faith.

In Otto's writings, the awe and attraction aroused in the creature by the numinous, drawing toward an ideal good known only in presentiment and yearning, are feelings awakened from the spirit, "and this spirit, this inborn capacity to receive and understand, is the essential thing."[78] He would perhaps recognize this innate capacity in Lonergan's "successive stages in the unfolding of a single thrust, the *eros* of the human spirit."[79] This can be either a sudden or a more gradual surfacing in awareness of the powerful attraction of the Divine.

The second way of attending to our own desire is to reflect on our development over time and to notice patterns of actions and shifts in attitudes that have occurred. The love of God poured out in our hearts may be operative in consciousness without being known, because it is never adverted to, queried, and understood, and thus never before accorded significance in any system of meaning by which our lives are interpreted:

> A person can be religiously mature yet have to recall to mind his past life and study it in its religious moments and features before he can discern in it a direction, a pattern, a thrust, a call to unworldliness. Even then his difficulties may not be at an end: he may be unable to associate any precise meaning with the words I have used; he may be too familiar with the reality of which I speak to connect it with what I say; he may be looking for something with a label on it, when he should simply be heightening his consciousness of the power working within him and adverting to its long-term effects.[80]

Like Moses on the mountain, we may be able to see God from behind (Exod 33:23). Unable to identify what God is doing in us in the present moment, we may more readily see what God has accomplished in us in the past. We notice only what is within our horizon, but it is possible that we will discover desire for value as the *eros* of the human spirit where we find attitudinal changes occurring within. Changes in our way of acting will alert us to the significance of the quiet pull drawing us to attentiveness, to courageous pursuit of truth, to actions for the good of others. With enlightenment from the Spirit, we can recognize even the inner suffering of dryness and darkness we have been going through as a real God experience. Journaling has been found by many to be one way of observing the movements of our thoughts and feelings over time, and discovering their patterns and leadings, though the unstructured diary method is somewhat less effective than the intensive writing advocated by Progoff.[81]

For this recognition, we may need guidance from a spiritual companion or mentor, or at least the fellowship of those who have shared the experience, and the third way of attending in order to appropriate the desire that we are is available to us in community.

> For however personal and intimate is religious experience, still it is not solitary. The same gift can be given to many, and the many can recognize in one another a common orientation in their living and feeling, in their criteria and their goals. From a common communion with God, there springs a religious community.[82]

We receive feedback from others that draws attention to aspects of our own focus, our own development. Others can so incarnate values in their way of life, their words, their deeds, their whole meaning, that we can become aware of the inner stirring of our own desire for goodness beyond criticism. Those whose hearts are also caught and held by this goodness can teach us to attend to our own heart's longing.

This is data and our exploration produces further data. Christians may find it in the "quickening of the word," the familiar experience of finding a passage of Scripture more alive and speaking right into the heart of our situation in a way it never has before. The psalms of longing (e.g., Pss 42, 43, 63, 107, 119), which were and are the prayers of Israel, now form part of the official prayer of the church in the Office of the Hours, and often find new resonance in the religiously converted who use them for prayer. We find ourselves drawn to this data and other passages in Scripture that speak of God's desire for us engendering and meeting our own desire for God.

The fourth dimension of the imperative, "Be attentive," is that of attending to the outer word of faith. We have seen how human love within family or friendship has the power to enlarge horizons, to engender trust, and to motivate generous self-transcendence for the sake of the beloved.

The transcendental notions, that is, our questions for intelligence, for reflection, and for deliberation, constitute our capacity for self-transcendence. That capacity becomes an actuality when one falls in love. Then one's being becomes being-in-love. Such being-in-love has its antecedents, its causes, its conditions, its occasions. But once it has blossomed forth and as long as it lasts, it takes over. It is the first principle. From it flow one's desires and fears, one's joys and sorrows, one's discernment of values, one's decisions and deeds.[83]

The love of God working within us because of religious conversion has similar effects. We are invited also to attend to "knowledge born of religious love,"[84] the data of religious experience as interpreted by others, and as opening to us in a life of prayer and reflection.

Before it enters the world mediated by meaning, religion is the prior word God speaks to us by flooding our hearts with his love. That prior word pertains, not to the world mediated by meaning, but to the world of immediacy, to the unmediated experience of the mystery of love and awe. The outwardly spoken word is historically conditioned; its meaning depends upon the human context in which it is uttered, and such contexts vary from place to place and from one generation to another.[85]

The prior word that God speaks to us by flooding our hearts with his love is preparing us for the word of faith transmitted within the tradition that nurtures us. This tradition is the one in which we recognize the proclamation of the "outer word" that enables us to make sense of our inner experience. This outer word within Christianity is preeminently the incarnate value of Christians living in the Spirit, the living tradition, and the written word of the Judeo-Christian Scriptures, and teaching authority within the church family:

The word, then, is personal. *Cor ad cor loquitur*: love speaks to love, and its speech is powerful. The religious

93

leader, the prophet, the Christ, the apostle, the priest, the preacher announces in signs and symbols what is congruent with the gift of love that God works within us.[86]

Lonergan points out, however, that it extends also to the "word" enfleshed in art: painting, sculpture, architecture, music, poetry, and liturgy, all of which are expressions, transmitted within a culture, of the prior word received through the Spirit. These may speak to us of the new meaning into which we are invited. The attraction they hold for us has significance and is to be attended to. For the Christian, we come to know ourselves as members of the family of God's chosen ones, holy and beloved, "in order that you may proclaim the mighty acts of him who called you out of darkness into his marvelous light" (1 Pet 2:9), and called to be ministers of the reconciliation we have ourselves known (cf. 2 Cor 5:18–19), and sharers in the unconditional love of Christ for the world.

To welcome the newness of the horizon opened to us by this love and the world of faith into which we are invited, we need to attend to it and remain open to the further questions that will arise. This is to transcend ourselves-as-attending by inquiring, following the second transcendental precept: "Be intelligent!"

BE INTELLIGENT!

Few will not have experienced the appreciative response common in Western cultures on receiving a significant material gift. A person will open it, admire it, look at it from all angles, be interested to learn how the donor discovered it and thought of them, and then see how it works, try it out, express gratitude to the giver, before showing how greatly it is valued by regular and appropriate use. We are drawn to understand both the nature of the gift and the loving intentions of the donor.

Religious experience as experienced is ineffable, though we can and do seek understanding. Lonergan draws a contrast between the infrastructure denoted by the word experience, an infrastructure "that easily is unnoticed until it is rounded off in combination with a manifold of further elements,"[87] and the suprastructure that is built on it by subsequent inquiries. The infrastructure is pure experience, the data before it is named, classified, appealed to in support of a hypothesis. It provides, in every instance, the given:

> Its defining characteristic is the fact that it is presupposed and complemented by the level of intelligence, that it supplies, as it were, the raw materials on which intelligence operates, that, in a word, it is empirical, given indeed but merely given, open to understanding and formulation but by itself not understood and in itself ineffable.[88]

The empirical level is the first level of consciousness, the level on which ordinary experience occurs, but the basic orientation of human knowing is dynamic, and experience is addressed, engaged, interrogated by intelligence, the second level. Questions arise, moving us to ask what and why, how and what for, and to look for some pattern of intelligibility in the data presented to us in experience. "Observing lets intelligence be puzzled and we inquire."[89] We imagine possibilities and seek "the idea or form, the intelligible unity or relatedness that organizes data into intelligible wholes,"[90] the desired insight or flash of understanding. We may then have a concept, which we can formulate and probably need to, lest the insight get lost again. Insight is the fruit of inquiry, which promotes us from attention to experience to intelligent understanding.

After a transforming experience of the love of God breaking through into awareness, nothing can ever be quite the same again. However, it is not always attended to or understood because it is not looked for in the ordinary encounters of life, which is where the Spirit works incarnationally. In some cultures, religious experience leading to conversion is held in high esteem and anticipated as the entry requirement for full adult membership of a given faith community.[91] This is close to our contention here too, since it may be considered a prerequisite for the theologian, and we have accordingly considered some ways of owning this experience and developing its possibilities for a full human flowering. In the following chapter, we will explore deprivational neurosis, the scotosis resulting from deep trauma and guilt, as blockages affecting these possibilities to some extent. At this stage, it is helpful to consider human formation as the nurturing ground for transformation or as being either too poor to be an adequate basis for change or too strong and thus stifling humanizing transformation.

There are different understandings of the role played by formation and by transformation in the salvation experiences of humankind. Since the Reformation, these two elements that have a different but complementary role have been separated and only recently has a valuable dialectic between them begun. Where the Reformed tradition placed high value on the transformative conversion experience that has enabled many Christians to be "born again" and live by faith, in total trust that they are saved, Catholicism placed excessively high reliance on formation, education, and socialization into the faith community after baptism to produce high principled, moral citizens living the sacramental life.

For the Reformed tradition, the expectation that those who had been converted were thereafter saints and to be recognized by their saintly behavior has led in the past to separatist movements of various kinds and made the achievement of community hazardous. There was the temptation in a culture in which formation was irrelevant and "works" held in low esteem, for individuals to try desperately to prove that they were among the elect by rigorous attention to the law and judgmental surveillance of others in the church to the detriment of both personal development and community. Within Catholicism, overreliance on formation over centuries led to dogmatism and hierarchical structures of control allowing insufficient room for the action of the Spirit in charismatic and more everyday paths to holiness; the church was described as a "perfect community" though it lacked elements of interpersonal engagement, and the expectation seems to have been that human effort to follow precept and doctrine, supplemented by sacramental grace working in ways that left feelings unaffected, would suffice.

Breakthroughs of Grace

English theologian and mother of ten Rosemary Haughton has made a challenging study of these issues in her book *The Transformation of Man: A Study of Conversion and Community*.[92]

Lonergan valued highly her insights into the action of God's Spirit in human experience and spoke of her with some reverence as "a mystic." This work develops its terms and relations in the light of recognizable human encounters, and witnesses to the incarnational presence of the Spirit where good human formation breaks down and transformation occurs:

> The theological categories studied here grow directly and verifiably out of actual and common human experiences. Everyone has them in some way, so that anyone who is searching for ways to understand God's love affair with human kind can recognize its words and actions in his or her (and also their) experience.[93]

Not every religious experience or conversion is on the scale of Paul's blinding encounter on the road to Damascus, Augustine's quotation, "Late have I loved Thee," or Wesley's experience of a "heart strangely warmed." The breakthroughs of grace that Rosemary Haughton uses to ground what she teaches in her seminal work in readily recognizable human experience are those of a children's quarrel, a lovers' first sexual encounter, and the change in a family man's social and religious consciousness. In each situation, there is "transgression," the breakdown of human formation, but in each she sees the power of the same spirit acting through self-giving love to effect a humanizing—and saving—transformation.

In the first situation, a boy of twelve—"imaginative, touchy, withdrawn"—has an angry quarrel with his little sister—"aged eight, obstinate, impulsive, generous."[94] She has helped herself, in his absence, to the precious brushes and paints on which he had depended for a peaceful time of solitude in finishing a painting. The blast of his disappointment and anger opens many doors in the boy's mind and releases much that he doesn't understand. The girl is half prepared for his attack—she knows the importance this activity has for him and is irritated by it since it excludes her. She also sensed that he would have refused had she asked to borrow these objects—but she is obscurely moved by a housewifely responsibility for her run-down doll's house, half-understood guilt for past neglect, and so she defends herself. The anger is fierce, insults fly; each sees the other as the aggressor, the enemy. "To each, the other symbolizes the destructive power of the unknown world—not merely the outside world of baffling other people, but the inner world of the unknown and terrifying self."[95] Donald Winnicott (1896–1971), an English pediatrician and psychoanalyst with whose theories Haughton was familiar, held that parents did not need to be perfectly attuned, but just "ordinarily devoted" or "good enough" to protect their little ones from often experiencing overwhelming extremes of discomfort and distress, emotional or physical.[96] In this case, however, the mother doesn't just suppress the disturbance and separate her furious offspring so that she can continue dinner preparations. That would have been an intervention and bought temporary peace but "the fears and desires and needs that blew up into a quarrel will be unaffected."[97] In this case, the intervention is that of someone with a feel for the quality of human relationships so that the children are guided by the loving quality of their mother's peacemaking to repentance and reconciliation, to new insight into their own individual gifts and needs, and into the demands of love in their relationship:

> Real knowledge of oneself is something people can only dare to accept when love has broken through. Without love, self-knowledge must be rejected because it weakens the defences against the outside world…in the light of love self-knowledge is bearable, even welcome. So one of the effects of reconciliation is greater individuation, a more complete awareness of oneself as distinct, yet not cut off.[98]

Within the security of the mother's love, there was established in each child new self-understanding, new appreciation of each other's distinctiveness and value, and a new "community" within the family. The episode was salvific. The Spirit was present, grace was involved, and a transformation effected where each child grew in capacity for love, received and given. Haughton attended to the strong desire for belonging and self-realization in each child and invites us into her understanding. She is appropriating their desire for them, and for her readers.

The second new community of which Haughton writes is established in the sexual encounter of a young doctor and a dutiful single woman who has given up all thoughts of marriage. Haughton invites us to reach out for the intelligibility to be found in their desire for love. The woman, on the one hand, has hitherto unquestioningly devoted her life and wages to the care and support of her more attractive younger siblings and their needy mother, who subordinates the older sister's prospects to theirs. The doctor, on the other hand, has been repelled by the cozy domesticity of his parents' marriage, and in serving his patients with all his heart, has rejected any thought of a committed romantic relationship for himself. When the two meet at an office party, both are initially attracted by this apparent indifference in the other. As they continue to see each other, their discovery of their own growing attraction is resisted, but they go on meeting regularly. One day, they are drawn to give themselves to each other in a sexual encounter that for each was a disruption, not the way they had previously foreseen their personal futures, since each is seriously limited by their inner entanglements. Their genuinely loving mutual gift of self brings about a transformation that enlarges and completes what has begun in their formation. Though they don't quite realize the significance of their encounter, it is an experience of love and grace, the existential appropriation of their own desire. It is transformational, bringing out in each a new sense of themselves as loving and beloved, a new awareness of their own capacity for love and sacrifice, a new ability to make changes in their way of living. Each has mediated Christ to the other. Both have fears and habits to overcome and a distance to travel before they can follow through completely, but they are on the way. Their previous formation had made of them individuals capable of the change love called for, though this represented a clear discontinuity in each case:

> Just as the children's mother in the first example was able, by her real love, to provide the conditions for a decision of love in her children, so, in the lives of the lovers, their own realized love can provide the conditions for formation towards their own further decisions.[99]

They could not name their change as Haughton does, but they may well come to be able to. Their ongoing lovemaking provides a type of celebration, a liturgy, for expression.

The third situation is that of a middle-aged research scientist whose first conversion remained unexplained in any language that did justice to it and was lost to some extent in that its good effects faded, and yet he was left with a "bad conscience." It began when he picked up and began to read the pacifist, communist pamphlets left around by his intensely irritating sixteen-year-old daughter. He did this with some sense of atoning for his inability to do anything but clash with her, and gradually, some of his assumptions are challenged as he reads. One day, he goes so far as to ask her about her political opinions and "since she is generous as well as enthusiastic she conquers a desire to crow over this apparently sudden change in his attitude, and answers his questions with sense and an unaccustomed humility."[100] He learns about a practical initiative she and others are involved in, offering a drop-in club in a squalid area for people with nowhere to go in the evenings. It is the initiative of a young man who has bought the premises for this purpose and himself lives there in poverty, offering the needy of the neighborhood a loving welcome and tender interest. The father is moved by her sharing and his relationship with her is changed for the better. He accepts her invitation to visit the club and is shaken by his confrontation with the place, the helpers, and most particularly, the "ugly and intense" young founder, who is passionate and brusque with his followers but "gentle, infinitely adaptable and undemanding" toward a suspicious old tramp, "with an apparently infallible sense of when to speak and when to be silent."[101] As the man leaves with his daughter, he receives a smile and a simple, "Come back. We need you." This encounter with committed love and vital concern for human beings is life changing. The father sees his life as a futile succession of evasions of reality, drifting, avoiding the sharp edges of decision. He is able to see this and not run away from the knowledge of it because of the challenge presented by the young man who ran the place and a decision made during that first visit as a result of which he becomes a regular there.

> The kind of self that he has discovered is realized gradually, later on, but it is in this moment that he actually sees, and seeing, repents, and repenting, is reconciled. He reconciled to *himself*, to this newly stripped

and worthless and unlovely self, for it is in realizing the complete worthlessness of all that he had thought worthwhile…that he discovers his real value. And this value is not something he *has*, not a possession—great or little—but precisely something that is given, and is only realized in being given.[102]

There was joy in his new self-awareness. The change was manifested in his efforts to see his wife and children more as people than as adjuncts to himself; he had more physical energy, more sexual adventurousness with his wife; he became less of a "featherbed" to his work colleagues when they discussed issues with him. "In these early days he is carried on by the sheer power of his new experience of life. Everything seems easy and delightful; he does not ask himself what he ought to do but just does it."[103]

However, while the transforming action of the Spirit is clearly recognizable through the changed feelings and ways of acting, it is not so recognizable to the man himself. He has no guide other than his transformed conscience to assist him, no language in which to express his conversion except that of political realities such as *poverty, working class, self-sacrifice*—words that have new color and life for him within the group of helpers he meets regularly once a week. The young founder has no real interest in his helpers, only in the poor they serve, so the group has no corporate sense, no explicit self-awareness. The man has a feeling he can't express that something more ought to change in his life, but it doesn't, and finally the decision to accept a social invitation that entails missing his weekly commitment marks the beginning of a real letdown, a loss that has a deleterious effect on self, family, and work relationships. For transformation, when it happens, cannot be undone.

It seems important to realize that when the personality has been transformed it stays transformed. Whatever happens, the definition of personality thus achieved continues. It can be refused admittance, refused acknowledgement, but it is still there.…So the repentant awareness becomes a remorseful awareness, and the unbearable knowledge of what one is like is faced not in love, but in hatred and despair and rejection of what cannot be rejected because it is oneself.[104]

Later, after an accident, lonely and in pain, he responds to the evangelizing material provided by a night nurse and his felt need for love recognizes the love offered by Christ. "And the self-awareness with which he responds to this invitation is so total and so peaceful that the agony often indicated by the word 'repentance' is almost unnoticed....His self-discovery is primarily a discovery of himself as loved."[105] In the light of his new self-discovery, he knows what he must do and determines to do it. He is alone but will be able to find a Christian fellowship—or draw others into one by the power of his love—and there he will find a "liturgy" in which to celebrate his conversion and the love he discovered in Christ. He can find a name for what has happened, and that is significant because even without a community and a liturgy, if he has a language for his conversion, he has begun to understand and that is a key step toward appropriation. It helps that the language of his conversion uses words that already have meaning in his surrounding world and recalls the Christian teachings and stories of a well-loved nanny, although for him, this meaning is irradiated by the new love he has found.

The focus of the desire Haughton invites us to appropriate in each story is different because each represents a different stage in coming to be ourselves. The desire is clear, but its realization is purely existential. Haughton sees more clearly than can any of her characters what is afoot. The language with which the two children can express their conversion is through actions and words that have to do with being a family and individual giftedness. "The two lovers used a language which also, because of the way they thought of themselves as related to others, included and affected their other human relationships, not merely the all-important community between the two of them";[106] formation affects transformation not only in giving some grounding in love, but in providing the basis of this language in which it can become intelligible. In each transformative event, the whole personality—insofar as it is aware of itself—is transformed. The decision for love makes further formation more likely to be fruitful.

The goal of questions for intelligence is to reach an insight that confers intelligibility on experience—in the case of desire and love for God, religious experience. When we fully advert to what is happening, when we become aware of "the unlimited, infinite goodness that whispers in our limitless questioning,"[107] many people struggle to do justice to the experience and can only resort to figurative language, using the imagery of light, warmth, of abundant and overflowing life, or of an overwhelming sense of beauty and wonder. As Lonergan wrote, surely about his own experience of being-in-love with God,

> It is as though a room were filled with music though one can have no sure knowledge of its source. There is in the world, as it were, a charged field of love and meaning; here and there it reaches a notable intensity; but it is ever unobtrusive, hidden, inviting each of us to join. And join we must if we are to perceive it, for our perceiving is through our own loving.[108]

However, the community of faith helps us to find a "liturgy" in which to express, celebrate, and reenact what has happened to us, the outer word of God's revelation to put words on it, and the fellowship of others who call it by the same name.

BE REASONABLE!

It is essential that the insight into what has happened in religious experience be affirmed, if it is to be truly known and appropriated: "Experience and understanding taken together yield not knowledge but only thought."[109] Yet, how can we truly give rational assent to an interpretation of our religious experience, which posits more than natural and physiological reasons for our new outlook on this world and our place in it; requires us to rely on the outer word of a received wisdom in order to plumb the depths of our own loving desire; and reexpresses our sense of self-worth in terms of a wondrous divine predilection beyond imagining and a destiny out of this world? Assent, after all, is "virtually unconditioned" where there are no unanswered questions, and we transcend ourselves in affirming that this understanding of what has happened is more than just what we might hope or see as possibly true; it truly *is* the case.

Lonergan invites us, in following the dynamism of conscious intending, to rely on belief and the self-correcting process of learning. We choose to believe what is speaking to us through the demands of the human spirit, to advance toward moral maturity by giving our assent to what the eyes of religious love have revealed to us, and to allow subsequent growth and development to refine and adjust where we are not quite there yet.

> As our knowledge...*increases*, our responses...*are strengthened*...our freedom may exercise its *ever increasing thrust* toward authenticity. *So we move* to the existential moment....Then is the time for the exercise of vertical freedom.[110]

Five Steps of Belief

It is not unreasonable to believe the truths of faith, since for Lonergan belief involves five steps. We are not in a position to be the one immanently generating the knowledge of supernatural realities:

> What no eye has seen, nor ear heard,
>   nor the human heart conceived,
> what God has prepared for those who love him.
>
> (1 Cor 2:9)

However, the first step in belief is taken not by the person believing but by the authentic subjects whom we believe. What they truly know they transmit. The second step is a general judgment of value: it is appropriate that there be a division of labor in acquiring knowledge, both in the historical and the social dimensions.[111] For example, we trust the GPS system to get us where we want to go, though we ourselves may be technologically challenged; we find the periodic table reliable, even though we did not develop it ourselves. Renaissance man may have aspired to a truly general knowledge of all reality, but in our age of specialization, we have prudently given up that ambition and agree to be experts in our own fields of competence, learning from others in theirs. The third step is also a value judgment, this time a specific rather than a general one. It regards the trustworthiness of the source of the information, the competence of the expert, or the sound judgment of the authority. We decide whether they merit our reliance, and then we are self-aware enough to admit that it could be true even if it seems counterintuitive:

> Finally, when everything favors belief except the intrinsic probability of the statement to be believed, one can ask oneself whether the fault is not in oneself, whether it is not the limitations of one's own horizon that prevents one from grasping the intrinsic probability of the statement in question.[112]

The fourth step is precisely this decision to believe, and the fifth, the act of believing.

Where the authority revealing is God and the Son who alone knows the Father and makes him known; where the witnesses are faithful in transmitting his message and the community develops, on these bases, genuine expressions of the love that unites its members, it is not unreasonable to believe, even if it seems "too good to be true."[113] Furthermore, the self-correcting process of learning is still functioning through the "passionateness of being," the *eros* of the human spirit, and can gradually help us sort out distortions. Crowe says that Lonergan agrees with Newman in holding that it is more constructive in general to believe than to doubt:

> Of the two, I would rather have to maintain that we ought to begin with believing everything that is offered to our acceptance, than that it is our duty to doubt of everything. The former, indeed, seems the true way of learning. In that case, we soon discover and discard what is contradictory to itself, and error having always some portion of truth in it, and truth having a reality which error does not, we may expect, that when there is an honest purpose and fair talents, we shall somehow

make our way forward, the error falling off from the
mind, and the truth developing and occupying it.[114]

This assumes steps one to three in the process of believing,
these being implied in the "honest purpose and fair talents" that
Lonergan requires of us. Tad Dunne[115] tells us that he has never
had an overwhelming sense of God's love for him such as may
occur in religious experience; yet for him believing that God loves
us is a judgment worth embracing with all one's heart. It is an act
of faith, a judgment of value born of religious love.

> As it happened, it was Lonergan who helped me under-
> stand the remarkable character of the evidence on God's
> love for me. The word of love from God is everything
> that the word of a friend is, plus a very different kind
> of word. A friend uses words, gestures, gifts; a friend
> shows up in time of need. God too, in Christ Jesus, uses
> words, gestures, gifts; Jesus showed up in our time of
> need. But God also takes up residence in the heart and
> loves from there. Lonergan calls this the "inner word" in
> hearts matched by the "outer word" of Jesus in history.
> Most poignantly, I realized that my love for God is the
> quintessential evidence that God must love me too.[116]

Dunne has attended to the reality of his own loving experience, understood and affirmed it. To affirm these beliefs involves
accepting the self-knowledge made possible by the new light
through a repentance that is not destructive but rather constructive of the new self. This also means assenting to a change that
has happened, accepting the new values—the new horizon—in
a self-surrender that can appreciate its enlargement. The eyes of
religious love open us to the possibility of belief in revealed truth
as transmitted by our faith community, and Christians assent to
its word: "For God so loved the world that he gave his only Son,
so that everyone who believes in him may not perish but may
have eternal life" (John 3:16); "Let the same mind be in you that
was in Christ Jesus" (Phil 2:5). With this understanding of the
reasonable way in which belief can function, we can affirm our
self-understanding as forgiven sinners, beloved in ourselves and in

Christ, sent with his exemplary mission to build a friendlier world and become ourselves a word of hope and love.

BE RESPONSIBLE!

The gracious gift of God's love is operative in us at the level that controls, by its choices, what we will attend to, understand, and verify, so we can move into the realms of interiority and transcendence, and return with new insight and commitment to the service of God and neighbor. As we come to know our own religious experience and affirm our own being-in-love, we are more likely to "seek the One who calls us by this gift of desire."[117]

> It also gives rise to man's quest for the otherworldly loveableness with which he is in love, and the fruits of that quest vary greatly as one moves from earlier to later stages of human meaning.[118]

Religious experience, surfacing within consciousness, has always this invitational dimension.

The invitation is to a subject-to-subject relationship with God. God honors the autonomy and full human functioning of human beings, creating them with the capacity to seek and find the divine fullness of Being to which they are oriented, but fully respecting their freedom. The very restlessness of the human heart in face of anything less than complete understanding, truth, reality, value, and love is a cry for completion. The unease of conscience resulting from unauthenticity in thought and action calls to repentance and redemption. But God does not coerce. In religious experience, we may come to know the infinite love that affirms our being, and the responsive love for God with which we are gifted, but nothing compels us. The invitation as formulated for the Christian is to be beloved, to love in return, and to honor the sovereign freedom and goodness of the God who calls us into the conversational heart of God's own inner life.[119] Being-in-love is a participation in the trinitarian relations.

The outward expression of love is not incidental, Lonergan reminds us: it has a constitutive role. When a man and a woman love each other, but do not avow their love, they are not yet in love. Their very silence means that they have not yet reached the point of self-surrender and self-donation. It is the love that each freely and fully reveals to the other that brings about the radically new situation of being-in-love and that begins the unfolding of its lifelong implications.[120]

It is the mutual acknowledgment of love received and love welcomed and returned that constitutes the joyous and liberating "change of state" that is being-in-love. While it lasts, there is glad subordination of one's own selfish inclinations to the well-being and joy of the other, a total willingness to be and do the best one can for the beloved's sake. Self-transcendence becomes not only possible but desirable. "Loved, forgiven, and with their subjectivity restored to its native capacity for self-transcendence, human beings can be 'origins of value' in themselves, and in their relationships with others."[121] There is a strong likelihood of their treating all other human beings as subjects also, as loved and accepted, and as invited into the same intimacy within the conversation of the Holy Three. Their transformed subjectivity helps to transform the world.

However, Lonergan writes not just of interiorly differentiated consciousness, but of religiously differentiated consciousness. This begins with religious experience and authentic human response to the transcendent invitation received in religious experience—religious conversion—but it seems that it can go further. Lonergan seems to be suggesting a continuum in this matter, which we may see as relating to the stages of the mystic way. Religiously differentiated consciousness, he says, is approached by the ascetic and reached by the mystic:

> In the latter, there are two quite different modes of apprehension, of being related, of consciously existing, namely, (1) the commonsense mode operating in the world mediated by meaning and (2) the mystical mode withdrawing from the world mediated by meaning into a silent and all-absorbing self-surrender in response to God's gift of his love.[122]

Like St. Teresa, following the mystic path in contemplative prayer while attending to the governance of her reform and the practicalities of administration, the mystic lives in two worlds. Both worlds are grounded in the love flooding the inmost heart. The world of common sense is suffused with God's values. But in the second world,

> it can also set up a different type of consciousness by withdrawing one from the world mediated by meaning into a cloud of unknowing. Then one is for God, belongs to him, gives oneself to him, not by using words, images, concepts, but in a silent, joyous, peaceful surrender to his initiative.[123]

This is a development in religiously differentiated consciousness: all gift, gathering up and sublating the lower levels of the human person in such a way that they are active rather than passive, yet enabling a progressive transcendence of self, and content with the negations of an apophatic theology, with the recognition that God is not anything we can conceive. For it is in love, and on its love there are no reservations or conditions or qualifications:

> By such love it is oriented positively to what is transcendent in lovableness. Such a positive orientation and the consequent self-surrender, as long as they are operative, enable one to dispense with any intellectually apprehended object. And when they cease to be operative, the memory of them enables one to be content with enumerations of what God is not.[124]

How one may grow in religiously differentiated consciousness, in ever deepening intimacy with the Holy Three, is the matter of Benedict XVI's encyclical letter *Deus Caritas Est* (2005). He tells us that the command to love is less a command, and hence extrinsic to us, than something intrinsic to us. We are made for love and to fulfill ourselves is ultimately to give ourselves to another.

> Yet *eros* and *agape*—ascending love and descending love—can never be completely separated. The more the two, in their different aspects, find a proper unity in the one reality of love, the more the true nature of love in

general is realized....The element of *agape* thus enters into this love, for otherwise *eros* is impoverished and even loses its own nature. On the other hand, man cannot live by oblative, descending love alone. He cannot always give, he must also receive. Anyone who wishes to give love must also receive love as a gift. Certainly, as the Lord tells us, one can become a source from which rivers of living water flow (cf. *Jn* 7:37-38). Yet to become such a source, one must constantly drink anew from the original source, which is Jesus Christ, from whose pierced heart flows the love of God (cf. *Jn* 19:34). (*Deus Caritas Est* 7)[125]

In *Complacency and Concern in the Thought of St. Thomas*,[126] Crowe writes of love in us, as in the Trinity, as a term before it is a principle of motion toward the good, looking back to its source before it looks ahead to a goal. His description of the state of being-in-love is as resting in God's love, *complacentia boni*, "consent to being, harmony with all that is, peace with the universe."[127] The Holy Spirit in this context is to be thought of "as an activity which is a state like joy and happiness, as an eternal, restful joy-ing that corresponds to the divine is-ing by which I have heard a philosopher describe God's being. Something analogous is true of God's image, in the successive stages of earthly affection and heavenly beatitude."[128]

Human capacity for self-transcendence meets its fulfillment, human desire turns to joy, when religious conversion transforms the existential subject into a subject in love, "a subject held, grasped, possessed, owned through a total and so an other-worldly love."[129] Then there is a new basis for doing the good, seeking the true, and sharing whatever understanding of the mysteries can be reached in a painstaking search. We are given a context, which is the cosmos, and a purpose, which is the reign of God on earth, "righteousness and peace and joy in the Holy Spirit" (Rom 14:17).

We have now considered how Lonergan fulfilled his lifetime desire in producing *Method in Theology*. Lonergan had nineteen more years of life rather than the five he thought he was to expect, and he continued to teach and to develop his thought on matters theological and methodological. He sometimes gave papers at the annual Lonergan Workshops held in the summer at Boston College and listened with his heart as well as his keen mind to those presented by his students. The consummate dialectician himself, he appreciated their considerable achievements and was willing at times to ask the apposite developing question. He was free also in these later years to follow a second consuming interest— economics. He wanted to contribute further to the good of human society by finding a new economic model "so that the widows and orphans can eat."[130] We will not follow him there[131] because it is beyond the scope of this study, but in the following chapter, we will seek further insight into his mature reflection on the affective dimension of intentionality; affective conversion in his writings and those of some former students by now teaching others; and interiority as a realm or stage of meaning. We will further explore how vertical finality as evolutionary enters into human consciousness in the experience of grace and the role of interiority, natural and religious, in the appropriation of desire.

5

DEVELOPMENT IN RELIGIOUS INTERIORITY

This chapter examines difficulties that can be encountered in appropriating the "love without restriction," which is received as gift in religious conversion, and in finding healing and effective freedom to live the demands of intellectual and moral conversion in a way commensurate with our desire for goodness and truth. We will consider further the question of the interrelatedness of the "way up" and the "way down" in the later writings of Lonergan, and ask whether a fourth conversion may be required to live in the third stage of meaning.[1] We will also find a helpful expansion of the notion of desire and its appropriation in the work of former students of Lonergan. We will then consider how the authenticity of the individual is involved in concern for the major authenticity of the tradition that nurtures communities, and note the need for commitment and ongoing development for the sake of human attentiveness, intelligence, reasonableness, responsibility, and loving kindness in the building of a friendlier world.

SELF-APPROPRIATION

Following the publication of *Method*, Lonergan continued to teach, often in response to invitations and questions from his readers. In lectures and papers of this period, he regularly uses phrases already familiar from that work, but at times, responds further to questions asked for elucidation of its key ideas. Such deepening and expanding on themes continued for nearly a decade. In an interview at the First International Lonergan Congress held in Florida during Easter 1970, Lonergan gives a clear and succinct statement on the extent and significance of the self-appropriation he is advocating. Asked whether his generalized empirical method is a way or a theory, he suggests that it is a way, though that way can be clarified theoretically:

> But that self-appropriation can be objectified. It's a heightening of consciousness—as one moves from attention to intelligence, to reasonableness, to responsibility, to *religious experience*. These modalities of consciousness, the *a priori* that they constitute, *that* can be objectified. Not in the sense of subject-object—in here now, out there now—but in the sense that objectivity is the fruit of authentic subjectivity. That self-appropriation can be objectified and its objectification is theory.[2]

Self-appropriation is coming to understand and affirm and act out of, not only one's experiencing, understanding, and knowing, but also one's existential decision-making. Together these are the way to live a fully human life. In this personal appropriation of the way we are made, Lonergan now includes really owning the saving experiences that have opened new horizons for human persons in the realm of grace and religious faith. These are at work in us to extend and support our authentic living and are to be welcomed because they give us a better sense of where we are heading. As he says,

> The exercise of self-appropriation gives you the structure that generates horizons. And because you have the structure that's generating horizon, because that structure is heuristic, you're anticipating. If the intelligible, being, the good—what you mean by those terms—is what is correlative to the desire to understand, to be reasonable, to be responsible; then, in yourself, you have the subjective pole of an objective field. You have also,

in intelligent reasonable responsibility, norms, built-in norms, that are yourself.

They are not propositions about yourself; but yourself, in your spiritual reality, to guide you in working out what that objective horizon is, the objective pole of the horizon. It's normative, it's potential. Not absolute, in the sense that you have it all tucked away.[3] But you have the machinery for going at it, and you know what happens when you do.[4]

We are not guaranteed that any self-knowledge we attain will be free of illusion, even delusion, but we do have the wherewith to "go at it." Lonergan acknowledges that some individual "may get caught in some sort of cul-de-sac and that's his misfortune," but since what he is talking about is a way, a dynamism, he identifies the way out of such an apparently dead end as the dynamic of asking further questions or, even more significantly, of really listening to and accepting the questions that stir one within.

Questioners were interested in the horizon set up in us by God's gift of love that grounds religious conversion—did it transcend the horizon of being?[5] Lonergan said no—the good goes beyond, is more comprehensive than the intelligible, the true, and the real, just as religious conversion takes you beyond both intellectual and moral conversion:

But it's not beyond being, if this being in love, total commitment...is the full actuation of the movement towards the intelligible, towards the true, towards the real, towards the good. This is the ultimate step in it. It's what you are *a priori*, what your authentic subjectivity is open to. It occurs, insofar as it does, through God's grace.[6]

In this interview, Lonergan does not go on to speak of God in this context as Being Itself, but he has always contended that human intending, human questioning, human desire is up to and including God. Clearly, the new horizon of religious conversion is even more open to a goodness beyond criticism, which is wholly transcendent beauty and truth. We come to know ourselves as longing for this. The text that Lonergan likes to use from this time on to demonstrate the undeserved, unexpected nature of this horizon shift is Ezekiel 11:19. As Lonergan states, "God plucking out the heart of stone which has no desire whatever to be a heart of flesh and putting in the heart of flesh, totally beyond the deserts, ambitions even, of the heart of stone."[7] Once the gifted change has happened, however, "being in love is a fact, and it's what you are, it's existential. And your living flows from it. It's the first principle, as long as it lasts, and…it's the source of all one's desires and fears, all the good one can see."[8]

The good now within the scope of our desiring is the ultimate in goodness, the truly worthwhile. As clarified by the outer word of the Christian faith community, it is to "let the same mind be in you that was in Christ Jesus" (Phil 2:5), where we follow the gaze of the Son to the Father, and in the Spirit, embrace the Father's comprehensive plan for human flourishing in a friendly universe. Lonergan sets out clearly some of the issues raised by this appropriation task in "Mission and the Spirit" (1976), which was written for a *Concilium* Festschrift in honor of Edward Schillebeeckx for his sixtieth birthday.[9]

In this article, Lonergan brings together in a compendious way key themes from *Insight* and *Method* to address this question: What in terms of human consciousness is the transition from the natural to the supernatural? He also revisits vertical finality as another name for self-transcendence, and the human subject in the context of human community and the divine self-communication of the Son and the Spirit. We are invited to consider the experiential dimension of grace and the way in which, through faith-filled reflection, we can affirm the redemptive action of God within a life of flawed and inconsistent response to the *eros* of the human spirit.

The self-appropriation advocated here is grounded in the reality of an evolutionary view of the universe: "As man's being is being-in-the-world, his self-understanding has to be not only of himself but also of his world."[10] This includes a more developed understanding of the roles vertical finality, probability/Providence[11] and the absolutely supernatural play in human and social progress when the evolutionary process is within the comprehensive design of the omniscient and omnipotent cause of the whole universe.

We see a new relevance in Lonergan's concept of emergent probability, which he was later to characterize casually as "not as the way God knows, but as what God's knowledge causes. It's the intelligibility *to us* of Divine Providence."[12]

In the physical universe, any higher order of being is beyond the proportion of lower orders and can be regarded as relatively supernatural to them, but "the divine order is beyond the proportion of any possible creature and so is absolutely supernatural."[13] Yet, we affirm within the Christian faith community that for the human person, vertical finality is to God, "so that man is not merely subordinate to God but also enters into the divine life and participates in it."[14] In the perspective of Rublev's icon of the Trinity, we are invited to take our place at the divine table and be at home there. What is fully human in us is subsumed into the communion of love at the heart of the Trinity, losing nothing of its humanness. But that humanness is enriched, transformed; through the Spirit it is God's life and love that empowers our self-transcendent operations in the world. This vertical finality does not operate inevitably. Lonergan points out that its ends may or may not be reached, and it remains multivalent and obscure. Its obscurity lies largely in the fact that it is only in the measure that it has been attained that it can be recognized. At the outset, there are intimations of it, perhaps aspirations, but many questions remain. Only as God's self-revelation is progressively recognized—the meaning of our strivings and groanings interpreted—can these intimations be known as announcing "a new and higher birth."[15]

> Vertical finality enters into evolutionary perspective. It does so inasmuch as emergence, unfolding, development, maturity follow the analogy of evolutionary process. Such process is to be understood in accord with emergent probabilities and under divine planning and action. By the analogy of that process is meant, not some basis for *a priori* prediction, but only a basis for *a posteriori* interpretation. Here as elsewhere, things are known insofar as they are in act.[16]

Our capacity for self-transcendence and its unrestricted openness to all that is intelligible, true, and good, our orientation to Divine Mystery, can be known to some extent as we reflect on our own living out of what it means to be authentically human and "in Christ."[17] The qualification is necessary. Lonergan had noted earlier that it can be difficult for a theologian to discern the patterns operative in mature religious living because he or she is too close to it. Even in recalling and studying their past, a theologian may find that

> even then his difficulties may not be at an end: he may be unable to associate any precise meaning with the words I have used; he may be too familiar with the reality of which I speak to connect it with what I say; he may be looking for something with a label on it, when he should simply be heightening his consciousness of the power working within him and adverting to its long-term effects.[18]

The tendency to look for something "with a label on it" is understandable, but grace, as the love with which God floods our hearts by the Holy Spirit given to us, is operative long before it is recognized.[19] Our own loving has much to teach us of the wonderful works of God.

It can also be known in our experience "of a twofold frustration of that capacity: the objective frustration of life in a world distorted by sin; the subjective frustration of one's incapacity to break with one's own evil ways."[20] As we encounter the egoism of ourselves and others, and what Lonergan tellingly calls "the securer egoisms of groups,"[21] shortsighted failure to attend to expert advice and to see beyond immediate satisfactions, sophisticated rationalizations of situational and personal impotence, we can be moved to seek the deliverance, redemption, and salvation we need. The awareness of this need is an important part of self-appropriation, and we know ourselves and the plan of God better when we realize that salvation, when it comes, always comes "as the charity that dissolves the hostility and the divisions of past injustice and present hatred; it comes as the hope that withstands psychological, economic, political, social cultural determinisms; it comes with the faith that can liberate reason from the rationalizations that blinded it."[22]

This experience of healing and growth can bring further insight into the compassion and patience of God's evolutionary plan for the universe and for each of us; as an invitation to accept our own and each other's slow development with similar patience and compassion. There is a gradual change effected in us by grace for which we can take no credit, but that is experienced as a deeper sense of our orientation to the divine and to the divine purposes for the universe of which we are part. We come to see things differently, want to love as we are ourselves beloved, and can accept the pain involved in accepting the consequences of sin, our own and others', walking the pathway of sacrificial love that the Son has recommended by his own exemplary living. Increasingly, we can know ourselves to be incorporated in this movement of the Spirit, despite occasional relapses:

> It is experience of a transformation one did not bring about but rather underwent, as divine providence let evil take its course and vertical finality be heightened, as it let one's circumstances shift, one's dispositions change, new encounters occur, and—so gently and quietly—one's heart be touched.[23]

In his treatment of vertical finality at this stage, Lonergan speaks frequently of the passionateness of being as a way to envisage the whole extent of the working of the *eros* of the human spirit. We have learned that he sees the dynamism of human intentionality resting on operators that promote activity from one level to the next. These operators[24] are questions for intelligence with respect to data; for reflection with respect to our guesses, insights, inventions, and discoveries; and for deliberation asking whether proposed courses of action resulting from them are feasible and worthwhile. In each case, the lower level, preparing for the next that sublates it, is an instance of vertical finality, which is realized when the higher levels function.

By 1976, Lonergan is writing of the *eros* of the human spirit—the passionateness of being—as being on a par with questioning as the operator moving us to self-transcendence. He speaks of it as a "quasi-operator." It is akin to the powerful dynamism of questioning but it has a further dimension of its own: "it underpins and accompanies and reaches beyond the subject as experientially, intelligently, rationally, morally conscious."[25] When we recollect the "dreams of the morning," which can reveal the truth of some of our deepest fears and desires in symbolism and metaphorical scenarios, and our own better judgment on courses of action we are engaged on or may be planning, we may be moved to admire the "inner film director" who is so skillfully on the side of our health and flourishing.[26] This is an example of the transition from the neural to the psychic, which "ushers into consciousness not only the exigencies of unconscious vitality but also the exigencies of vertical finality." When a person is self-actualizing, this "underpinning" will bring deficiency needs to awareness, but it goes further:

> It shapes the images that release insight; it recalls evidence that is being overlooked; it may embarrass wakefulness, as it disturbs sleep, with the spectre, the shock, the shame of misdeeds. As it channels into consciousness the feedback of our aberrations and our unfulfilled strivings, so for the Jungians it manifests its archetypes through symbols to preside over the genesis of the ego and to guide the individuation process from the ego to the self.[27]

We will find this quasi-operator not just *underpinning* our conscious and intentional operations, but also *accompanying* them, providing "the mass and momentum of our lives, the color and tone and power of feeling,"[28] as we have considered earlier. It also *overarches*:

> There it is the topmost quasi-operator that by intersubjectivity prepares, by solidarity entices, by falling in love establishes us as members of community. Within each individual, vertical finality heads for self-transcendence. In an aggregation of self-transcending individuals there is the significant coincidental manifold in which can emerge a new creation.[29]

Vertical finality is natural to us as human beings, and it is natural for us to love not only our families, our affective partners, our friends and our country, but even to love God above all else. In fact, however, we also live under the reign of sin and redemption lies "not in what is possible to nature but in what is effected by the grace of Christ."[30] Lonergan maintains that vertical finality is heightened precisely by our own "revulsion from the objective reign of sin"[31] and our experience of our personal impotence, our inability consistently to live as we are called to by our anticipation of a goodness beyond criticism.

In his evolutionary perspective, this moves us to seek deliverance, opens us to the outer word of the economy of grace and salvation that comes with the sending of the Word and the mission of the Spirit.

> So the self-communication of the Son and the Spirit proceeds through history by a communication that at once is cognitive, constitutive and redemptive: it is cognitive, for it discloses in whom we are to believe; it is constitutive, for it crystallizes the inner gift of the love of God into overt Christian fellowship; it is redemptive, for it liberates human liberty from thralldom to sin, and it guides those it liberates to the kingdom of the Father.[32]

The underpinning, accompanying action of this quasi-operator cooperates with the influence of grace and increases the possibility and probability of its overarching building of the reign of Christ in human communities. The experience of grace "is the experience of a new community, in which faith and hope and charity dissolve rationalizations, break determinisms, and reconcile the estranged and the alienated, and there is reaped the harvest of the Spirit that is "love, joy, peace, patience, kindness, goodness, faithfulness, gentleness, and self-control" (Gal 5:22–23).[33]

In this way, grace heals faltering achievement and gives a new impetus to authentic living out of our full human potential. The desire within us, the passionateness of being, is the quasi-operator drawing us into communion with the very life of the Trinity, our greatest joy now, our future beatitude and all gift.

What has come to be called, none too felicitously, "the way up and the way down," is formulated explicitly in several papers presented between 1974 and 1980. The dynamism of the upward

movement as the *eros* of the questioning human subject is complemented and completed by the new "downward" direction where
the dynamism is not simply subjective, it is intersubjective—the
intersubjective in its full range from spontaneous intersubjectivity
to persons in community.[34] In "Healing and Creating in History"
(1975),[35] Lonergan clarified his key idea of the healing action of
the "development from above downwards" as complementing the
upward trajectory of human creativity in all human living. Progress happens in human societies and economies as the result of an
ongoing learning process:

> The creative task is to find the answers. It is a matter of
> insight, not of one insight but of many, not of isolated
> insights but of insights that coalesce, that complement
> and correct one another, that influence policies and
> programs, that reveal their shortcomings in their con-
> crete results, that give rise to further correcting insights,
> corrected policies, corrected programs, that gradually
> accumulate into the all-round, balanced, smoothly func-
> tioning system that from the start was needed but at the
> start was not yet known.[36]

However, if the flow of fresh insights dries up, and circumstances
continue to change, the initially successful system can well become
a frustrating and unworkable imposition enforced by a dominant
minority in thrall to the bias of group egoism, "blind to the fact
that the group no longer fulfills its once useful function and that it
is merely clinging to power by all the maneuvers that in one way or
another block development and impede progress."[37] The advance
of progress is halted and decline sets in as a result of the distortions
of bias.

> Increasingly the situation becomes, not the cumulative
> project of coherent and complementary insights, but the
> dump in which are heaped up the amorphous and incom-
> patible products of all the biases of self-centered and
> shortsighted individuals and groups. Finally, the more the
> objective situation becomes a mere dump, the less is there
> any possibility of human intelligence gathering from the

situation anything more than a lengthy catalogue of the aberrations and the follies of the past.[38]

Just as an individual can get stuck in a rut—resisting any further challenge, settling for a personal status quo that becomes familiar and manageable despite its obvious anomalies because that individual is no longer open to the inquiring spirit of the "passionateness of being"—so too the way we have always done things becomes, for groups, the enemy of the call to serve others by recognizing the needs of the times.

But human development is of two quite different kinds, Lonergan insists. The way to the fore in *Insight*, and to a lesser degree also in *Method*, and here called *creating*. He characterizes it as "from below upwards," and it proceeds "from experience to growing understanding, from growing understanding to balanced judgment, from balanced judgment to fruitful courses of action, and from fruitful action to the new situations that call forth further understanding, profounder judgment, richer courses of action."[39]

It is complemented by the *healing* trajectory. There is a second way, "a development from above downwards,"[40] also implicit in *Method* as the guiding principle of the last four functional specialties, and, in fact, prior in the life of a human being. At birth, we are all potential, plasticity[41] in its most remarkable form, and able, in the measure of the love that surrounds us, to learn an amazing amount—language, ideas, facts, skills, attitudes, and values. This is the childhood learning that occurs in the ambiance of parental love and guidance, the warmth and friction of family relationships, in schooling, and by gradual socialization into culture and the community of faith. The major part of all human knowledge is transmitted in these ways and held as beliefs long before they are tested in the field of human trial and error. It is in this heritage of traditional learning and in this context of affective development that the ability to function intellectually and morally is progressively developed. It flowers when an individual falls in love: "the domestic love of family, the human love of one's tribe, one's city, one's country, mankind; the divine love that orients man in his cosmos and expresses itself in his worship."[42] Just as in the life of individuals, so also in the life of societies and economies there is a need for the love that reveals values:

At once it commands commitment and joyfully carries it out, no matter what the sacrifice involved. Where hatred reinforces bias, love dissolves it, whether it be the bias of unconscious motivation, the bias of individual or group egoism, or the bias of omnicompetent, shortsighted common sense. Where hatred plods around in ever narrower vicious circles, love breaks the bonds of psychological and social determinisms with the conviction of faith and the power of hope."[43]

Here, Lonergan affirms the working out in human affairs of the principle he expressed in *Insight*: "A man or woman knows that he or she is in love by making the discovery that all spontaneous and deliberate tendencies and actions regard the beloved."[44] The healing trajectory is at its most evident in "other-worldly falling in love" that, as we saw in *Method*, is "total and permanent self-surrender without conditions, qualifications, reservations."[45]

It is being-in-love with God…the basic fulfilment of our conscious intentionality. That fulfilment brings a deep-set joy that can remain despite humiliation, failure, privation, pain, betrayal, desertion. That fulfilment brings a radical peace, the peace that the world cannot give. That fulfilment bears fruit in a love of one's neighbour that strives mightily to bring about the kingdom of God on earth.[46]

It is perhaps only in the personal appropriation of the love poured out in our hearts by the Holy Spirit that we come anywhere near to living out the potential for the fullness of humanity which is made visible in the life and work of Jesus of Nazareth.

From a superficial reading of such passages in Lonergan, we could see that self-appropriation at the level of feelings is a straightforward affair, as accessible to our attention, understanding, and naming as are the cognitive operations, but there are passages that show that he can also envisage complications. Unrecognized and unacknowledged feelings sometimes cloud the judgment and skew decision-making. There may be need for skilled therapeutic treatment where confusion and distress are beyond the capacity of an individual or their friends within the community to lift, and Lonergan instances Carl Roger's client-centered therapy as one way of coming to know ourselves at the feeling level:

> What can be done for insights, can also be done for feelings. Feelings as simply felt pertain to an infrastructure. But as merely felt, so far from being integrated into an equable flow of consciousness, they may become a source of disturbance, upset, inner turmoil. Then a cure or part of a cure would seem to be had from the client-centered therapist who provides the patient with an ambiance in which he is at ease, can permit feelings to emerge without being engulfed by them, come to distinguish them from other inner events, differentiate among them, add recognition, bestow names, gradually manage to encapsulate within a superstructure of knowledge and language, of assurance and confidence, what had been an occasion for disorientation, dismay, disorganization.[47]

The hitherto unrecognizable feelings are subsequently less able to shape conduct in undesirable ways. However, there is also a gap, even after religious conversion, between aspiration and actual achievement of existential authenticity, for "human authenticity is never some serene and secure possession. It is ever a withdrawal from unauthenticity, and every successful withdrawal only brings to light the need for further withdrawals."[48] This is not, in and of itself, a barrier to growth. Just as our growth toward truth involves the elimination of oversights and mistakes in the self-correcting process of learning, so our moral development is through recognition of failure and repentance, and religious development is likewise open to aberration: "of itself, self-transcendence involves tension between the self as transcending and the self as transcended."[49] However, this dialectical development in our being-in-love in an unrestricted manner with someone transcendent in lovableness can be rendered more than normally problematic for some, and those whose human affective development is less than adequate can find themselves in difficulties.

THE WORK OF FORMER STUDENTS OF LONERGAN

Following the publication of *Method in Theology*, some of Lonergan's former students were already trying to integrate his thinking into current psychological systems: relevant here are Robert Doran, SJ, who wrote on "psychic conversion," bringing Jungian dream analysis and depth psychology into dialogue with Lonergan's intentionality analysis; and Bernard Tyrrell, with his treatment of neurosis, both deprivational and repressive, by means of twofold "affectional conversion." Lonergan spoke and wrote respectfully[50] of their efforts to understand the difficulties experienced by those with emotional and psychological problems in entering fully into the effective freedom to which love is calling them. In *Insight*, dramatic bias had been identified as a flight from understanding caused by a "psychic wound"[51] resulting in the suppression of questions that would expose it and therefore leading to irrational behavior. In *Method*, he commented,

> Besides the immediate world of the infant and the adult's world mediated by meaning, there is the mediation of immediacy by meaning when one objectifies cognitional process in transcendental method and when one discovers, identifies, accepts one's submerged feelings in psychotherapy.[52]

Lonergan recognized the value of advances in the human, psychological, and social sciences,[53] and as he began to speak of "development in the way down" as complementary to his cognitional process from below upward, he acknowledged the key significance of human affectivity in human growth:

> The handing on of development…works from above downwards: it begins in the affectivity of the infant, the child, the son, the pupil, the follower. On affectivity rests the apprehension of values. On the apprehension of values rests belief. On belief follows the growth in understanding of one who has found a genuine teacher and has been initiated into the study of masters of the

past. Then to confirm one's growth in understanding comes experience made mature and perceptive by one's developed understanding.[54]

This is the desirable progression: love is the key factor, and experiences of safety and "good enough parenting" during the first three years of a child's life have definite impacts on subsequent ability to recognize and respond to nurture.[55] Lonergan was also aware of the damage that can occur to developing affectivity, and its consequences, which can be severe:

> One's affectivity can have things go wrong with it before you even know what affectivity is, and it keeps getting worse. There is an affective conversion and there is affective liberation.[56]

Lonergan uses the term *affective conversion* in "Natural Right and Historical Mindedness," an address to the American Catholic Philosophers Association in 1977: "But in the contemporary context it is such self-transcendence as includes an intellectual, a moral, and an affective conversion." Here he continues, after speaking of the other two, "Finally, as affective, it is commitment to love in the home, loyalty in the community, faith in the destiny of man."[57] It would seem here, however, to be almost synonymous with or in place of the term *religious conversion*, since the formulation is very close to that used in *Method* for being-in-love.[58] In general, Lonergan's own preferred manner of tackling imperfection was that of the traditional purgative and illuminative way:

> We have no choice but to follow the advice of John Henry Newman—to accept ourselves as we are and by dint of constant and persevering attention, intelligence, reasonableness, responsibility, strive to expand what is true and force out what is mistaken in views that we have inherited or spontaneously developed.[59]

It is the constant turning away from unauthenticity as it is recognized that is the nearest human beings come to authenticity for Lonergan, though this recognition comes more readily, more reliably to some than others. The study of the healing of psychic wounds he left to others, such as Robert Doran, SJ.[60]

One of Doran's main concerns in developing his insights into the need for further "conversion" at the affective, psychic level—what he called "psychic conversion"—was to generate explanatory categories connecting psychotherapy with the self-appropriation of the existential subject, as a dimension of theological foundations.[61]

He saw depth psychology as able to bring about the identification of affective aberration by the study of symbolic images evoked by or evoking feelings, and then the needed "transformation of the psychic component of what Freud calls 'the censor' from a repressive to a constructive agency in a person's development."[62] Where feelings have become dissociated from repressed images, skilled therapists enable clients to attend to symbolism in language and analysis of dreams "to mediate a capacity to disengage the symbolic or imaginal constitution of the feelings in which values are apprehended."[63] This makes depth psychology a way of addressing at another level the neglect or truncation of the subject with which Lonergan was dealing at this period in writings such as "the Subject."[64] Doran writes,

> It is with respect to the existential subject that we may
> turn to reflection on the body, on image and feeling, on
> symbol and story, on intersubjectivity, companionship,
> collaboration, friendship and love. It is also the existen-
> tial subject who brings into being, maintains, and trans-
> forms the world mediated by meaning.[65]

We become normal human beings, Lonergan suggests, "only by mastering vast systems of symbols and adapting our muscles, our nerves, our cerebral cortex, to respond to them accurately and precisely."[66] Human beings are the subjects of symbolic systems that mediate the world by meaning. "What happens," Doran asks, "when self-appropriating subjectivity, carefully tutored by Lonergan's intentionality analysis, becomes psychically self-appropriating subjectivity?"[67] He envisages a time when there will emerge a new unity-differentiation of philosophy, depth psychology, and theology through our knowledge of the transcendental infrastructure of human subjectivity:

Psychotherapy as we have known it is clearly a transitional stage, not only in the life of individuals but also in the evolution of Western culture. It must be relativized, not only by method, but also by the "soul beyond psychology," the soul in dialogue and concert with the God of love, the soul that is the life to which both method in its entirety and psychotherapy in particular point and which both method and psychotherapy mediate in a new way.[68]

Doran reports that, in 1974, he saw the aim of his psychic conversion as "the healing of a psychic rift," and by *psychic rift* he meant "not only dramatic bias from below but also something very like what Heidegger is perhaps naming when he speaks of the forgetfulness of Being, at least if he means the forgetfulness of an already given, temporally and historically conditioned facticity that is mediated by meaning 'from above.'"[69]

In 2003, the form this healing takes in his thinking and writing is "a habitual being-at-home with, not being alienated from, the stream of an empirical consciousness that receives data mediated by meaning,"[70] the retrieval or reestablishing of a link between the inquiring and critical spirit and the mediated immediacy of that empirical consciousness. To be healed is to be at ease with the true functioning of one's spiritual being in its God-given openness, a condition that would greatly facilitate appropriation of the desiring self.

Bernard Tyrrell developed his teaching on *affectional conversion* as a way of addressing the problem of neurosis encountered regularly in clinical practice. He distinguished two kinds, deprivation neurosis and repressive neurosis, because neurosis consisted in either one of two states:

(1) a person's deeply felt sense of being unlovable and worthless, and (2), severe repression in a person and/or other destructive effects and expressions of miseducation which cause great psychic discomfort, and impair the ability to function well in the give and take of everyday life.[71]

Though he acknowledged that deprivation neurosis at its worst can be severe enough to lead to repressive neurosis,[72] Tyrrell focused mainly on the love deprivation of the first state described in the above definition and what he saw as the conversion process that is the core of its healing.

> Primal affectional conversion consists in a shift on the level of sensitive awareness from the felt sense of frustration of the pleasure/love/desire appetite to a felt sense of fulfilment of this appetite. It is a shift from a felt sense of affectional deprivation to a felt sense of affectional acceptance and fulfillment. Primal affectional conversion occurs on the first level of consciousness, which Lonergan designates as the level of experiencing. Upper level affectional conversion consists in a healing transformation of a consolidated, on-going affective-deprivation insofar as this deprivation is at work and negatively impacting the individual on the levels of understanding, judging, deciding, loving in Lonergan's model of consciousness.[73]

Clearly, therapeutic intervention can help free an individual from the distortion that prevents them from knowing themselves to be deeply loved and desired by the God they long for, the God whose love is surfacing in their religious experience, and thus their capacity to be fully themselves in loving service to others. Depth psychology may be the only way to unmask deeper dissociations and work to heal the wounds of trauma. Affectional conversion is either sought for its own sake or to be expected as a by-product of successful analysis and skillful depth psychology. Either way, it can provide the availability for love to be acknowledged and welcomed as empowerment for self-transcendence.

John Dadosky of Regis College, Toronto, is appreciative of both Doran and Tyrrell, and their call for the integration of the theological and the psychological aspects of conversion:

> An integral theological and psychological understanding of conversion offers the promise of preserving psychology from the blind alleys of reductionism while simultaneously

challenging theologians and philosophers to "wrestle with their own demons" which can flow from the four-fold bias: dramatic, egoistic, group or general.[74]

However, he has sought to apply Occam's razor to the multiplying "conversions"[75] and suggests as a working hypothesis that psychic conversion and affectional conversion with their acknowledged overlap could be subsumed under a more generic term—using *psychological conversion* to cover both. We must be prepared to admit, as Dadosky does, that "perhaps we are all in need to some degree of psychic and/or affectional conversion."[76] The world has known two major world wars in the last hundred years, and there are evident scars of intergenerational dysfunction underlying the psychological woundedness of our time. While for some, the gradual empowerment to live as beloved and loving has been experienced as healing, others may pursue the question whether conversion or healing is the more appropriate explanatory term for this step toward authentic living out of the desire that moves us to appropriate our fullest human possibilities.

At this point, it would be profitable to examine both the nature of desire and other obstacles to its flourishing from the viewpoint of another good "nondisciple" of Lonergan,[77] Dom Sebastian Moore, OSB. Understanding that theology is "the sustained attempt to understand religious experience,"[78] "the story of the real self in all people,"[79] he learned from Lonergan, and in turn teaches his students, to attend to themselves as desiring beings. Desire defines us, he claims. It is who we are, created into a mystery toward which we yearn.

> What I have from Lonergan is a haunting, persistent and systematic conviction that the movement of my heart to the unknown God, a movement of which I am more certain than I am of anything else in my life, can be understood as felt-after by all my other desires as their fundamental direction: and therefore to help students to understand themselves as desiring beings is to move them towards the point where this fundamental direction of consciousness can show itself.[80]

In writing his classic *The Fire and the Rose Are One*, he set himself the task of identifying and naming "one universal human desire without some satisfaction of which our life would be unendurable, and total satisfaction of which would be perfect bliss."[81] Ernest Becker had made him aware of "the passionate sense of self-worth which characterizes human existence everywhere."[82] Traditionally, philosophers have claimed that we all desire to be happy; however, when he explored the notion of happiness, he found it usually defined by his students in terms of the absence of what threatens it or "the suspension of snags."[83] The feeling state more deeply desirable would be something that could sustain us even in a world beset by snags, and he found it in the feeling that whatever happens to me I am significant; I do have worth. I matter to someone who matters to me. The positive aspect of human self-absorption is, he claims, the one uncontested human proposition: "That we all desire to be desired by one we desire."[84] This is more than the cliché that we all need to be needed. It is the one on whom our desire is fixed, he would maintain, who alone can fulfill our desire by reciprocating.

We are invited to discover in ourselves the truth of that one uncontested proposition—that our overwhelming desire is to be significant and beloved in the eyes of the one our being longs for. The presence or fact of a need is known by its nonfulfillment, and the distress of the neglected child or ostracized adolescent or unrequited love of a lover is a clear sign of our human need to be significant for an important other, to be fully ourselves for that other and enhance their lives. But the full meaning of a need is recognized only in its fulfillment, "only reveals where it is going when the eyes of the beloved light up for the lover."[85] The eyes of the beloved light up in joy at the other's longed-for presence, and equally because of the new value he or she finds in themselves,[86] and that too delights and validates the lover.

> In other words, the elemental thrust of life in the human being, the need to feel significant, the essential appetite of self-aware being, finds its full meaning and satisfaction as an act of love which creates happiness in another.[87]

131

"The need which is the mainspring of the individual only shows its real meaning when the two come together in love and thus form the nucleus of the human community,"[88] and does so even more fully when groups of like-hearted people fashion an authentically human way of living together.

Furthermore, Moore suggests the possibility that our self-absorption and passionate pursuit of meaningfulness are, at root, our inner dialogue with our unknown origin:

> And if our experience with each other shows that self-absorption finds its meaning and release in knowing that I am significant for someone else, might it not be that my self-absorption is ultimately to find its meaning and release *in knowing that I am significant for the unknown reality that is my origin?*[89]

Our sense of dependence and hunger for meaning are two key realities of our human existence. In this way, the question *of* God becomes the question *to* God: "Is human self-awareness, when it finds its fulfilment in love, resonating, albeit faintly, with an origin that 'behaves,' infinitely and all-constitutingly, as love behaves?"[90] Does our human experience of attraction, desire, joy in love returned become revelatory of the truth that religion has been asserting and we are hesitant to believe—did we invent the story that God loves us? Moore suggests that today the God question[91] is inviting us to seek God with what is most intimately ourselves, "to use as probe our very selves."[92]

> The strange thing about the question to God is that it seems at first to be markedly less real than the question to the beloved, but on further reflection appears much more real. Of the beloved I ask more life, more meaning, more being in the eyes of another, while of this mysterious deeper other I am asking whether I have *any* meaning in his/her/its scheme of things. It is not easy to catch yourself asking this question, but I think you do.[93]

It is because all our quest for human love and recognition is essentially an expression of our longing to find that the ground of our being—our mysterious origin and destiny—is in love with us, that religious conversion comes as the joyous release of the tension of desire: faith is hearing the answer of the beloved, accepting God's yes to the question we are, believing the good news that changes one's whole life.[94] If Moore is to be helpful to us in our quest for the full appropriation of our desiring self, it is precisely because he sees so clearly that

> the religious question nowadays has to conceive of the making, constitutive nature of God as some unimaginable, possible, bliss-giving "Yes'" to a question which the self-aware person increasingly learns himself to be. The religious question today is, quite simply, mystical. Religion as a decency is out. It is either transforming or it is nothing. It is a question of the availability or non-availability of a permanently transformed existence.[95]

We feel a growth in our worth when we know we are significant to our significant others because, by our very nature, we are "psychically wedded" to the significant Other who gives us our being. "Other-grounded, we are other-oriented."[96] Humankind has a prereligious orientation to mystery, to our origin in God who desires our love and created us within the context of "an erotic (desire-shaped) dependence which is pre-religious, universal, conscious at the deepest level, and shaping of all we think and do."[97]

> Only if man is in his self-awareness God-questioning as the lover questions the beloved can religious conversion, the received answer of the beloved, be the radical fulfilment of man, the release of all his energies....The power and glory of the Gospel, as the proclamation that God loved us before we loved him, consists precisely in liberating our pre-religious God-hunger.[98]

Moore had found his own way to write of desire as the *eros* of the human spirit, and so the completion of his first task: to discover the one universal desire without which human life would be unbearable, and the fulfillment of which leads to supreme happiness.

His second task was to discover the universal trait that acts as the counterpull to this desire, and then to "write the story of the liberation of desire from its crippling and interwoven companion."[99] He thought first about guilt, "our most important negative feeling,"[100] which had been preoccupying him for some time—distinguishing infantile from adult guilt:

> Infantile guilt is the shadow of the joyous infant eros, of the child "grasping at kisses and toys" (Eliot): the sudden stab of loneliness, of being left out, abandoned, of a power-cut in the generous adult current of love. It is the passive sense of being unloved. Adult guilt is the shadow of adult love. It is the active sense of being unloving.[101]

Guilt that comes from not meeting the expectations of others is a remnant of infantile guilt, not genuine adult guilt that accepts responsibility for wrongdoing, particularly in the failure to be ourselves, lovingly, for others. We are not able simply to opt out of this desire without being out of sync with our deepest drive, without it making us miserable. Guilt is "unhappy unlove."[102] However, Moore realizes that for our self-appropriation, "guilt is a slippery fish" and so offers some hooks for catching hold of it, including these:

> Guilt is the sense of failing another. It is the most personal sense of failure I experience, because my very feeling of personal worth is "in another's eyes." As my sense of worth is "worth to," so my sense of unworthiness is of "unworth to."…If love is feeling good in the presence of another, guilt is feeling bad in the presence of another….Guilt is an emotional impotence…. Guilt is when all that is left of another's calling on me is the "ought," the "should." "Should" plus "can't" equals guilt.[103]

There is a ring of truth, verifiable in experience, in these pointers, and especially in his next conclusion: "One very important aspect of the feeling of guilt is that the other, the person I am failing, appears strangely unattractive." The acrimony of many divorce proceedings witnesses to the fact that this sense of the ugliness of the other is particularly strong when it is an intimate relationship that goes wrong. The hatefulness of the other is due to the sudden failure of a normal love current—they have become alien. Moore continues this line of thought:

> Is there an "other" in our life who is *the* other to which our whole being looks for meaning, and whose becoming unlovable to us would thus constitute the most radical and universal form of guilt?...This guilt is the crippling in us of that in-love-ness with the all-powerful mystery which belongs to our very constitution as self-aware, self-fascinated, questing, questioning beings. It is an original cosmic love-affair gone sour. It is the all-embracing mystery experienced not as presence but as pressure.[104]

In this way, religion has all too often been associated with law, not love, and humankind has talked itself into perceiving divinities as ugly, alien, demanding all sorts of payment and self-abasement from humankind. Nowhere is the definition of guilt as "the inflated currency of love" more clear than in the history of religion. Moore thus shows that the shadow cast over humanity has come from the denial, repression, and derailment of the desire that we are. Shame and guilt, hopelessness and desolation, are the outcome, rather than the cause, of our loss of contact with the mystery on which or on whom our being and becoming depends.

In *The Fire and the Rose Are One*, and in subsequent publications such as *The Inner Loneliness* (1982)[105] and *Jesus, Liberator of Desire* (1989),[106] Moore's existential Christology demonstrates how God intervened in Jesus to liberate our desire from its "crippling and interwoven companion," initially in his disciples, and then through their witness and the therapy of the Spirit, in us. Jesus shows us what our existence would be without guilt. Able to hear unimpeded the voice of the Beloved: "This is my Son, the Beloved, with whom I am well pleased" (Matt 3:17; see also 17:5; Luke 3:22; Mark 1:11), Jesus showed in his way of being with his disciples what it was to live in intimate communion with the Father.

With this secret, which shapes his whole way of being in the world, Jesus lifts people up to hear in their hearts, in their fellowship and in the whole world of nature the Yes of the Beloved. With the failure of his mission, and in its bitter conclusion on a cross, he plunges them from this height into the original emptiness, the death of God. Coming to them again, *then*, in that awful gap in time, he is God, he is life, he is the unlocking of the Spirit, he is that Yes of the Beloved over which death, the great human pretext of guilt, has no more power.[107]

Their desolation after his death was an experience that, in its starkness, prepared them for the joyous discovery of Jesus's divinity and the meaning of their salvation in a risen life of friendship with self, God, and one another. Moore makes clear in the psychological perspicacity of all his later writings that God's solution to the problem of alienation, guilt, and sin is Jesus and his modeling of the Son who knows the heart of the Father and whose desire, whose food and drink, is to do the Father's will (cf. John 10:15, 4:34; Matt 11:27).

Jesus comes to be the liberator of our desire, the one enabling us to be who we really are: desire destined for a knowing, loving fulfillment. Jesus is free at the deepest level, his intimacy with ultimate mystery total and unimpeded, as might ours be also in the full human flourishing God desires for humankind:

> There would be no guilt in the relationship, no holding back and rendering the other fearsome and threatening. The self would flourish in its ultimate companionship with the infinite, in a total, grateful and joyful acceptance of one's being from the mystery, on which in consequence one casts no "shadow." There is a consciousness of the self as beloved of the mystery and of the mystery as unshadowed love and beauty. The sense of "I am not alone" would be overpowering.[108]

Jesus was fully open to other persons because no sense of unworth "snarled up" his relationships, and he saw as actually achievable, God's plan for a new order of relationships on earth, and with the earth, toward the full revelation of the reign of God in the eschaton. His disciples caught from him that sense of the beauty and goodness of nature, of the world, of life, of people, which is part of an open and guilt-free relationship with the mystery. "The God of Jesus promotes human flourishing and is evidenced by human flourishing."[109] Moore saw this understanding as the way of living into the effective freedom and increased self-appropriation as desiring lover to which Lonergan points.

> This is the place for me to acknowledge Bernard Lonergan as the master in whose school I have known something of this priceless awareness, as undeniable by him who has it as is the enjoyment of Mozart. We should surely expect that the transformation of the person in Christ would show up in the intellect as well as in the heart, and especially in the intellect's enlarged capacity to name what is in the heart.[110]

For many, Sebastian Moore's threefold inquiry into desire, guilt, and appropriation of our being-in-love with God as Christians has made Lonergan's contribution to spiritual theology more accessible. His insights into the "shadow" have helped to make sense of one factor affecting the probabilities of consistent and progressive human development for individuals and the communities they form.[111]

AUTHENTICITY, COMMITMENT, AND ONGOING DEVELOPMENT

Lonergan's good nondisciples continued during this period to explore other rich lines of questioning his methodology opened for them, and he was spending more time exploring methods for the apparently random and pseudoscientific area of macroeconomics—but our moving viewpoint on the question of the appropriation of desire notes three further developments during the post-*Method* years. They are not new insights, but rather expansions on existing ones. One concerns authenticity, the authenticity of the believer or

137

the theologian in face of the possible unauthenticity of a nurturing tradition; another the interdependent and developing nature of the conversions; and the third, which is linked to both, is the issue of commitment.

Lonergan continues to reflect on how God's love flooding our inmost heart is a human experience and how it fits into human consciousness.[112] He says again that consciousness is like a polyphony, or like a concerto that blends many themes in different ways:

> So too religious experience within consciousness may be a leading voice or a middle one or a low one; it may be dominant and ever recurrent; it may be intermittently audible; it may be weak and low and barely noticeable. Again, religious experience may fit in perfect harmony with the rest of consciousness; it may be a recurrent dissonance that in time increases or fades away; it may vanish altogether, or, at the opposite extreme, it may clash violently with the rest of experience to threaten disruption and breakdown.[113]

Just as there is a wide register of religious experience in the lives of individuals, it may develop in different ways over time in the experience of different people. Lonergan speaks of cultivating religious experience, whereby we bring the whole of our personal symbolic system into harmony with our loving desire for God, love increasingly "reconciling us, by committing us, to the obscure purposes of our universe, to what Christians name the love of God in Christ Jesus."[114] Commitment is the opposite of "just drifting through life."[115]

> Content to do what everyone else is doing, to say what everyone else is saying, to think what everyone else is thinking, where the "everyone else" in question is just drifting too. Out of that company of drifters one steps when one faces the problem of personal existence, that is, when one finds out for oneself that one has to decide for oneself what one is to do with oneself, with one's life, with one's five talents or two or lonely one.[116]

138

Specifically, it becomes a question of what it means for being-in-love to become the first and dominant principle in the way we live our intimate relationships, our membership of a faith community, and our civic responsibilities. Appropriation of this Love's desires and purposes invites and facilitates our complete surrender to the values of the reign of God. "The experience of being-in-love is an experience of complete integration, of a self-actualization that is an unbounded source of good will and good deeds."[117] When fully realized in authentic commitment, such self-actualization is very attractive.

Authenticity, however, is twofold, and the converted person or theologian becomes aware that apart from the minor authenticity resulting from his or her faithful adherence to the truths, ideals, and practices of the nurturing tradition, there is the question of the major authenticity of the tradition itself. To authentically appropriate a tradition rendered unauthentic by "devaluation, distortion, corruption" and not just in a few scattered individuals but over time and in the many, is a tragedy indeed.

> The words are repeated but the meaning is gone. The chair is still the chair of Moses, but it is occupied by scribes and Pharisees. The theology is still Scholastic, but the Scholasticism is decadent. The religious order still reads out the rules and studies the constitutions, but one may doubt whether the home fires are still burning.[118]

Thus, theologians may have a double price to pay. Not only do they have to undo their own falls from grace, but they have to "discover what is wrong in the tradition they have inherited and they have to struggle against the massive undertow it sets up."[119] It is heartening to note, however, that Lonergan is convinced that those who genuinely set themselves to achieve self-transcendence are usually aware of shortcomings, "while those that are evading the issue of self-realization are kept busy concealing the fact from themselves."[120] This results from the fact that the inner dynamism of human reality, the passionateness of being, is so strongly drawing human beings into self-transcendence that, in general, "one cannot but be aware when one is moving towards it and, on the other hand, one cannot but feel constrained to conceal the fact when one is evading the abiding imperative of what it is to be human."[121]

The greater problem with unauthenticity in the formation and transmission of tradition is that we have been socialized into one and share many of its biases. Even if we recognize where the unauthenticity lies as we follow the insistent questioning of our own conversions, large-scale change is difficult to effect because transformation will only be in single individuals, one at a time, and "however much we may react, criticize, endeavor to bring about change, the change itself will always be just another stage of the tradition, at most a new era, but one whose motives and whose goals—for all their novelty—will bear the imprint of their past."[122] Fred Lawrence advises us not to underestimate the extent to which we are shaped in our understanding of ourselves by the culture and worldview of our milieu, or to overestimate our effectiveness in contributing to transformation in others.[123]

Our self-appropriation and our struggle for authenticity will necessarily be affected by upbringing, education, and human community, as we have seen, and sometimes authenticity requires, when problems are intractable, that we seek a more fruitful place to grow and contribute. There is hope, however. Whenever we can move from a conflict of positions to an encounter of persons, we discover, as Lonergan reminds us, that

> every person is an embodiment of natural right. Every person can reveal to any other his natural propensity to seek understanding, to judge reasonably, to evaluate fairly, to be open to friendship. While the dialectic of history coldly relates our conflicts, dialogue adds the principle that prompts us to cure them, the natural right that is the inmost core of our being.[124]

The more we can be in touch with our own being-in-love, the more we will be apt to look for and find the same desire moving others toward truth and goodness. "Only through one's own experience of that dynamism can one advert to its working in others."[125] The more we live out the reality of our own conversion, the more we can walk in newness of life.

Two years before his death, Lonergan told those gathered at the ninth annual Lonergan Workshop at Boston College in 1982[126] that conversion involves a new understanding of oneself because, more fundamentally, it brings about a new self to be understood. A new mode of developing has begun too. The orientation of the three dimensions of conversion differs—intellectual conversion to the intelligible and the true; moral conversion to the good; religious conversion to God—so that conversion may occur in one or more dimension but not in another. "At the same time the three dimensions are solidary. Conversion in one leads to conversion in the others and relapse from one prepares for relapse in the others."[127] It is not to the initial stages of one or other that we are called, but to the ongoing development of all three, to the love of God "with all your heart, and with all your soul, and with all your mind, and with all your strength" (Mark 12:30):

> The authentic Christian strives for the fullness of intellectual, moral and religious conversion. Without intellectual conversion he tends to misapprehend not only the world mediated by meaning but also the word God has spoken within that world. Without moral conversion, he tends to pursue not what truly is good but what only apparently is good. Without religious conversion, he is radically desolate: in the world without hope and without God (cf. Eph 2:12).[128]

And yet, it is not exclusively or even predominantly because of intense personal effort that we can hope to reach the desired authenticity, fullness of loving union with Christ in the Spirit. Called to this fullness, welcoming this destiny, and cooperating with grace in the measure of our possibilities, we must recognize that its realization will remain gift and blessing to be received rather than won by right of conquest. It will come in a deepening relationship of intimacy and friendship with God and with other human beings.

In this chapter, we have followed the moving viewpoint of Lonergan's thought through his own writings and those of some of his "good nondisciples" up to the time of his death in Pickering, Ontario, on November 26, 1984. He was never slow to recognize that his generalized empirical method of conscious intentionality, discovered through assiduous attention to the way our human consciousness operates optimally, is not always easy to come to terms with: "And of the few that attempt this, even fewer succeed in mapping the interior of the 'black box' in which the input is sensations and the output is talk."[129] Yet, his insights are a gift of the Spirit to the church, and his theological enterprise to human development generally. The self-assembling creative process of "the way up," which was the major discovery of *Insight*, is complemented by the healing trajectory of "the way down," which *Method in Theology* shows to the fore in the divine gift of redemption and the undoing of decline, and in the transmission and expansion of the tradition in the functional specialties of the second, mediating phase of theology. The way down is also seen to be prior in time, involving the affective development of the child in the nurturing love of family, society, and education, as well as in the reception and development of faith traditions. It has been possible to estimate the significance of affectivity in human capacity to live the demands of intellectual and moral conversion and to appropriate the love without restriction that is poured into the human heart by the Holy Spirit and received in religious conversion.

6

THE *EROS* OF THE SPIRIT AS OUR DESIRE

Through these pages, we have sought to understand what is involved in the personal appropriation of our human desire to know and love God. It has required full cognizance of the yearnings of our own being and the need to make value decisions about their provenance and demands. Our guide has been the writings of Bernard J. F. Lonergan, SJ, whose lifelong quest to follow the movement of the Holy Spirit in and through his own questioning has been an invitation, a resource, and a springboard for our theological journey. This search began in the first chapter with his early discoveries and followed the moving viewpoint of his growth in understanding through a study of his writings on natural and religious interiority.

The young Bernard was intelligent and curious, eager to learn and understand the worlds of nature, culture, and faith. At this early stage, it was the powerful desire to know, obvious in his insistent questioning, that was most readily recognized and embedded in his early writings. His respect for the Society of Jesus during his college years at Loyola grew out of his encounter with the intelligence and trained minds of the Jesuits who taught him. Yet it was with reluctance and a certain dread that he followed a call to join them in a life of celibate consecration to God—his response to the drawing power of love not yet fully comprehensible and certainly not objectified. During his novitiate, his motivation was a puzzle, his heart clearly more mysterious than his mind until he could reach an adequate understanding of grace. Throughout his formation years of philosophy and theology, his inquiring mind remained dissatisfied unless he could identify elements of a theory of knowledge that were in accord with his own developing understanding of cognitional process and methodology: Plato reaching for answers anticipated in questions, "ideas" being akin to the definitions reached by understanding; the introspective perspicacity of Augustine; and Newman's insight into judgment as assent to truth. Yet, it was in "reaching up to the mind of Aquinas" during his doctoral studies in Rome that Lonergan reached the certainties he was to publish in the *Verbum* articles. These ten years represent, on the one hand, an example of engagement in what he will later call the functional specialties of *Research, Interpretation*, and *History*, and on the other, provide a recognizable example of the scholarly differentiation of consciousness. Lonergan traced the development of Aquinas's thought and language regarding a hitherto obscure article on operative grace in the *Summa Theologica* and brought new clarity to its interpretation.

In the *Verbum* articles, Lonergan explores the created participation in divine light that constitutes us as image of God, and explains the procession within the human intellect of the inner word of understanding as the best available analogy for the procession of the Word within the Trinity. Our longing is to understand all reality—created and uncreated—and to reach truth in so doing. The wonder of inquiry, the very restlessness of our unbounded questioning, is the sign and promise of a supernatural fulfillment awaiting us. We are oriented by our very nature into mystery, and the end of our searching is to be knowledge of our origin, in beholding face to face the mystery of God. At this stage, Lonergan is clear: the light of intellect leading to wisdom is the "highest in us and in God the most like us."[1] The heuristic quality of our learning is that questioning brings us nearer to the desired unknown to which we are tending. In the introduction to *Verbum*, Lonergan encourages us to follow Augustine's practice of psychological introspection and highlights the uncannily accurate introspective skill of Aquinas. Lonergan thematizes this self-appropriation in a way that neither Augustine nor Aquinas could, and in *Verbum*, he gives his first explanatory account of the intellectual operations of understanding and definition, and of reflection and judgment.

However, for Lonergan as for Aquinas, the second procession grounding a real relation of origin in the Trinity is one that involves the will as rational appetite. It is the act of love proceeding from the inner word in the intellect. As early as 1943, he is writing of love as key to the God-given direction of human life in *Finality, Love, and Marriage*. Vertical finality is at work in all world processes, moving all things, according to their nature, toward the ultimate in goodness. God draws our minds by the desire to know, but draws all things, by everything they are, to respond to love as ultimate good. This became a central focus in his later theological work.

We then considered how we can discover our own desire and capacity for objective truth, by exploring the way human consciousness works. Lonergan demonstrated in his classic philosophical work *Insight* that there is a way for ordinary human attentiveness and understanding to come to a true knowledge of our own knowing. Sustained effort is required, but the data of consciousness are available to scrutiny—we can be aware of ourselves attending to data, having the flash of insight that renders it intelligible, testing this explanation to ensure that it accounts fully for what we have observed and leaves no conditions for reality unmet, and finally according it a status: our insight is possible, probable, relatively certain, true—or not. By observing these processes recurring within our own minds, we can understand them as an invariant pattern, innate in human beings, essential for optimal human functioning, and valid across cultures and historical periods. With the help of Lonergan's step-by-step pedagogy, and following his moving viewpoint, we are able to affirm ourselves as knowers and this pattern as a method. Intentionality analysis explains this self-assembling pattern, given in consciousness, as one that recurs constantly, yielding results that are cumulative and progressive. It provides a key to all Lonergan's subsequent work and the foundation of his *Method in Theology*.

The desire that is celebrated in *Insight* is the *eros* of the human spirit, the pure, detached, disinterested, and unrestricted desire to know. Lonergan invites us to recognize and affirm it in our lives, and to see it as part of the divine plan for optimal human functioning, not only for individuals, but also for human society. We desire, and God desires for us, that we should operate, and collaborate,

145

intelligently and reasonably. The pure desire to know is a constitutive part of our affirming and of the self that is affirmed.

Optimal human functioning does not seem to be the norm, however. The flow of our dynamic conscious intentionality can be blocked. Consciously or unconsciously, we can stem the flow of questions to avoid unwanted answers and then our judgments and subsequent decisions are affected by biases of various kinds. The perspective of *Insight* is to grasp the overall intelligibility of the universe in terms of an evolutionary process where all natural processes, events, and developments will follow not only the classical laws of science and morality, but more frequently statistical laws of probability and survival. This reflection enables us to see slow progress in perspective: we desire total truth and total reasonableness within and for the universe as it is, and equally for each person as they are, but necessarily in the context of emergent probability. We are called to appreciate the long patience of God and the slow outworking of God's benevolent purposes. Consequently, we recognize in the call to discover ourselves as knowers, and the powerful inner pull of the desire to know, the first steps in the appropriation of desire. From that point all other longings and attractions we discover in ourselves can gradually be brought into focus in the light of the vertical finality that orients us toward the Divine Mystery.

Based on his investigation of cognitional theory, Lonergan then developed the formulation of a methodology for the study of theology. In the years between writing *Insight* and *Method in Theology*, key articles show the direction of his inquiries, and take us deeper into existential questions on the fourth level of conscious intentionality. When the human person has reached the third-level assurance of judgment about what really is the case, the next step is to allow further questions to arise, to deepen reflection. We deliberate and question what the outcome in word or deed needs to be if we are to act responsibly in the light of what we know. We transcend ourselves as empirically aware by the questioning that promotes us to understanding. We transcend ourselves as understanding by our careful checking of assumptions and proceeding calmly to affirming that our interpretation of the data is correct. Now the focus is on the self-transcendence revealed in feelings and values, and involved in making responsible and moral decisions about how to proceed in the light of what we know. It is at this level that the person is self-constituting, by their choices and actions making themselves into who they will be.

The desire for genuine value, for total goodness, goes beyond the desire to know things by their essence, though it is continuous with it. We are attracted to the good, the beautiful, and the best expressions of love. Desire moves us to transcend ourselves in the operations of evaluation, choice, and decision-making and to act in a way that realizes the general good.

Lonergan invites us to consider the question of authenticity in the subject who will progressively constitute him- or herself by existential choices, and establish the personal horizon, the world-view within which freedom will be exercised. If our God-given conscious intentionality and the adequate human formation we receive conspire together to draw us to live as responsible moral beings, it is still in the experience of love that our best hope of authenticity lies. Love of another human being, partner or child, the domestic love within families or patriotic love of our homeland, all these increase our chances of transcending ourselves with some consistency. When we discover that God's love is poured out in our hearts by the Holy Spirit, we taste a new and joyous freedom at the fourth and highest level of our being to follow our desire for truth, for goodness, and for the fullness of love. The secure openness to truth and goodness that comes as a redemptive gift from God enlarges our horizon and heals faltering achievement so that we can live out of the desire we are.

Desire as a massive thrust toward self-transcendence is available in some measure for our appropriation. To live authentically in the light of it, we need to pay attention to the inner movement of our mind and heart at the level of deliberation, choice, and pursuit of what is truly worthwhile, where we are forging personality and character. Others in our communities can assist us to grasp better what is driving us by their responses to our actions and inactions, and often their generous living of true values can draw us to incarnate these in our own lives. In our fidelity to practices of prayer, it is possible to grow in discernment of the action of the Spirit who moves in our deepest desires.

In *Method in Theology*, we discovered how the appropriation of desire is operative in the three conversions required for theology to be a fully collaborative and creative exercise. Functional specialties would follow the pattern of generalized empirical method given in transcendental consciousness, four in receptive and four in transmission modes, and foundational in the enterprise is the threefold conversion of the authentic subjects doing theology. Vitally important is that theologians welcome their own being-in-love with God in an unrestricted manner that is the essence of religious conversion. In the light of this loving openness, moral conversion to true value is easier to embrace, and the theologian can work with, not against, the pattern of human consciousness in the search for truth as revealed in intellectual conversion. A genuine interdependence of exchange and mutual enrichment can then be facilitated among the theologians working in the eight functional specialties.

The two functional specialties on the existential fourth level of evaluation, decision, and choice are Lonergan's distinctive contribution to theology. As specialists in Research, Interpretation, and History mine the meanings and traditions of the past, there have always been disagreements about research findings, variant meanings identified, and historical conflicts over what was going forward at a given time. Dialectic evaluates and works on such conflicts, thus offering a deeper understanding of the issues presented and a choice for the theologian in the transforming light of the three conversions. Foundations, in this new way of doing theology, makes these conversions thematic, and the foundation of the theological enterprise is no longer certain key doctrinal propositions, but rather the authentic believer, the converted theologian passing on in intellectual honesty and moral integrity what has been gleaned from the past. This treasure is then formulated in Doctrines, explored in Systematics, and proclaimed in Communications.

Clearly, a large degree of self-knowledge is required for these tasks, so the self-appropriation of the religiously converted person doing theology is a prerequisite for fruitful work, particularly in the specialties of the second phase. Conversion is not a once-and-for-all phenomenon. Though it effects a significant change in the reality of who the theologian is, all three conversions will be progressively deepened and extended over a person's lifetime. Objectivity is not sacrificed in the joyful personal response of a theologian to God's love. Objectivity is the result of authentically following the inbuilt truth-seeking method of our inmost being, "the method we are." Being-in-love with God is the best situation for attentiveness, intelligence, reasonableness, and responsibility to be exercised freely. However, as we have reiterated, authenticity is never a serenely secure possession. It requires continual withdrawal from unauthenticity as this is uncovered, and continual repentance and growth to ensure active cooperation with the Lord who is Spirit and who whispers in our persistent questioning. When our questions dry up, so do we.

The pure and unrestricted desire to know, which we have recognized in ourselves, has been swept up into the passionateness of being in the perspective of *Method*. With Lonergan's help and using the attentiveness, intelligence, reasonableness, responsibility, and love that are the mark of God's image in us, we seek to appropriate the love without restriction that is moving us to authenticity in knowing and loving, to involvement in God's plan for human flourishing in a friendly universe.

In the years following the publication of *Method*, Lonergan continued to teach and expand on themes already contained in that remarkably dense and allusive work, notably, for our purposes, further consideration of the affective dimensions of intentionality and the conversions. In their explorations of this topic, some of his former students saw its relevance to depth psychology and other therapeutic interventions to heal psychic wounds that block full human functioning and the experience of God's loving invitation into the fellowship of the Trinity. We noted, especially, Sebastian Moore's insightful unpacking of the relationship between the desires we have and the desire we are. He named incisively some of the defenses we put up against the intimacy with God to which we are called by divine longing, and presented Jesus as the liberator of our desire. We are desirous, precisely because our destiny is to recognize God's love of predilection in the need we have to be desired by a significant other. We are created this way in order to discover our deepest fulfillment in the yes of the Beloved Other to the question we are.

Interiority is a key differentiation of consciousness and closely linked to the appropriation of desire. Common sense enables us to interact with our environment and cultural setting, learning by precept and example or even more vividly by trial and error and adding insight to insight to build up a competence in work situations and an ease in getting along with others within human systems of commerce and leisure. This is a satisfyingly rich domain for many human beings. In Lonergan's framework, this domain is called undifferentiated consciousness. Still this provides the rock on which human well-being can be built, "the subject in his conscious, *unobjectified* attentiveness, intelligence, reasonableness, responsibility. The point to the labor of objectifying the subject and his conscious operations is that thereby one begins to learn what these are and that they are."[2] Lonergan's objectifying brought consciousness into the realm of theory where we can write of an invariant pattern of operations, but he first discovered it in his interiority.

Sufficient psychological interest to question and get in touch with the movements of our feelings and thought patterns is the entry point for the realm of interiority, where those who have taken the trouble to appropriate their own conscious intentionality are most at home. It is not the exclusive domain of philosophers and theologians. Lonergan holds that the most common differentiation of consciousness across the planet and down the ages has been the combination of common sense with the realm of transcendence. The reach of our intending, if not that of our attainment, is unrestricted. Human beings are by nature worshipers, however varied the objects of that worship. The love drawing them to their mysterious and numinous Other will move many to inquire and discover the action of spirit in their being. Hence interiority, both natural and religious, proves to be of special interest and importance in the search for the appropriation of desire.

Lonergan has often been categorized as an intellectualist, though he would claim rather to be a critical realist. Certainly, he placed very high value on the power of human reason to pursue truth and attain considerable knowledge of reality as it is. He had a formidably acute mind, honed by education and wide-ranging inquiry. Yet Lonergan's moving viewpoint brought him to the point where he regarded love as the key criterion for a true understanding of all reality, especially within the world of faith. In his teaching, love came to replace reason as "that which is highest in us and in God the most like us."[3] The viewpoint moved because he was faithful over his lifetime to the insistent drive of his own desire and questioning. In his life of prayer, he drew upon the "love without restriction for Someone transcendent in lovableness" that he found had been poured out into his own heart by the Holy Spirit. To this love, he invites each of us to attend.

If Lonergan's most significant contribution was initially in the world of philosophy, with his transposition of Aristotelian metaphysics and Thomist faculty psychology into generalized empirical method based on intentionality analysis, his greatest achievement overall is his specifically methodological vision of the way theology is to be done—one day—for the glory of God and the coming of the reign of God on earth. When theologians appropriate their own desire for truth, and gradually take the measure of the love that is drawing them to seek God in a study of their faith tradition, they will want to engage in this enterprise wholeheartedly in a spirit of cooperation and ecumenical collaboration. Wonder and awe, longing and gratitude are good equipment for a theological journey. These attitudes can only continue to intensify, and through their living, writing, and teaching, particularly in the functional specialty of Communications, theologians will touch the lives of many self-aware believers, leading them also to appropriate the desire they are.

Lonergan had been sure as a young man that *nihil amatum nisi praecognitum*—knowledge precedes love. Faculty psychology maintained that it is the intellect that pronounces something reasonable and good—the two were, at one stage, synonymous for Lonergan—and commends it as such to the rational appetite or will, which is then moved to pursue it. His discovery of the God-given dynamism involved in coming to experience, understand, know, and decide, completed by his experience of falling in love with God, taught Lonergan that we only know truly what we love and when we love, particularly but not exclusively in religious matters.

> But the major exception to the Latin tag is God's gift of his love flooding our hearts. Then we are in the dynamic state of being in love. But who it is we love, is neither given nor as yet understood. Our capacity for moral self-transcendence has found a fulfilment that brings deep

joy and profound peace. Our love reveals to us values we had not appreciated, values of prayer and worship, of repentance and belief. But if we would know what is going on within us, if we would learn to integrate it with the rest of our living, we have to inquire, investigate, seek counsel. So it is that in religious matters love precedes knowledge and, as that love is God's gift, the very beginning of faith is due to God's grace.[4]

As we have noted, human beings are created with a capacity for and drive toward transcendence. Because God desires "everyone to be saved and to come to the knowledge of the truth" (1 Tim 2:4), God's gift of his love flooding human hearts is a universal experience, offered to all human beings, though not always adverted to or recognized, and issuing in adherence to many world religions when it surfaces into full awareness. It underlies and supports the fervor and generous self-transcendence of many faithful Hindu, Jewish, Christian, Muslim, Buddhist, and other believers, and proves to be the bond between them when, in interfaith dialogue, they can share their deepest desires and religious experience. This dialogue would be greatly enriched, and so would their personal faith journey, if they would inquire, investigate, and seek counsel, as Lonergan suggests, and so learn what is going on within them.

To know what is going on within us is the task of self-appropriation, the key to the world of interiority. It is my contention that human beings can come to appreciate their own desire to know, and understand the steps by which reality is known; they can be encouraged to recognize religious experience and to value the lack of restriction in God's love received, returned, and expressed. For philosophers and theologians, it is particularly significant that they do appropriate their own desiring, but it is not their exclusive prerogative. For everyone, it is good news that human beings are desirous, desiring to be and to become, to know and to love, enhancing the lives of those they love.

That human beings are desired by their God, the Significant Other, is a reality assented to in faith. Our destiny is, in some mysterious way, to enter into the communion of love within the Trinity, to hear, even now, the affirming response of the mystery for which our whole being yearns, telling us that we are desired, loved beyond measure by the Creator of our desiring selves. This is something we can come to understand and live in joy and ever-increasing freedom.

This conviction that desire is life enhancing and able to be personally appropriated by many people is shared by others. Notably, there are the Fellows of the Woodstock Theological Centre, Georgetown University, who also chose Lonergan as their guide in a collaborative revision of the living practice of the Ignatian Spiritual Exercises. In *The Dynamism of Desire* (2006), they demonstrate how Lonergan's writings illuminate the Ignatian "exercises of self-awareness, the dialectic between good and evil, conversion to a Christian 'horizon,' loving choice as determinative of a responsible life and service of others as the continuing fruition of Christian mysticism."[5] The writers see that self-appropriation is one of a retreatant's key fruits following through the steps of the Exercises, and self-transcendence its whole meaning; the primary role of the retreat is to foster the dynamism of desire. The founder of the Society of Jesus, a man of desire himself, saw the presence of a great desire as the unmistakable sign that a retreatant would profit much from the Exercises. This is a rich and insightful handbook for retreatants and directors, but its key focus is the four weeks of the thirty-day retreat, not just the extended study of desire and its appropriation.

In the same year, another Jesuit, Ravi Michael Louis, SJ, brought Lonergan's perceptive writing on desire and self-transcendence into dialogue with Indian philosophy, as well as that of Heidegger, Levinas, and the European postmodernists.[6] A complex and culturally rich study, Louis's work brings together and relates the operations of human imagination, human affectivity, human morality, and human historicity, and the attunement into alterity fostered by being-in-love. He thus sets a wider compass and, with Doran's assistance, explores more fully than this book the ontological role played by *psychic conversion* in the appropriation of the transcendental-historical mechanisms of human desiring; its position at the very heart of the relationality between the sciences, philosophy, and theology; and its relevance for the much-needed grounded dialogue between *philosophia* and *dar'sana*.

By contrast, we have the comparatively straightforward task of showing the personal self-appropriation of the human desire to know and love God as it unfolded in the life and writings of

Bernard Lonergan, SJ, and offering it as a source of hope and spiritual growth. We *can* know ourselves as questioning, persistent seekers of truth and Truth itself. We *can* recognize the desires that move us in feelings and motivations and evaluate them in terms of the greatest desire of all exerting its steady pull within us toward transcendence. As human even before we are Christian, we are called to nothing less.

To the seemingly bleak world of questions with which we began, we can now offer something like a *Babette's Feast* of possibilities: the realization that human creativity and artistry, and human love and collaboration in society are the outworkings of the same desire that moves us to be dissatisfied with anything but the best and to want to do our utmost. By exploring natural and religious interiority, we can discover the power and passionateness of being at work in this universe, in which the Infinite Act of Understanding Love has placed us. The same Spirit that moves in the emergent probabilities of our evolutionary world, moves in our desires, and will meet us there.

AFTERWORD

When we embarked on our theological journey, we identified only longing as a key component. That the longing was the "the drawing of this Love"[1] is no longer in doubt, though we have not yet ceased our exploration.

For myself, I valued the longing, seeing it as "a thirst for God," and praying anxiously not to be deprived of it, sensing that my desire for God was my one redeeming feature. I manifestly did not understand it even so, much less appropriate it.

In understanding and appropriating this longing, I realized that this desire is no transitory, haphazard acquisition but rather an integral part of my humanness, the deepest drive of my being. It is Truth for which I thirsted, and to which I pursued a persistent search for answers, which, in the world of knowledge, were opened for me by formal education. Therefore, I read everything I could lay my hands on, age appropriate or not, and spent hours on the floor of the boarding school library reading the entire McHardy family Bible before I was fifteen, making startling discoveries that were sometimes not age appropriate. The Walter Farrell commentary on the *Summa Theologica*[2] captured me during my secondary school years as I tried to understand the being of God, the meaning of life, and why each angel was, necessarily, a separate species. I did not know then that this insistent drive to find out "everything about everything" was the way all human beings are made, and unless the questions are knocked out of the child or stifled by deadening forces over which the child has little or no control, that is the way each person will come to know the world and can contribute to it. Learning has always been deeply satisfying for me. During this research, I have come to understand not only that it is, but that it is meant to be an engrossing, challenging, lifelong activity. The reason for this wellspring of questions is that we are created into mystery, and our longing is to know God even as we are ourselves known by God.

That it is not so for some, but was for me, relates to the context in which learning occurs best. At the age of eight, I moved from a punitive and fearful state school classroom in which spelling was taught with the strap, to a school where the mission of the teachers was "to make known the Love of the Heart of Jesus by the work of education." The contrast between these two schools was also something I sought to understand, and seeds of a vocation to religious life were sown. In the affirming security of being loved, a child is open to learn and grow. In the expansion of loving, one is moved to learn and grow even more.

Therefore, it was providential rather than accidental, and quite understandable in hindsight, that I joined the religious congregation of the Society of the Sacred Heart of Jesus, with its educative charism and a spirituality of seeking to know the heart of God by studying the heart of God made man in the Gospels, "in order to unite and conform ourselves to him."[3] A blessing then and since, and one for which I will always be grateful.

This work has brought me into conversation with many individuals whose spiritual and theological journeys demonstrate a genuine and growing intimacy with the desire that moves them to love God and to develop as thinkers. The wise counsel of spiritual advisors and personal therapy has aided affective healing, and brought a gradual opening to the joy of self-discovery— reconciliation with a desirous and incomplete selfhood and the loving patience of our evolutionary God who does not "fix everything on the spot," even though so entreated. Desire can be an integrating force in our lives. Welcomed for what it really is, the impulse of God's Spirit reinforcing sweetly and powerfully the image of God that moves in our human consciousness, it enables us to love ourselves and everyone else in the love of God. Through this research, the possibility of owning one's deepest desires has been the goal and hope.

NOTES

INTRODUCTION

1. The Danish film *Babettes gæstebud* (*Babette's Feast*) was made in 1987 by Gabriel Axel based on a story by Isak Dinesen, also writing as Karen Blixen. It won an Academy Award for Best Foreign Language Film in that year. The Norwegian village of Berlevaag, where Dinesen set his story, turned out to be too picture-book pretty for the filmmaker, who moved it to a Danish setting.

2. Isak Dinesen, "Babette's Feast," in *Babette's Feast and Other Anecdotes of Destiny* (New York: Vintage Books, 1988), 6.

3. Ibid., 18.

4. Ibid., 48.

I. TO KNOW ONESELF AS DESIRER AND KNOWER

1. Pierrot Lambert, Charlotte Tansey, and Cathleen Going, eds., *Caring About Meaning: Patterns in the Life of Bernard Lonergan* (Montreal: Thomas More Institute Papers, 1982), 22–23. In recorded conversations, Lonergan quotes more than once Voegelin's use of this image from the puppeteer in Plato's *The Laws*.

2. Bernard J. F. Lonergan, *Insight: A Study of Human Understanding*, CWL 3, ed. Frederick E. Crowe and Robert M. Doran (Toronto: University of Toronto Press, 1992). First published in London, 1957, by Longmans, Green & Co. Hereinafter, references will be made to *Insight*, and page numbers for both the 1st and 2nd editions will be given, respectively.

3. Subsequently this work will be referred to as *Caring About Meaning.*

4. Richard M. Liddy, *Transforming Light: Intellectual Conversion in the Early Lonergan* (Collegeville, MN: Liturgical Press, 1993).

5. William Mathews, *Lonergan's Quest: A Study of Desire in the Authoring of Insight* (Toronto: University of Toronto Press, 2005). See also "Lonergan's Apprenticeship," *Lonergan Workshop 9*, ed. Fred Lawrence, Boston College, 1993; "On Becoming Oneself in the World," unpublished paper presented at Boston College, June, 2003.

6. *Caring About Meaning*, 132–33.

7. Ibid., 133.

8. Ibid., 141.

9. Ibid.

10. Lonergan was to comment on his disappointment that they didn't "know how to make one work, that working was unnecessary to pass exams" in a letter to his provincial, John L. Swain, on May 5, 1946, quoted by Frederick E. Crowe in *Lonergan* (Collegeville, MN: Liturgical Press, 1992), 5.

11. *Caring About Meaning*, 142.

12. Ibid., 131.

13. Ibid., 145.

14. Bernard J. F. Lonergan, *Method in Theology* (Toronto: University of Toronto Press, 1996), 113. First published in Great Britain by Darton Longman & Todd, 1971. Further references will be to *Method.*

15. Bernard J. F. Lonergan, "*Existenz* and *Aggiornamento*," in *Collection*, CWL 4, ed. Frederick E. Crowe and Robert M. Doran (Toronto: University of Toronto Press, 1988), 230.

16. *Caring About Meaning*, 145.

17. Ibid.

18. Ibid., 146.

19. Lonergan, "*Existenz* and *Aggiornamento*," 230–31.

20. *Caring About Meaning*, 145.

21. Ibid., 10.

22. Bernard J. F. Lonergan, "Theories of Inquiry," in *A Second Collection*, ed. William F. J. Ryan, and Bernard Tyrrell (Philadelphia: The Westminster Press, 1974), 38.

Notes

23. Liddy, *Transforming Light*, 12.

24. *Caring About Meaning*, 14.

25. Liddy, *Transforming Light*, 38.

26. John Alexander Stewart, *Plato's Doctrine of Ideas* (Oxford, 1909). See Lonergan, *Second Collection*, 264–65.

27. *Caring About Meaning*, 44.

28. Ibid., 49.

29. Augustine, *De Beata Vita*, translation from The Fathers of the Church, *Writings of St. Augustine* 1, ed. Ludwig Schopp (New York: Cima Publishing Co., 1948), 4.

30. Interview with Bernard Lonergan in *Curiosity at the Center of One's Life* (Montreal: Thomas More Institute Papers, 1987), 403–4.

31. Lonergan, "Insight Revisited," in Ryan and Tyrrell, *Second Collection*, 265.

32. Frederick E. Crowe, "Obituary for Fr. Bernard J.F. Lonergan, S.J.," *Newsletter of the Upper Canada Jesuit Province* 60 (May–June 1985): 16.

33. Lonergan, *Insight*, 4/28.

34. Crowe, *Lonergan*, 19.

35. Lonergan, *Insight*, 185/209.

36. Ibid., 4/28.

37. Transcript by Nicholas Graham of discussions at the Lonergan Workshop, June 13, 1978.

38. Liddy, in *Transforming Light*, 118, suggests that Lonergan tries in *Insight* to mediate for readers a shorter way around. Liddy gives an extended and more adequate account of the intellectual content of this breakthrough.

39. Lonergan, "Insight Revisited," 265.

40. The confident energy and enthusiasm engendered in Lonergan are expressed in a personal letter to his Jesuit superior.

41. Charles Boyer pointed him toward the article on *gratia operans* in *Summa Ia IIae*, saying that neither he nor those he consulted were able to interpret it.

42. Completed in 1940 as *Gratia Operans: A Study of the Speculative Development in the Writings of St. Thomas of Aquinas*, it was subsequently published as four articles in *Theological Studies* (1941–42) and later in book form as *Grace and Freedom: Operative Grace in the Thought of St Thomas Aquinas*, ed. J. Patout Burns

(New York: Herder and Herder, 1971). Quotations below are taken from the CWL edition of the same name, edited by F. E. Crowe and R. M. Doran, republished in 2000 by the University of Toronto Press.

43. Taken from an unpublished lecture, "The Scope of Renewal," The Larkin-Stuart lectures at Trinity College in the University of Toronto, 1973, 2. Cited by Liddy, *Transforming Light*, 125.

44. Liddy, *Transforming Light*, 124.

45. Lonergan, *Insight*, 748/770. We are indebted to Fr. Crowe for the number, referring to the years 1938–49, from the beginning of this study until the completion of the *Verbum* articles.

46. Lonergan, *Insight*, 748/770.

47. Crowe, *Lonergan*, 47.

48. Ibid., 48.

49. Pope Leo XIII, in his encyclical letter of 1879, *Aeterni Patris*, had recommended a return to Aristotelian Thomism for philosophical and theological formation in seminaries.

50. Bernard J. F. Lonergan, *Verbum: Word and Idea in Aquinas*, CWL 2, ed. Frederick E. Crowe and Robert M. Doran (Toronto: University of Toronto Press, 1997).

51. Lonergan, "Insight Revisited," 266–67, and *Caring About Meaning*, 51, 98.

52. Following Aristotle and Aquinas, Scholasticism acknowledged intellect and will as the highest faculties of the rational human soul. Intellect presided over the external activities of the senses, the internal work of memory and imagination in cognitional processes to arrive at truth. In the appetitive dimension, will as rational appetite directed choice to the recognized truth or desired goodness. Lonergan's intentionality analysis involves understanding of the cognitional and existential process: from experiencing to understanding, from verifying insight to rational assent, and from thence to responsible decision-making and action based on love; it is less concerned with faculties than with a dynamic, self-assembling process of conscious, intentional operations, which is the way human beings function spontaneously.

53. Lonergan, "Insight Revisited," 266–67.

54. Lonergan, *Verbum*, 11.

55. Ibid., 105.

56. "For then a word is most like the known thing from which it is brought forth and most an image of that thing, since from the vision of knowledge a vision of thought arises, which is a word of no language, a true word of a true thing, having nothing of its own, but everything from that knowledge from which it is born," Augustine, *De trinitate*, XV, xii, 22.

57. Lonergan, *Verbum*, 109.

58. Ibid., 85. Lonergan cites Aquinas: "*Ipsum enim lumen intellectuale quod est in nobis, nihil est aliud quam quaedam participata similtudo luminis increati.*" *Summa theologiae*, 1, q. 84, a. 5c.

59. Crowe, *Lonergan*, 49.

60. Ibid., 92.

61. Ibid., 185.

62. Ibid., 104.

63. Aquinas quoted "endlessly," according to Lonergan, the Aristotelian commonplace that intellect as active is *potens omnia facere* and as passive *potens omnia fieri* (able to make or become all things). Ibid., 96.

64. Ibid., 98.

65. Ibid., 104.

66. Ibid., 66.

67. Ibid., 97. *Summa theologiae*, 1-2, q. 3, a. 8c.

68. Lonergan, *Verbum*, 87.

69. "We know by what we are; we know we know by knowing what we are; and since even the knowing in 'knowing what we are' is by what we are, rational reflection on ourselves is a duplication of ourselves." Ibid., 99. This reduplication is spelled out in *Insight* 274–75/299–300, and even more explicitly in *Method*, 14–15.

70. Lonergan, *Verbum*, 24.

71. Ibid., 6.

72. Ibid., 90.

73. Cf. the stage depicted at *Conf.* 7.9.13–15.

74. Lonergan, *Verbum*, 48.

75. Bernard J. F. Lonergan, "The Natural Desire to See God," in Crowe and Doran, *Collection*, 81–91. The paper was first published in the *Proceedings of the Eleventh Annual Convention of the Jesuit Philosophical Association*, Boston College, 1949, 31–43.

76. Ibid., 81. An editorial note comments that this pair of questions had been referred to in *Verbum*, but there the main concern

was to transform "what" questions into "why" questions: "What is refraction?" is reducible to "Why does light refract?" Later, as Crowe remarks, Lonergan will recognize a third, the operator for fourth-level evaluation and choice.

77. Lonergan, *Verbum*, 82.

78. Lonergan, *Insight*, 10–11/35–36. Here, Lonergan's affinity with Newman is evident.

79. Crowe sees in the distinction Lonergan makes in this article between the proportionate object of intellect (specifying the essence of a material being) and the adequate object, which is being, a clarification of notions already appearing in *Verbum*. Editorial note d, *Collection*, 270.

80. The three ways involve first transferring to the divinity created perfections, then denying created imperfections, then understanding that these perfections are attributed to God only in an analogous and eminent sense.

81. Humanity does not exist in a vacuum, separate from the grace that opens understanding to ultimate questions and to grasp the truth of mysteries beyond proportionate human understanding.

82. Lonergan, "The Natural Desire to See God," 82.

83. Ibid., 83.

84. Synonymous terms, as Crowe points out in editorial note f, Crowe and Doran, *Collection*, 270.

85. Lonergan, "The Natural Desire to See God," 84.

86. On the objective side, static essentialism precludes the possibility of natural aspiration to a supernatural goal. On the subjective, closed conceptualism precludes the possibility of philosophy being confronted with paradoxes that theology can solve. Ibid., 84.

87. Ibid., 84–85.

88. Lonergan enters here, though indirectly, into the controversy around Blondel's conservative response to Henri de Lubac's new approach to the relation of natural and supernatural in *Surnaturel*.

89. Bernard J. F. Lonergan, SJ, "Finality, Love, Marriage," in Crowe and Doran, *Collection*, 17–52.

90. Lonergan had reviewed an article on marriage by von Hildebrand in *The Canadian Register*, 1942, and in this article, takes up, in depth, issues related to the ends of marriage that had

emerged in the ensuing correspondence. Lonergan's invitation at the end of the 1943 article to an ongoing discussion could not be followed up because the Holy Office ruled in 1944 against the suggestion that secondary ends were not essentially subordinate to the primary end of marriage, the generation and education of children.

91. See chapter 3, "Heightening Self-Appropriation to the Existential Level" and beyond.

92. Commonly, when Scholastic philosophy was the staple diet in Catholic formation, intelligibility was sought in terms of causality: anything could be understood in terms of material cause (what it is made of), efficient cause (how it comes to be made), formal cause (what makes it the sort of thing it is), and final cause (that for which it is made.) In a world of faith, created by God, the formal cause of human beings was understood to be the spiritual soul, and the final cause union with God.

93. "Appetition" is, for Lonergan, the capacity to respond.

94. Lonergan, "Finality, Love, Marriage," 19.

95. Ibid., 19.

96. Kathleen M. Williams, "Friendly Authenticity in a Fractured World" (paper presented at the Lonergan Workshop, Boston, 2004). This was also stressed by Lonergan in "Mission and Spirit," in *A Third Collection: Papers by Bernard J. F. Lonergan*, ed. F. E. Crowe (New York: Paulist Press, 1985), 21–33.

97. Aquinas, *De veritate*, q. 22, a. 2.

98. Aquinas, *Summa contra Gentiles*, 3, c. 19.

99. Lonergan, "Finality, Love, Marriage," 20.

100. Ibid.

101. Ibid.

102. Ibid., 22.

103. Notably in *Insight*, 237–42; *Method*, 50–55, 359–61; "Healing and Creating in History," in Crowe, *A Third Collection*, 100–109.

104. Lonergan, "Finality, Love, Marriage," 22.

105. Lonergan's developed understanding of sublation is when he states, "What sublates goes beyond what is sublated, introduces something new and distinct, puts everything on a new basis, yet so far from interfering with the sublated or destroying it, on the contrary needs it, includes it, preserves all its proper features and

properties, and carries them forward to a fuller realization within a richer context." *Method*, 241.

106. Lonergan, "Finality, Love, Marriage," 22.

107. Ibid., 49.

108. Ibid., 46.

109. This analysis is expressed in terms of the faculty psychology of the day, language Lonergan will continue to use into the 60s, even when his actual method has become intentionality analysis.

110. Thomas Aquinas, *Summa theologiae*, 1-2, q. 25, a. 2c.

111. Aquinas's understanding of these first two modes of love is comprehensively treated by Crowe in "Complacency and Concern," a three-part study that appeared initially in *Theological Studies* 20, and is currently available as chs. 3–6 in *Three Thomist Studies*, by Frederick E. Crowe, a supplementary issue of *Lonergan Workshop*, vol. 16, ed. Fred Lawrence, 2000.

112. Lonergan, "Finality, Love, Marriage," 23–24.

113. Aristotle, *Ethics*, VIII, 3–7; esp. 4, 1157a 16—9; IX, 4, 1166b 2–29; IX, 8, 1169a 12–15.

114. Aquinas was able to see, as Aristotle was not, that objective lovableness involves an absolute good. *Summa Theologiae*, 1-2, q. 109, a. 3c.

115. Lonergan, "Finality, Love, Marriage," 25.

116. Ibid., 26.

117. Ibid., 27.

118. Ibid., 29.

119. Ibid., 30.

120. Ibid.

121. Ibid., 32.

122. Ibid., 31.

123. Ibid., 32.

124. Ibid., 33.

125. Ibid., 33–34.

126. Ibid., 35.

127. Ibid., 36.

128. Ibid., 39.

129. St. Augustine of Hippo, *Confessions*, bk. 1, ch. 1: "You have made us for yourself, O Lord, and our hearts are restless till they rest in you."

130. Lonergan, "Finality, Love, Marriage," 39.

131. Fred Lawrence, "The Human Good and Christian Conversation," in *Communication and Lonergan: Common Ground for Forging the New Age*, ed. Thomas J. Farrell and Paul A. Soukup (Kansas City, MO: Sheed & Ward, 1993), 267. See also ch. 5.

2. SELF-AFFIRMATION AS A KNOWER IN *INSIGHT*

1. Bernard J. F. Lonergan, *Insight: A Study of Human Understanding*, 2nd ed. (London: Longmans, 1978). First published in 1958 and most recently in the fully annotated critical edition by Lonergan Research Institute of Regis College, Toronto, by University of Toronto Press in 1992. Page numbers will be given for both 1st and 2nd editions, respectively.

2. Bernard J. F. Lonergan, "Insight Revisited," in *A Second Collection*, ed. William F. J. Ryan and Bernard J. Tyrrell (Philadelphia: Westminster Press, 1974), 269.

3. In Scholastic philosophy, transcendentals are those qualities that are common to all things whatsoever, and to all differences between things. They are not restricted to any category, class, or individual. The classic transcendentals are thing (*res*), being (*ens*), something (*aliquid*), the one (*unum*), the true (*verum*), the good (*bonum*), and according to some philosophers, the beautiful (*pulchrum*).

4. Richard M. Liddy, *Transforming Light: Intellectual Conversion in the Early Lonergan* (Collegeville, MN: Liturgical Press, 1993), 179.

5. See their most recent publication in translation in Bernard J. F. Lonergan, *Grace and Freedom: Operative Grace in the Thought of St Thomas Aquinas*, CWL 1, ed. Frederick E. Crowe and Robert M. Doran (Toronto: University of Toronto Press, 2000). Part 1 of this volume comprises four articles written in 1941–42, and part 2 is Lonergan's doctoral dissertation, *Gratia Operans*, submitted to the Gregorian University in 1940. He maintained that commentators on Aquinas from the sixteenth century onward lacked historical consciousness, raising questions that Aquinas had never considered and generally obnubilating the issues. Lonergan reconstructed Aquinas's intellectual development on grace and added a unique diagnosis of the mistakes made by modern Scholastic authors on this subject.

6. Lonergan, *Insight*, 744/769.

7. Ibid., xvii/11. Lonergan wrote before the concern about inclusive language was in vogue: all humanity could be safely subsumed under the label *man* and the third-person singular could be routinely *he//him/his* without giving offense to half the English-speaking world. I have not sought to alter it in direct quotes, even though Lonergan had himself become sensitive to the issue before his death in 1984.

8. Lonergan, "Insight Revisited," 269.

9. Bernard J. F. Lonergan, *Method in Theology* (Toronto: University of Toronto Press, 1996), 7. This is a characteristically respectful statement. Though Hans-Georg Gadamer's *Wahrheit und Methode* was published in 1960 and aimed also to uncover the nature of human understanding, his emphasis is more concerned to critique approaches to the human sciences and demonstrate that human consciousness is affected by ambient culture in the historical period—that it is "historically affected consciousness," *Wirkunggeschichtlichesbewußtsein.*

10. For naïve realists, knowing is a matter of taking a good look; objectivity is a matter of seeing just what is there to be seen. This is what Lonergan was to call "the myth of the eyeball."

11. Lonergan, *Insight*, xi/4.

12. Ibid., xx/14.

13. Ibid., xx–xxi/15.

14. Lonergan, unpublished notes in the possession of the Toronto Lonergan Research Institutes archives and cited by Frederick E. Crowe, in *Lonergan* (Collegeville, MN: The Liturgical Press, 1992), 75.

15. Lonergan, *Insight*, 242/267.

16. In this study, we are following the same pattern, by following the moving viewpoint of Lonergan's own life discoveries as mediated for us in his writings and the writer's own gradual appropriation of the desire we are.

17. This idea is elaborated on in the next page.

18. Terry J. Tekippe, *Bernard Lonergan's Insight: A Comprehensive Commentary* (Lanham, MD: University of America Press, 2003), xiii–xxiv. Later in his life, Lonergan used these epistemological questions: What do I do when I know? Why is doing that knowing? What do I know when I do it?

19. Lonergan, *Insight*, xxviii/22.

20. Lonergan, *Method*, 260.

21. Lonergan, *Insight*, xxiii/17.

22. See Lonergan, *Method*, 38, 66.

23. Lonergan, *Insight*, xxviii/22.

24. Lonergan's transcendental philosophy as applied to cognitional theory is comprehensively covered in his *Method*, 3–25, as well as in *Insight*.

25. Lonergan, *Insight*, 333/358.

26. Ibid., 183/206.

27. Ibid., 185/208. Lonergan maintains that art (musical, graphic, kinesthetic, poetic, etc.) is an expression of the human spirit that seeks to mean, to convey, to impart something that is to be reached, not through science or philosophy, but through a participation, and in some fashion a reenactment of the artist's inspiration and intention.

28. Ibid., 331/355–356.

29. Ibid., 4 (old), 28 (new), quoted by Beth Beshear, "The Problem of Desire in Human Knowing and Living," *METHOD: Journal of Lonergan Studies* 20, no. 2 (Fall 2002): 155–73.

30. Lonergan, *Insight*, 474/498.

31. Ibid., 9/34.

32. Ibid., 349/373.

33. Ibid., 596/619.

34. Ibid., 380/404. The questions of bias and the dialectical nature of human development are given fuller treatment in ibid., 214–27.

35. Ibid., 701/723.

36. Ibid., 218/244.

37. Ibid., 221–22/247.

38. Ibid., 223/248.

39. Lonergan, "Mission and Spirit," in *A Third Collection: Papers by Bernard J. F. Lonergan*, ed. F. E. Crowe (New York: Paulist Press 1985), 31.

40. Kathleen M. Williams, "Lonergan and the Transforming Immanence of the Transcendent: Towards a Theology of Grace as the Dynamic State of Being-In-Love with God" (PhD thesis, Melbourne College of Divinity, 1998), 126.

41. Lonergan, *Insight*, 623–24/646–47

42. Ibid., 693/715.

43. Lonergan speaks of one further form of bias, "general bias," which privileges common sense (concerned with the immediate, concrete situation) to the point of disregarding larger issues, theoretical insights, and long-term results. Ibid., 225/251.

44. "The reign of sin is the expectation of sin." Ibid., 693.

45. It is shortsighted because, as Aristotle understood, "the wicked are true friends neither to themselves nor to others." *Ethics*, VIII, 5, 1157a 16ff.What is implicit in Aristotle's assertion that being a true friend to oneself requires choosing the best, namely knowledge and virtue, is made explicit by Aquinas's affirmation that human beings and, as well, all creatures according to their mode, naturally love God above all things. Aquinas, *Sum. Theol.*, 1-2, q. 109, a. 3c; *Qodl.* 1a. 8c. & ad 3m.

46. The dramatic pattern of experience and its relevance to the constitution of self and one's own worldview will be treated in the following chapter.

47. Notably in "Healing and Creating in History" and "Mission and Spirit," in Crowe, *A Third Collection*, though it pervades his writings from *Method in Theology* onward, as we will discuss in chs. 4 and 5.

48. Lonergan, *Insight*, 352/376.

49. Ibid., 638/661.

50. As we noted in the preceding chapter, the distinction is between proportionate and adequate attainment of the desired understanding. We desire more than we can attain on earth.

51. Lonergan, *Insight*, 639/662.

52. Ibid., 640/663.

53. Ibid.

54. Ibid., 374/398.

55. Ibid., 701/723.

56. Ibid., 637–38/661.

57. Ibid., 665/688.

58. The term *conjugates* is used by Lonergan with a specific meaning: terms are conjugate when they are fixed by their relations. He draws here on mathematics where the term is used in this sense.

59. Lonergan, *Insight*, xix/13–14.

60. Ibid., 380/404.

61. Ibid., 745/766.

62. Ibid., 470/495.

63. Ibid., 297/322.

64. Ibid., 599/622.

65. Ibid., 602/625.

66. Ibid., 473/498.

67. Ibid., ch. 4, "The Complementarity of Classical and Statistical Investigation," 103–39/126–62.

68. When acts occur in sequence with a certain predictable regularity, such as the rotation of the planets, the return of the shearwaters from their annual migration north, or an irritated reaction to "I told you so," we can speak of a scheme of recurrence.

69. In Australia, terrestrial placental mammals disappeared early in the Cenozoic (their most recent known fossils being 55-million-year-old teeth resembling those of condylarths) for reasons that are not clear, allowing marsupials to dominate the Australian ecosystem. *Wikipedia*, accessed October 7, 2011, http://en.wikipedia.org/wiki/Marsupial.

70. Lonergan, *Insight*, ("Space and Time") 171/195.

71. Lonergan, *Insight*, 693–96/716–25. In the section "The Heuristic Structure of the Solution," he proceeds step by step to deduce the reasonableness of a suitable solution.

72. Genetic method concerns the sequences in which correlations and regularities change and sequential development over time. Dialectic methods concern linked but opposing principles of change. *Insight*, 486/509, 708.

73. A surd is an instance of the absence of intelligibility. For Lonergan, sin is a surd. A social surd is a situation in human affairs that makes no sense at all.

74. Lonergan, *Insight*, 698/721.

75. Ibid., 210/235–36.

76. Faculty psychology and common parlance both speak of "having free will," as does Lonergan on occasion for, though he has made the transition to intentionality analysis and facilitated this for us, old habits die hard.

77. Lonergan, *Insight*, 619/643.

3. THE APPROPRIATION OF DESIRE

1. This classic was finished in haste and published in 1972, but key themes appear in papers before that date. The moving viewpoint of this study follows that of Lonergan.

2. Bernard J. F. Lonergan, "Openness and Religious Experience," in *Collection*, CWL 4, ed. Frederick E. Crowe and Robert M. Doran (Toronto: University of Toronto Press, 1988), 186.

3. Lonergan, "Cognitional Structure," in Crowe and Doran, *Collection*, 219.

4. Bernard J. F. Lonergan, *Insight: A Study of Human Understanding*, CWL 3, ed. Frederick E. Crowe and Robert M. Doran (Toronto: University of Toronto Press, 1992), 375.

5. Bernard J. F. Lonergan, "The Subject," in Crowe and Doran, *Collection*, 73.

6. Ibid., 79.

7. Ibid., 80.

8. Ibid., 81.

9. Ibid., 80.

10. Bernard J. F. Lonergan, *Method in Theology* (Toronto: University of Toronto Press, 1971, reprinted in paperback 1996), 241.

11. Lonergan, "The Subject," 80.

12. Ibid., 81.

13. Lonergan, *Method*, 9.

14. Ibid., 10.

15. Bernard J. F. Lonergan, "The Response of the Jesuit as Priest and Apostle in the Modern World," in *A Second Collection: Papers by Bernard J. F. Lonergan, S.J.*, ed. William F. J. Ryan and Bernard Tyrrell (Toronto: University of Toronto Press, 1987), 169.

16. Bernard J. F. Lonergan, "Cognitional Structure," in Crowe and Doran, *Collection*, 221. Lonergan had commented to Philip McShane that in *Insight*, "My purpose was not a study of human life but a study of human understanding." *Language, Truth and Meaning* (Notre Dame, IN: University of Notre Dame Press, 1972), 310.

17. Lonergan, "The Response of the Jesuit," 170.

18. Ibid.

19. Lonergan, "Insight Revisited," in Ryan and Tyrrell, *A Second Collection*, 271–72.

20. Bernard J. F. Lonergan, "Openness and Religious Experience," in Crowe and Doran, *Collection*, 198–201.

21. Ibid., 199.

22. Lonergan, "The Response of the Jesuit," 170.

23. Ibid., 14.

24. Frederick Lawrence, *On Being Catholic* (unpublished talk, Boston College), 4. (Author's emphasis.)

25. Lonergan, "Openness and Religious Experience," 200.

26. Ibid.

27. Aquinas, *I Sent.*, d. 39 q. 2, a. 2, ad 4m.

28. Lonergan, *Method*, 240.

29. Lonergan, *Insight*, 473/501.

30. Ibid., 625/648.

31. From the much-quoted monologue in Shakespeare's *As You Like It*.

32. Lonergan, *Insight*, 187/210.

33. Ibid., 191/214. This is the area familiar to us as Freud's censor, which excludes some insights and the further questions that would help give us a comprehensive viewpoint.

34. Lonergan, *Method*, 121, 240.

35. Lonergan, *Insight*, 623/646. Lonergan says that, for human beings to live a fully successful, authentic life, the "universal antecedent willingness" that leaves us open to embrace the good, wherever it may reveal itself, must complement the pure and unrestricted desire to know.

36. Ibid., 627/650.

37. Ibid., 666/689.

38. Aquinas, *I Sent.*, d. 39 q. 2, a. 2, ad 4m. Lonergan endorses Aquinas on this point.

39. Bernard J. F. Lonergan, "Openness and Religious Experience," 186.

40. Anthony Kelly, *The Trinity of Love: A Theology of the Christian God* (Wilmington, DE: Michael Glazier, 1989), 104.

41. Rudolf Otto's *mysterium fascinans et tremendum*, in *The Idea of the Holy* (London: Oxford, 1923). Cited by Lonergan, *Method*, 106.

42. This expression is Fred Lawrence's expansion of Lonergan's "infinite act of understanding" as a way of naming God in chapter 20 of *Insight*, 684. According to verbal reports received from those who had known both Lonergan and Professor Lawrence, Lonergan accepted that Lawrence truly represented his later thought in so speaking and writing.

43. Lonergan, "Healing and Creating in History," in *A Third Collection*, ed. Frederick E. Crowe (New York: Paulist Press, 1985), 106.

44. Ibid., 106.

45. Ibid., 106.

46. Charles C. Hefling Jr., *Why Doctrines?* (Boston, MA: Cowley Publications, 1984), 18. (Author's emphasis.)

47. Lonergan, *Method*, 32.

48. Lonergan, "Openness and Religious Experience," 187.

49. Lonergan, "*Existenz* and *Aggiornamento*," in Crowe and Doran, *Collection*, 230.

50. Ibid.

51. Ibid., 231.

52. Ibid., 230. This list also omits what was to become the first imperative, corresponding to the level of experience: Be attentive.

53. Bernard J. F. Lonergan, "Theology in a New Context," in Ryan and Tyrrell, *A Second Collection*, 65–66.

54. Lonergan, "The Future of Christianity," in Ryan and Tyrrell, *A Second Collection*, 153.

55. Ibid., 153–54.

56. Ibid., 156.

57. Ibid., 161–62.

58. See ch. 1. The word belongs to Frederick E. Crowe, who noted this key difference between the "early Lonergan" and the later one in "Early Jottings on Bernard Lonergan's Method in Theology," *Science et Esprit* (1973): 121.

59. At the Jesuit Institute at Fuscz Memorial, St. Louis. Published as "The Response of the Jesuit."

60. Ibid., 173.

61. Ibid., 171.

62. Bernard J. F. Lonergan, "Horizons," in *Philosophical and Theological Papers 1965–1980*, CWL 17, ed. Robert C. Croken and

Robert Doran (Toronto: University of Toronto Press, 2004), 22–23, 12.

63. As well as critical history and hermeneutics through extended contact with European *Geisteswissenschaften*.

64. According to Vatican I, *Constitutio dogmatica "Dei Filius" de fide catholica*, cap. 4. Lonergan's former students attest to his frequent use of this article.

65. Lonergan offered doctoral courses: *De intellectu et methodo, De systemate et historia, De methodo theologiae*.

66. Lonergan, *Insight*, 639/662.

67. Lonergan, "*Insight*: Preface to a Discussion," in Crowe and Doran, *Collection*, 148.

68. Lonergan, "Cognitional Structure," 210–11.

69. Lonergan defines introspection in 1964 as adverting to the data of consciousness, a shift of attention from the object to the subject. "Philosophical Positions with Regard to Knowing," in Croken and Doran, *Philosophical and Theological Papers 1965–1980*, 222–23.

70. Lonergan, "Cognitional Structure," 277.

71. Lonergan, "Horizons," 14.

72. Ibid. Much work on feelings and the *ordo amoris* has been done by Patrick Byrne. Note especially, "What Is *Our* Scale of Value Preference?" in *Lonergan Workshop*, vol. 21, and *The Ethics of Discernment: Lonergan's Foundations for Ethics* (Toronto: University of Toronto Press, 2016).

73. Lonergan, "Horizons," 15. (Author's emphasis.)

74. Lonergan, "The Response of the Jesuit," 172.

75. Lonergan, "Cognitional Structure," 220.

76. Lonergan, "*Existenz* and *Aggiornamento*," 229.

77. He does so in both "*Existenz* and *Aggionamento*" and "The Response of the Jesuit."

78. Bernard J. F. Lonergan, "Time and Meaning," in *Philosophical and Theological Papers 1958–1964*, CWL 6, ed. Robert C. Croken, Frederick E. Crowe, and Robert Doran (Toronto: University of Toronto Press, 1996), 114.

79. Ibid.

80. Ibid., 115.

81. Ibid., 116. Father Eric O'Connor comments on the significant change Lonergan has made here when preparing the paper for

publication in 1975. Originally, it read, "a means through which God is present to one *in an exceptional manner.*" See *Bernard Lonergan: 3 Lectures* (Montreal: Thomas More Institute Papers 75, 1975), 48. (Author's emphasis.) Republished in the first edition of *A Third Collection.*

82. Lonergan, "The Mediation of Christ in Prayer," in Croken, Crowe, and Doran, *Philosophical and Theological Papers 1958–1964*, 178–79.

83. Ibid., 179–80.

84. Ibid., 180.

85. Pierrot Lambert, Charlotte Tansey, and Cathleen Going, eds., *Caring About Meaning: Patterns in the Life of Bernard Lonergan* (Montreal: Thomas More Institute Papers, 1982), 145.

86. Lonergan, "*Existenz* and *Aggiornamento*," 224, 222.

87. For Diogenes, the *Eureka* moment was in a hot bath.

4. THE APPROPRIATION OF DESIRE IN *METHOD IN THEOLOGY*

1. William Matthews, "A Biographical Perspective on Conversion and the Functional Specialties in Lonergan," *Method: Journal of Lonergan Studies* 16 (1998): 133–60.

2. According to one of his ablest students, Frederick Lawrence, "'*Cor ad Cor Loquitur*': Bernard Lonergan S.J.," *Compass: A Jesuit Journal* (Spring 1985): 19–20.

3. Bernard J. F. Lonergan, *Method in Theology* (London: Darton Longman & Todd, Ltd., 1972), reprinted 2003 by University of Toronto Press for the Lonergan Research Institute, 4.

4. And yet there are many of these, differing in a variety of ways!

5. Lonergan, *Method*, 4.

6. Transcendental method is the basic pattern of conscious and intentional operations involved in all human knowing, the dynamic functioning of our questioning moving us from experiencing, to understanding, to judgment, to decision...ultimately to response in love to the love God pours out in our hearts.

7. Lonergan, *Method*, 18.

8. Ibid., 14.

9. Ibid., 4.

10. The first four specialties involve the theologian in learning, "the theologian listens." Lonergan also refers to this first phase of theology as being *in oratione obliqua*.

11. Lonergan, *Method*, 127.

12. Ibid., 178.

13. In the second phase, the listening theologian speaks, teaching, *in oratione recta*.

14. Lonergan, *Method*, 132.

15. Ibid.

16. Ibid., 134.

17. Ibid., 24.

18. Ibid., 141.

19. Frederick E. Crowe, *The Lonergan Enterprise* (Cambridge, MA: Crowley Publications, 1980), 58.

20. Lonergan, *Method*, 130.

21. Philip McShane, ed., *Foundations of Theology: Papers from the International Lonergan Congress 1970* (Dublin: Gill and MacMillan Ltd., 1971), 209.

22. Lonergan, *Method*, 235.

23. Crowe, *The Lonergan Enterprise*, 90.

24. Vernon Gregson, "Theological Method and Collaboration II," in *The Desires of the Human Heart*, ed. Vernon Gregson (Mahwah, NJ: Paulist Press, 1988), 100.

25. Lonergan, *Method*, 270.

26. Ibid., 238.

27. Michael L. Rende, *Lonergan on Conversion: The Development of a Notion* (Lanham, MD: University Press of America, 1991), 183.

28. Ibid., 187.

29. Lonergan, *Method*, 240.

30. Ibid., 252.

31. Ibid., 254.

32. Ibid., 104.

33. Ibid., 240.

34. Ibid., 110.

35. Ibid., 364.

36. Ibid., 10.

37. Crowe, *The Lonergan Enterprise*, 90.

38. In *Insight*, Lonergan essayed to show that the proofs for the existence of God were not unreasonable. Now he is more inclined to look at the existence of the question as more significant. "In the measure that we advert to our own questioning and question it, there arises the question of God." Lonergan, *Method*, 103.

39. Ibid., 101–3.

40. Ibid., 103.

41. Denise Lardner Carmody, "The Desire for Transcendence: Religious Conversion," in Gregson, *The Desires of the Human Heart*, 59.

42. Lonergan, *Method*, 240.

43. Bernard J. F. Lonergan, *Philosophy of God and Religion: The Relationship between Philosophy of God and the Functional Specialty, Systematics* (London: Darton, Longman & Todd, 1973), 17.

44. Ibid., 38.

45. Lonergan, *Method*, 268.

46. Crowe, *The Lonergan Enterprise*, 116. In a footnote, Crowe quotes from "Bernard Lonergan Responds," *Foundations of Theology*, ed. Philip McShane, 227.

47. Gregson, *The Desires of the Human Heart*, 99.

48. Fred Lawrence, quoted in lecture notes.

49. Lonergan, "Bernard Lonergan Responds," in McShane, *Foundations of Theology*, 229.

50. Crowe, *The Lonergan Enterprise*, 88.

51. Lonergan, *Method*, 268.

52. Crowe, *The Lonergan Enterprise*, 93.

53. That is, in doctrines, systematics and communications.

54. Lonergan, *Method*, 331.

55. Gregson, *The Desires of the Human Heart*, 117.

56. Lonergan, *Method*, 9.

57. Bernard J. F. Lonergan, "The Subject," in *Collection*, CWL 4, ed. Frederick E. Crowe and Robert M. Doran (Toronto: University of Toronto Press, 1988).

58. Lawrence, "*Cor ad Cor Loquitur*," 20.

59. Bernard J. F. Lonergan, "Religious Experience," in *Trinification of the World: A Festschrift in Honor of Frederick E. Crowe*, ed. Thomas A. Dunne and Jean-Marc Laporte (Toronto: Regis College Press, 1978).

60. Lonergan, *Method*, 55, 231. Lonergan lists only the first four at this juncture, but it is clear that in making religious conversion foundational for the study of theology, he has effectively joined "Be in love" to the earlier four transcendental precepts.

61. Ibid., 122–23.

62. Ibid., 14–15. Self-appropriation involves the objectification of transcendental method; that is, attending to, inquiring about, understanding, conceiving, and affirming one's attending, inquiring, understanding, conceiving, and affirming.

63. For Lonergan, interiority is a third realm of meaning, going beyond the realms of common sense and theory. "The aim of *Insight*, self-appropriation, is a movement to the world of interiority. One wants to know just what it is that happens when one understands, and all the different ways in which one understands. The exigence of critical philosophy is this: one should not talk about what one does not know, and still less should one talk about what one cannot know." "Time and Meaning," in *Philosophical and Theological Papers 1958–1964*, CWL 6, ed. Robert C. Croken, Frederick E. Crowe, and Robert Doran (Toronto: University of Toronto Press, 1996), 114–15.

64. Fred Lawrence, in lectures, 2003.

65. In the *Spiritual Exercises of Ignatius of Loyola*, retreatants learn the rules for the discernment of spirits: in those earnestly seeking to serve God, assenting to a proposal that will advance them in the spiritual life leads to feelings of peace and joy, whereas choosing what is not truly good leads to heaviness and sadness. They are encouraged to make an election and then observe the feelings that arise. A Jesuit learns to pray for the feeling responses appropriate to passages or texts chosen for meditation and to distinguish, in himself and those he directs, "consolation and desolation."

66. Lonergan, *Method*, 31.

67. Ibid., 30.

68. Manfred Frings, *Max Scheler* (Pittsburgh: Duquesne University Press, 1965) and Dietrich von Hildebrand, *Christian Ethics* (New York: David McKay, 1953). Lonergan directs his reader to the wealth of analysis of feelings in these works.

69. This influence is comprehensively treated by Mark J. Doorley in *The Place of the Heart in Lonergan's Ethics: The Role of*

Feelings in the Ethical Intentionality Analysis of Bernard Lonergan (Lanham, NY: University of London Press, 1996.)

70. Lonergan, *Method*, 30–31.

71. *States*, such as fatigue or irritability, have causes; *trends*, such as hunger or sexual arousal, have goals. Neither category relates a person directly to an object as do intentional responses such as fear, trust, or desire.

72. Lonergan, *Method*, 30–31.

73. Ibid., 32. See also Patrick H. Byrne, "Analogical Knowledge of God and the Value of Moral Endeavour," *METHOD: Journal of Lonergan Studies* 2 (Fall 1993): 103–36.

74. This question is comprehensively treated by Rosemary Haughton in *The Transformation of Man: A Study of Conversion and Community* (Springfield, IL: Templegate Publishers, 1967, 1980).

75. William James, *Varieties of Religious Experience,* Fontana Library Theology and Philosophy ed. (London and Glasgow: Collins Clear-Type Press: 1960/1974), 397–98. James acknowledges his debt to Professor Leuba for the term *faith state*.

76. Ibid., 398n16.

77. Pure experience can be "without content and structure." What Lonergan is talking of is the *prior* word God addresses to us by the Spirit, before any interpretation. See also Lonergan, "Openness and Religious Experience," in Crowe and Doran, *Collection*.

78. Otto, *The Idea of the Holy* (London: Oxford, 1923), 61.

79. Lonergan, *Method*, 13.

80. Ibid., 290.

81. A theorist in this matter, Ira Progoff developed and refined the Intensive Journal Method in the mid-1960s and 1970s to provide a way to mirror the processes by which people find healing and personal growth. Lonergan was interested in his work and the workshops he was conducting throughout the United States and Canada. *At a Journal Workshop: The Basic Text and Guide for Using the Intensive Journal Process* (New York: Dialogue House, 1975).

82. Lonergan, *Method*, 118.

83. Ibid., 105.

84. Ibid., 115. This is Lonergan's definition of faith.

85. Ibid., 112.

86. Ibid., 113.

87. Bernard J. F. Lonergan, "Religious Experience," in *A Third Collection: Papers by Bernard J. F. Lonergan*, ed. F. E. Crowe (New York: Paulist Press 1985), 127.

88. Bernard J. F. Lonergan, *Insight: A Study of Human Understanding*, CWL 3, ed. Frederick E. Crowe and Robert M. Doran (Toronto: University of Toronto Press, 1992), 273.

89. Lonergan, *Method*, 13.

90. Ibid., 10.

91. For the Amish in Pennsylvania, youth are accorded a period of freedom known as the "rum springa" (from the German *herumspringen*, "to jump around"), during which wild oats can be sown, and only after a conversion "rebirth" do they make an adult commitment to the exacting "living plain" of the *Ordnung*. In the Baptist tradition and most of the evangelical and Pentecostal churches, it is the experience of being born again, or baptized in the Spirit (or both) that are deemed to constitute full membership of a denominational gathering.

92. Haughton, *The Transformation of Man*, 282. In a prefatory statement to the second edition, she describes the significance of this work in her own journey as a theologian: "It was the 'place' where I discovered a whole new set of concepts which helped me to understand what Christianity is all about: a language for human experience, and therefore a community of people using it and changing it, but the language of word, symbol, relationship, itself growing from the community, yet shaping the community as it does so, in a kind of dialectic progression through the centuries. The language identifies for people what is going on in their lives as they try to learn in themselves God's presence and work. It helps, therefore, to find out how to cooperate with that work in ways fuller and faster and more far-reaching than they could discover without it. They need to understand it accurately and live it obediently. Most of us don't."

93. Ibid.

94. Ibid., 15.

95. Ibid., 20.

96. Simon Grolnick, *The Work and Play of Winnicott* (Northvale, NJ: Aronson, 1990), 44.

97. Haughton, *The Transformation of Man*, 22.

98. Ibid., 38.

99. Ibid., 70.

100. Ibid., 91.

101. Ibid., 94.

102. Ibid., 97.

103. Ibid., 98.

104. Ibid., 105.

105. Ibid., 110.

106. Ibid., 136–37.

107. Carmody, "The Desire for Transcendence," 61.

108. Lonergan, *Method*, 290.

109. Ibid., 213.

110. Ibid., 240. (Italics mine.) I am indebted to Frederick E. Crowe, SJ, longtime friend, editor, and interpreter of Lonergan's works for these insights into the significance of the self-correcting process of learning as a key concept in both *Insight* and *Method*. See Crowe, *Appropriating the Lonergan Idea*, ed. Michael Vertin (Washington, DC: Catholic University of America Press, 1989), 62.

111. Lonergan, *Method*, 41–47.

112. Ibid., 46.

113. Lonergan acknowledges in *Method* that, as well as the authenticity of the subject, there is also the need for the authenticity of the tradition that nurtures him or her, and this is not guaranteed. However, the same process of questioning, the same self-correcting process of learning can challenge and correct the major inauthenticity of institutions where subjects remain open. *Method*, 80, 162, 299.

114. John Henry Newman, *An Essay in Aid of a Grammar of Assent* (London: Longmans, Green, 1930 [1870]), 337, cited by Crowe, *Appropriating the Lonergan Idea*, 60.

115. Tad Dunne is a former student of Lonergan, certainly religiously converted, and now an associate professor of philosophy at Siena Heights University.

116. Tad Dunne, "Being-in-Love," in *METHOD: Journal of Lonergan Studies* 13, no. 2 (Fall 1995): 161–75.

117. Tad Dunne, "Experience," in *The New Dictionary of Catholic Spirituality*, ed. Michael Downey (Collegeville, MN: Liturgical Press, 1993), 368.

118. Bernard J. F. Lonergan, *The Pilgrim People: A Vision with Hope*, ed. Joseph Papin (Villanova, PA: Villanova University Press, 1970), 60.

119. A treatment of Lonergan's understanding of the trinitarian life as intrinsically conversational is to be found in "The Human Good and Christian Conversation" by Frederick Lawrence, in *Communication and Lonergan: Common Ground for Forging the New Age*, ed. Thomas J. Farrell and Paul A. Soukup (Kansas City, MO: Sheed & Ward, 1993), 249–68; Philip McShane, *Music That Is Soundless: Introduction to God for the Graduate* (Washington, DC: University of America Press, 1977); and Kathleen Williams, *Lonergan and the Transforming Immanence of the Transcendent: Towards a Theology of Grace as the Dynamic State of Being-in-Love with God* (PhD thesis, Melbourne College of Divinity, 1998), 228–53.

120. Lonergan, *Method*, 113.

121. Williams, *Lonergan and the Transforming Immanence of the Transcendent*, 251.

122. Lonergan, *Method*, 273.

123. Ibid., 266.

124. Ibid., 273.

125. Benedict XVI, *Deus Caritas Est*, 2005, accessed April 4, 2017, http://w2.vatican.va/content/benedict-xvi/en/encyclicals/documents/hf_ben-xvi_enc_20051225_deus-caritas-est.html.

126. Frederick E. Crowe, "Complacency and Concern in the Thought of St. Thomas," *Theological Studies* (March, June, September, 1959): 1–39, 198–230, 343–95. Father Crowe was a long-standing and trusted friend of Lonergan, who asked him to be an executor of the Lonergan estate. His work of editing and establishing annotated final texts of Lonergan's writing for the Collected Works of Bernard Lonergan series and unfailing support and resourcing for Lonergan scholars all around the world from the Toronto Centre for Lonergan Studies came to an end on Easter Sunday, April 8, 2012, when he entered into the joy of his Lord.

127. Ibid., 3, 347.

128. Ibid.

129. Lonergan, *Method*, 242.

130. Lonergan's response to an interviewer in Montreal when asked why he was giving so much thought to the matter.

131. For further information, see Collected Works of Bernard Lonergan, vol. 15, *Macroeconomic Dynamics: An Essay on Circulation Analysis* (Toronto: University of Toronto Press, 1999). Michael Shute, *Lonergan's Discovery of the Science of Economics* (Toronto: University of Toronto Press, 2010), has noted, "It is a central claim of this present work that Lonergan discovered the fundamental set of significant variables for economic science in 1942. It is my belief that if economists were to recognize what Lonergan discovered, the so far delayed scientific revolution in economics would be under way. Such a revolution would certainly have significant positive influence on the welfare of humankind."

5. DEVELOPMENT IN RELIGIOUS INTERIORITY

1. This term refers to a stage where differentiated consciousness is able to distinguish from common sense, not only the theoretical, the scientific, the scholarly, but also the realm of interiority. Lonergan's intentionality analysis places his work in this stage of meaning.

2. "An Interview with Fr. Bernard Lonergan S.J.," by Philip McShane, in *A Second Collection*, ed. William F. J. Ryan, SJ, and Bernard Tyrrell, SJ (Philadelphia: The Westminster Press, 1974), 214. (Emphasis mine.)

3. Note the telling expression used by Fred Lawrence in the title of his article, "The Fragility of Consciousness: Lonergan and the Postmodern Concern for the Other," *Theological Studies* 54 (1993). In the article, he comments, "Consciousness however as an internal self-presence or awareness has to itself not only a dimension of explicit, foreground awareness, but a tacit or background dimension—namely, the most radical presence of ourselves to ourselves—that can never be made explicit exhaustively," 59.

4. McShane, "An Interview with Fr. Bernard Lonergan S.J.," 214.

5. Being, for Lonergan, is "the universe, the world mediated by meaning. It's the answer to what you know when you answer questions that regard everything about everything." See McShane, "An Interview with Fr. Bernard Lonergan S.J.," 218.

6. Ibid., 228.

7. Ibid., 229.

8. Ibid., 228.

9. Peter Huizing and William Bassett, eds., *Experience of the Spirit: To Edward Schillebeeckx on His Sixtieth Birthday*, Concilium 9, no. 10 (1976): 69–78.

10. Lonergan, "Mission and the Spirit," in *A Third Collection: Papers by Bernard J. F. Lonergan, S.J.*, ed. Frederick E. Crowe (New York: Paulist Press, 1985), 23.

11. See also Bernard J. F. Lonergan, *Insight: A Study of Human Understanding*, CWL 3, ed. Frederick E. Crowe and Robert M. Doran (Toronto: University of Toronto Press, 1992), 25. Lonergan notes that while a theologian may think of divine providence as the key to evolution, he is in accord with a scientist such as Darwin in thinking of providence in terms of probabilities, probabilities of emergence and survival requiring "very large numbers and very long intervals of time."

12. Lonergan in Pierrot Lambert, Charlotte Tansey, and Cathleen Going, eds., *Caring About Meaning: Patterns in the Life of Bernard Lonergan* (Montreal: Thomas More Institute Papers, 1982), 253.

13. Lonergan, "Mission and the Spirit," 26.

14. Ibid. Aquinas held that the gift of God's love is the cause of our knowledge of God by connaturality. *Summa Theologica*, II-II, q. 45, a. 2c.

15. Lonergan, "Mission and the Spirit," 26.

16. Ibid., 27.

17. As noted earlier, Lonergan here regards vertical finality as another name for self-transcendence: ibid., 29. As vertical finality is always a relationship to the end rather than to just stages in self-transcendence, vertical finality for us is to the ultimate end and fulfillment of the universe in God and our own beatitude.

18. Bernard J. F. Lonergan, *Method in Theology* (Toronto: University of Toronto Press, 1996), 113, 290.

19. As in *Method* (268), Lonergan sees "the exception" to the old tag *nihil amatum nisi praecognitum*. Increasingly, during this period, he comes to realize how insecure is learning outside the ambit of love. We derive many of our convictions from our being-in-love.

20. Lonergan, "Mission and the Spirit," 32–33.

21. Ibid., 31.

22. Ibid., 31–32.

23. Ibid., 33.

24. Particularly in *Insight*, the "operator," the force moving us from one level to another, is the pure desire to know expressed in questioning. In *Method*, he often refers to the whole subject in the dynamism of conscious intentionality as the operator, 7.

25. Lonergan, "Mission and the Spirit," 29.

26. The author acknowledges her debt to Margaret Bowater for insights shared in dream workshops and her work *Dreams and Visions: Language of the Spirit* (Auckland: Tandem Press, 1997). On the function of dreaming, see also Lonergan, *Insight*, 218–20, 482. He distinguishes "dreams of the night," which allow for the appropriate release of unmet neural demands, and "dreams of the morning," which orient us to the new day. In so doing, he is following the thought of Ludwig Binswanger, *Le rêve et l'existence*, introduction and notes by Michael Foucault (Tournai: Desclée, 1954).

27. Lonergan, "Mission and the Spirit," 29–30.

28. Ibid., 30.

29. Ibid.

30. Ibid.

31. Ibid., 32.

32. Ibid.

33. Ibid., 33.

34. For the development of Lonergan's thinking during the period, see Frederick E. Crowe, "An Expansion of Lonergan's Notion of Value," in *Appropriating the Lonergan Idea*, ed. Michael Vertin (Washington, DC: Catholic University of America Press, 1989), 334–59.

35. Lonergan, "Healing and Creating in History," in Crowe, *A Third Collection*, 100–109.

36. Ibid., 103. Lonergan finds this creative process expressed well by Jane Jacobs in her *The Economy of Cities* as "repeatedly finding new uses for existing resources," and by Arnold Toynbee in his *Study of History*, "where the flow of fresh insights takes its rise from a creative minority, and the success of their implementation wins the devoted allegiance of the rank and file." In the last four volumes of this ten-volume work, Toynbee, like Lonergan,

sees the world religions and a new style of human development emerging from frustration and disgust amongst the internal proletariat.

37. Lonergan, "Healing and Creating in History," 105.

38. Ibid.

39. Ibid., 106.

40. Ibid.

41. Cf. Jean Jacques Rousseau, 1712–78, writing in *Emile: Or on Education*, who rather miscalculated our ability to shape this plasticity in his educational theory. A child preserved from temptation, as he tried to ensure, has no way of developing self-control. See translation, introduction, and notes by Alan Bloom (New York: Basic Books, 1979).

42. Lonergan, "Healing and Creating in History," 106.

43. Ibid.

44. Lonergan, *Insight*, 698/720–21.

45. Lonergan, *Method*, 240.

46. Ibid., 105.

47. Lonergan, "Prolegomena to the Study of the Emerging Religious Consciousness of Our Time," in Crowe, *A Third Collection*, 58. See also *Method*, 33–34.

48. Lonergan, *Method*, 110.

49. Ibid.

50. For example, in a letter to a publisher in support of a book proposal by Robert Doran, he wrote, "Intellectual, Moral, and Religious conversion of the theologian are foundational in my book on method in theology. To these Doran has added a psychic conversion in his book on *Psychic Conversion and Theological Foundations*. He has thought the matter through very thoroughly and it fits very adroitly and snugly into my own efforts." A2280 (File 490.1/6), Archives, Lonergan Research Institute of Regis College, Toronto. Cited with permission by John D. Dadosky of Regis College in his article "Healing the Psychological Subject," *Theoforum* 35 (2004): 73–91.

51. Lonergan, *Insight*, 214–17.

52. Lonergan, *Method*, 77.

53. Lonergan, "Theology in a New Context," in Ryan and Tyrrell, *Second Collection*, 62–63. Though well read in Freud at the time of writing *Insight*, and more inclined to quote Jung at the

time of *Method*, Lonergan claimed no particular competence in therapeutic psychology.

54. Lonergan, "Natural Right and Historical Mindedness," in Crowe, *A Third Collection*, 181.

55. Donald Woods Winnicott, 1896–1971, an English psycho-analyst and pediatrician, wrote of "the ordinary, devoted mother's attentive holding of her child" as creating a holding environment, laying down foundations of health, and needing to be replicated in healing by the psychotherapist. His best-known work is *Playing and Reality* (London: Tavistock, 1971).

56. From a verbatim transcript of a question and answer session from the 1978 Lonergan Workshop, Boston College, File #885 Archives, Lonergan Research Institute of Regis College, Toronto, 9.

57. Lonergan, "Natural Right and Historical Mindedness," 179.

58. Cf. Lonergan, *Method*, 105.

59. Lonergan, "Merging Horizons: Systems, Common Sense, Scholarship," *Cultural Hermeneutics* 1 (1973); See also *Method*, 159, 208–9.

60. Robert Doran, *Subject and Psyche*, 2nd ed. (Milwaukee, WI: Marquette University Press, 1994). Originally published in 1977 by University Press of America. Of it, Lonergan wrote in "Questions on Philosophy," *Method: Journal of Lonergan Studies* 2, no. 2 (1984): 31: "Following the method…is not a matter of deduction but of creativity; such creativity may enrich the thematization of experiencing, judgment, deliberation that has already been achieved; it may also add quite new dimensions to it, as has Robert Doran S.J. in his doctoral dissertation." Doran was appointed by Lonergan, with Frederick E. Crowe, SJ, to be a trustee of the Bernard Lonergan estate, and in that role, he has coedited the collected works and made a great deal of material available to scholars through the website www.bernardlonergan.com.

61. Doran maintains that "depth psychology is neither philosophy nor theology but methodologically related to both in the context of foundational subjectivity." *Subject and Psyche*, 14.

62. Robert Doran, *Theology and the Dialectics of History* (Toronto: University of Toronto Press, 1990), 59. The constructive censor works to sort relevant from irrelevant data so that the images necessary for insight are admitted, others screened. When

it is repressive, however, it blocks images that would allow needed insights to occur. This may be occasioned by trauma, victimization, abuse, or neglect.

63. Doran, *Subject and Psyche*, 115.

64. Lonergan, "The Subject," 69–86.

65. Doran, *Subject and Psyche*, 51.

66. Lonergan, "Religious Experience," in Crowe, *A Third Collection*, 127.

67. Doran, *Subject and Psyche*, 98.

68. Ibid., 99.

69. Robert Doran, *Reception and Elemental Meaning: An Expansion of the Notion of Psychic Conversion* (paper presented at a Lonergan Workshop, Boston College, 2003, and accessed through the Lonergan Centre at Boston College in that same year), 33.

70. Ibid., 33.

71. Bernard J. Tyrrell, *Christotherapy II* (Eugene, OR: Wipf & Stock, 1999), 55.

72. Bernard Tyrrell, "Affectional Conversion: A Distinct Conversion or Potential Differentiation in the Spheres of Sensitive Psychic and/or Affective Conversion?" in *METHOD: Journal of Lonergan Studies* 14 (1996): 1–35, at 16.

73. Ibid., 18.

74. John D. Dadosky, "Healing the Psychological Subject: Towards a Fourfold Notion of Conversion?" *Theoforum* 35 (2004): 75–76.

75. Others working within a Lonerganian frame of reference to explore the concept of conversion include Walter Conn in *Christian Conversion* (Mahwah, NJ: Paulist Press, 1986); "Affective Conversion: The Transformation of Desire," in *Religion and Culture: Essays in Honor of Bernard Lonergan* (Albany: State University of New York Press, 1987); *The Desiring Self: Rooting Pastoral Counseling and Spiritual Direction in Self-Transcendence* (Mahwah, NJ: Paulist Press, 1998); and Donald Gelpi, *Experiencing God* (New York: Paulist Press, 1978), 179–81.

76. Dadosky, "Healing the Psychological Subject," 81.

77. Tom Halloran reminds us in his paper "Finality, *Insight* and Method: My Stand on Lonergan's Contribution to Philosophy and Theology," in *Fifty Years of Insight*, ed. Neil Ormerod, Robin Koning, and David Braithwaite (Hindmarsh, SA: ATF Theology,

2011), 206, that "Lonergan did not intend to found a school of 'Lonerganians'; and he would not rejoice at such founding....I recall Lonergan's *parting words* at the first Lonergan Workshop at Boston College in 1974: 'Be good non-disciples.'" Sebastian Moore attended that workshop and annually thereafter until 2003, when his health prevented it.

78. Sebastian Moore, *The Fire and the Rose Are One* (London: Darton, Longman & Todd, 1980), 3.

79. Ibid., 4.

80. Sebastian Moore, "For Bernard Lonergan," *Compass: A Jesuit Journal* (Spring 1985): 9.

81. For Moore, this endeavor formed a continuation of his lifelong quest to understand the depths of the mystery of the crucifixion and resurrection of Christ, which he wrote about also in *The Crucified Jesus Is No Stranger* (San Francisco: HarperSanFrancisco, 1983).

82. Ernest Becker, *The Denial of Death* (New York: Free Press, 1973) cited by Moore, *The Fire and the Rose Are One*, xii.

83. Moore, *The Fire and the Rose Are One*, 6.

84. Ibid., xii.

85. Ibid., 8–9.

86. In addition to Charles Hefling's comment about Dante being in love not only with but through Beatrice, he also claims that in and through this experience of loving her, "Dante has to become the thing he has seen in Beatrice, and has, for the moment, seen in himself." Charles C. Hefling Jr., *Why Doctrines?* (Boston, MA: Cowley Publications, 1984), 14. The transforming effect of love and religious experience makes the person aware of the values possible for his self-constitution.

87. Moore, *The Fire and the Rose Are One*, 9.

88. Ibid., 10. Moore privileges human sexual love, as does Rosemary Haughton, and for the same reason—because it is so easily recognizable there—but it is operative also in the way we come to be ourselves for our friends.

89. Ibid., 13. (Italics in the original.)

90. Ibid., 15.

91. Anne Henderson notes that the question of God is at the heart of our deepest longings and desires, and as we struggle to name and live their truth, we struggle to return to the heart, to

the invitation that it extends to us to celebrate the place where the human and the transcendent meet in the experience of being-in-love. Until we arrive at this place, God must remain a question that we seek to answer in our living. "Reclaiming the Question of God in a Contemporary Context: Bernard Lonergan's Transcendental Method and the Transforming Power of the Poetic Word" (MTh thesis, Melbourne College of Divinity, 2002), 115.

92. Sebastian Moore, *The Fire and the Rose Are One*, 16.

93. Ibid., 17. (Italics in the original.)

94. Ibid., 36.

95. Ibid., 16. This concept will be developed further in the following chapter. For Rosemary Haughton, too, religion as a decency is out; it means transformation or it means nothing.

96. Ibid., 23. Furthermore, Moore writes, "We only live by desire. We only desire out of a sense of being desirable. We only feel desirable absolutely because we are absolutely desired." *Let This Mind Be in You: The Quest for Identity from Oedipus to Christ* (New York: Harper and Row Publishers Inc., 1986), xi.

97. Moore, *The Fire and the Rose Are One*, 34.

98. Ibid., 34–35.

99. Ibid., xii.

100. Ibid., 58.

101. Ibid., 58.

102. Ibid.

103. Ibid., 60.

104. Ibid., 64–65.

105. Sebastian Moore, *The Inner Loneliness* (New York: Crossroad Publishing Company, 1982).

106. Sebastian Moore, *Jesus, the Liberator of Desire* (New York: Crossroad Publishing Company, 1989).

107. Moore, *The Fire and the Rose Are One*, xiii.

108. Ibid., 78.

109. Moore, *The Inner Loneliness*, 82.

110. Moore, *The Fire and the Rose Are One*, xiv.

111. Moore expands further on the maxim "Desire is love trying to happen" in his most recent book, *The Contagion of Jesus: Doing Theology as If It Mattered*, ed. Stephen McCarthy (London: Darton, Longman & Todd, 2007), 120–41.

112. Notably in three lectures given as The Donald Mathers Memorial Lectures 1976 at Queen's University in Kingston, Ontario: "Religious Experience," "Religious Knowledge," and "The Ongoing Genesis of Methods," all now available in Crowe, *A Third Collection*, 113–65.

113. Lonergan, "Religious Experience," 125.

114. Ibid., 127.

115. Cf. *Method*, 40, which states, "Drifting on to an ever less authentic self-hood." See also "A Post-Hegelian Philosophy of Religion," in Crowe, *A Third Collection*, 208.

116. Lonergan, "Religious Experience," 123.

117. Ibid., 133.

118. Ibid., 121.

119. For a recent fine study of this reality, see Alan Wade, "The Theologian as Authentic Subject: Lonergan and the Centrality of Method" (PhD diss., MCD University of Divinity, 2012), esp. 253–58.

120. Lonergan, "Religious Knowledge," 133.

121. Ibid., 133–34.

122. Ibid., 122.

123. Lawrence, "The Fragility of Consciousness," 65.

124. Lonergan, "Natural Right and Historical Mindedness," in Crowe, *A Third Collection*, 182.

125. Lonergan, "Theology and Praxis," in Crowe, *A Third Collection*, 195.

126. In a paper titled "Unity and Plurality: The Coherence of Christian Truth," subsequently published in Crowe, *A Third Collection*, 239–49.

127. Ibid., 247.

128. Ibid., 248.

129. Bernard Lonergan, "Theology and Praxis," in Crowe, *A Third Collection*, 197.

6. THE *EROS* OF THE SPIRIT AS OUR DESIRE

1. Bernard J. F. Lonergan, *Verbum: Word and Idea in Aquinas*, CWL 2, ed. Frederick E. Crowe and Robert M. Doran (Toronto: University of Toronto Press, 1997), 90.

2. Bernard J. F. Lonergan, *Method in Theology* (Toronto: University of Toronto Press, 1996), 20. (Author's italics.) People do *not* have to be able to name the operations of their consciousness in order to live authentically as attentive, intelligent, reasonable, and responsible human beings, particularly if they are in love. It just helps sometimes!

3. Whereas the younger Lonergan was completely in accord with Aquinas as to the primacy of intellect, by this stage he is expressing a more Augustinian awareness of love as uniquely constitutive of God's likeness in us and the chief work of grace.

4. Lonergan, *Method*, 122.

5. James L. Connor, *The Dynamism of Desire: Bernard J.F. Lonergan S.J. on The Spiritual Exercises of Saint Ignatius of Loyola* (Saint Louis: The Institute of Jesuit Sources 2006), vii.

6. Ravi Michael Louis, "Appropriating Human Desiring: The Fate of Historical Transcendence" (master's thesis, Regis College, Toronto, 2006).

AFTERWORD

1. T.S. Eliot, "Little Gidding," *Four Quartets*, 1942 (London: Faber and Faber, 1959), 59.

2. Walter Farrell, "My Way of Life" was the short version, corresponding to *The Companion to the Summa*, IIIA and Supplement.

3. Constitutions of the Society of the Sacred Heart, no. 17.

BIBLIOGRAPHY

WORKS OF LONERGAN

Verbum: Word and Idea in Aquinas. Vol. 2 of Collected Works of Bernard Lonergan, edited by Frederick E. Crowe and Robert M. Doran. Toronto: University of Toronto Press, 1997. First published 1967.

Insight: A Study of Human Understanding. 2nd ed. London: Longmans, 1978. First published 1958.

Collection: Papers by Bernard Lonergan. Edited by F. E. Crowe. New York: Herder and Herder, 1967. Republished as Vol. 4 of Collected Works of Bernard Lonergan, edited by F. E. Crowe and R. M. Doran. Toronto: University of Toronto Press, 1993.

———. "Finality, Love, Marriage." First published, *Theological Studies* 4 (1943).

———. "The Natural Desire to See God." 1949.

———. "Openness and Religious Experience." First published, *Il Problema dell'esperienza religiosa*. Atti del XV Convegno del Centro di Studi Filosofici tra Professori Universitari. Gallarate, 1960.

———. "Cognitional Structure." First published in *Continuum* 2 (1964).

———. "*Existenz* and *Aggiornamento*." 1964.

———. "Dimensions of Meaning." 1965.

"Religious Commitment." In *The Pilgrim People: A Vision of Hope*, edited by Joseph Papin. Villanova, PA: Villanova University Press, 1970.

Philosophical and Theological Papers 1958–1964. Vol. 6 of Collected Works of Bernard Lonergan, edited by Robert C. Croken, SJ, et al. Toronto: University of Toronto Press, 1971.

A Second Collection: Papers by Bernard J.F. Lonergan, S.J. Edited by W. F. J. Ryan and Bernard J. Tyrrell. Philadelphia: The Westminster Press, 1974. Republished Toronto: University of Toronto Press, 1987.

———. "The Transition from a Classicist World-View to Historical-Mindedness." 1966.

———. "Theories of Inquiry." 1967.

———. "Natural Knowledge of God." 1968.

———. "The Subject." 1968.

———. "Theology in its New Context." 1968.

———. "The Future of Christianity." 1969.

———. "The Response of the Jesuit as Priest and Apostle in the Modern World." 1970.

———. "An Interview with Fr. Bernard Lonergan, S.J." 1971.

———. "Insight Revisited." 1972.

Grace and Freedom: Operative Grace in the Thought of St Thomas Aquinas. New York: Herder and Herder, 1971. Republished as Vol. 1 of Collected Works of Bernard Lonergan, edited by F. E. Crowe and R. M. Doran. Toronto: University of Toronto Press, 2000.

Method in Theology. London: Darton, Longman & Todd, 1972. Reprinted in paperback, Toronto: University of Toronto Press, 1996/2003.

Philosophy of God and Theology: The Relationship between Philosophy of God and the Functional Specialty, Systematics. London: Darton, Longman & Todd, 1973.

"Religious Experience." In *Trinification of the World: A Festschrift in Honour of Frederick Crowe*, edited by Thomas A. Dunne and Jean-Marc Laporte. Toronto: Regis College Press, 1978.

A Third Collection. Edited by Frederick E. Crowe. New York: Paulist Press, 1985.

———. "Healing and Creating in History." 1975.

———. "Prolegomena to the Study of the Emerging Religious Consciousness of our Time." 1975.

———. "Mission and Spirit." 1976.

———. "The Ongoing Genesis of Methods." 1976.

————. "Religious Knowledge." 1976.

————. "Natural Right and Historical Mindedness." 1977.

————. "Theology and Praxis." 1977.

————. "A Post-Hegelian Philosophy of Religion." 1981.

————. "Unity and Plurality: The Coherence of Christian Truth." 1982.

Understanding and Being: The Halifax Lectures on Insight. Vol. 6 of Collected Works of Bernard Lonergan, edited by E. and M. Morelli. Toronto: University of Toronto Press, 1990.

Topics in Education. Vol. 10 of Collected Works of Bernard Lonergan, edited by Robert Doran and Frederick E. Crowe. Toronto: University of Toronto Press, 1993.

SECONDARY SOURCES

Beshear, Beth. "The Problem of Desire in Human Knowing and Living." *Method: Journal of Lonergan Studies* 20, no. 2. (2002).

Byrne, Patrick H. "The Thomist Sources of Lonergan's Dynamic World View." *The Thomist* 46 (1982): 108–45.

————. "Analogical Knowledge of God and the Value of Moral Endeavour." *Method: Journal of Lonergan Studies*, 11, no. 2 (1993).

————. "Consciousness: Levels, Sublations, and the Subject as Subject." *Method: Journal of Lonergan Studies* 13 (1995): 131–50.

————. "…and God's Own Glory, in Part, Is You: What Aspect of the Lonergan Legacy Needs to Be Stressed Right Now?" *Lonergan Workshop* 21 (2009).

————. "Which Scale of Value Preference? Lonergan, Scheler, von Hildebrand and Doran." In *Meaning and History in Systematic Theology: Essays in Honour of Robert M. Doran, S.J,* edited by John Dadosky, 19–49. Milwaulkee, WI: Marquette University Press, 2009.

Carmody, Denise Lardner. "The Desire for Transcendence: Religious Conversion." In *The Desires of the Human Heart: An Introduction to the Theology of Bernard Lonergan,* edited by Vernon Gregson. New York: Paulist Press, 1988.

————. "Lonergan's Transcendental Precepts and the Foundations of Christian Feminist Ethics." In *Lonergan and Feminism,* edited by Cynthia S. W. Crysdale, 134–45. Toronto: University of Toronto Press, 1994.

Conn, Walter E. *Conscience: Development and Self-Transcendence*. Birmingham, AL: Religious Education Press, 1981.

———. "Passionate Commitment: The Dynamics of Affective Conversion." *Cross Currents* 34 (1984): 329–36.

———. *Christian Conversion*. Mahwah, NJ: Paulist Press, 1986.

———. "Affective Conversion: The Transformation of Desire." In *Religion and Culture: Essays in Honor of Bernard Lonergan, S.J.*, edited by Timothy P. Fallon and Philip Boo Riley, 261–76. Albany: State University of New York Press, 1987.

———. *The Desiring Self: Rooting Pastoral Counseling and Spiritual Direction in Self-Transcendence*. New York: Paulist Press, 1998.

Connor, James L., and Fellows of the Woodstock Theological Center. *The Dynamism of Desire: Bernard J. F. Lonergan S.J. on The Spiritual Exercises of Saint Ignatius of Loyola*. Saint Louis: The Institute of Jesuit Sources, 2006.

Crowe, Frederick E. "Complacency and Concern in the Thought of St. Thomas." *Theological Studies* 20 (1959): 1–39; 198–230; 343–95.

———. "Early Jottings on Bernard Lonergan's Method in Theology." *Science et Esprit* 25 (1973): 128–38.

———. "An Exploration of Lonergan's New Notion of Value." *Science et Esprit* 29 (1977): 123–43.

———. *The Lonergan Enterprise*. Cambridge, MA: Cowley Publications, 1980.

———. "Obituary for Fr. Bernard Lonergan, S.J." *Newsletter of the Upper Canada Jesuit Province* 60 (May–June 1985).

———. "An Expansion of Lonergan's Notion of Value." *Lonergan Workshop* 7 (1988).

———. "Rethinking Moral Judgments: Categories from Lonergan." *Science et Esprit* 40 (1988): 137–52.

———. "Rethinking the Religious State: Categories from Lonergan." *Science et Esprit* 40 (1988): 75–90.

———. "Rethinking God-with-Us: Categories from Lonergan." *Science et Esprit* 41 (1989): 167–88.

———. *Lonergan*. Collegeville, MN: The Liturgical Press, 1992.

Crysdale, Cynthia. *Lonergan and Feminism*. Toronto: University of Toronto Press, 1994.

Dadosky, John D. "Healing the Psychological Subject: Towards a Fourfold Notion of Conversion." *Theoforum* 35 (2004): 73–91.

Doorley, Mark J. *The Place of the Heart in Lonergan's Ethics: The Role of Feelings in the Ethical Intentionality Analysis of Bernard Lonergan*. London: University of London Press, 1996.

Doran, Robert M. *Theology and the Dialectics of History*. Toronto: University of Toronto Press, 1990.

———. "Consciousness and Grace." *Method: Journal of Lonergan Studies* 11 (1993): 51–76.

———. *Subject and Psyche*. 2nd ed. Milwaukee: Marquette University Press, 1994.

———. "Revisiting 'Consciousness and Grace.'" *Method: Journal of Lonergan Studies* 13 (1995): 151–60.

———. "Reception and Elemental Meaning: An Expansion of the Notion of Psychic Conversion." Paper presented at the Lonergan Workshop, Boston College, Boston, MA, June 16–20, 2003.

Dunne, Tad. *Lonergan and Spirituality. Toward a Spiritual Integration*. Chicago: Loyola University Press, 1985.

———. "Experience." In *The New Dictionary of Catholic Spirituality*, edited by Michael Downey, 366–69. Collegeville, MN: The Liturgical Press, 1993.

———. "Authentic Feminist Doctrine." In *Lonergan and Feminism*, edited by Cynthia S. W. Crysdale, 114–33. Toronto: University of Toronto Press, 1994.

———. "Being in Love." *Method: Journal of Lonergan Studies* 13 (1995): 161–76.

Dunne, Thomas A. and Jean Laporte, eds. *Trinification of the World: A Festschrift in Honour of Frederick E. Crowe*. Ontario: Regis College Press, 1978.

Fallon, Timothy P. and Philip Boo Riley, eds. *Religion in Context: Recent Studies in Lonergan*. Lanham, MD: University Press of America, 1988.

Flanagan, Joseph. *Quest for Self-Knowledge: An Essay in Lonergan's Philosophy*. Toronto: University of Toronto Press, 1997.

Gelpi, Donald. *Experiencing God*. New York: Paulist Press, 1978.

Gregson, Vernon. *Lonergan, Spirituality, and the Meeting of Religions*. Lanham, MD: University Press of America, 1985.

———., ed. *The Desires of the Human Heart*. New Jersey: Paulist Press, 1988.

Halloran, Tom. "Finality, *Insight* and Method: My Stand on Lonergan's Contribution to Philosophy and Theology." In *Fifty Years of Insight*, edited by Neil Ormerod, Robin Koning, and David Braithwaite. Hindmarsh, SA: ATF Theology, 2011.

Hefling, Charles C., Jr. *Why Doctrines?* Boston: Cowley Publications, 1984.

———. "Grace, Christ, Redemption, Lonergan (in That Order)." *Lonergan Workshop* 14 (1998): 99–113.

Henderson, Anne. *Reclaiming the Question of God in a Contemporary Context: Bernard Lonergan's Transcendental Method and the Transforming Power of the Poetic Word*. Master's thesis. Melbourne: Melbourne College of Divinity, 2002.

Hosinski, Thomas. "Lonergan and a Process Understanding of God." In *Religion and Culture: Essays in Honor of Bernard Lonergan, S.J.*, edited by Timothy P. Fallon and Philip Boo Riley, 63–78. Albany: State University of New York Press, 1987.

Kelly, Anthony. *The Trinity of Love. A Theology of the Christian God*. Wilmington, DE: Michael Glazier, 1989.

Lamb, Matthew L. *Creativity and Method: Essays in Honor of Bernard Lonergan, S.J.* Milwaukee: Marquette University Press, 1981.

Lambert, Pierrot, Charlotte Tansey, and Cathleen Going, eds. *Caring About Meaning: Patterns in the Life of Bernard Lonergan*. Montreal: Thomas More Institute Papers, 1982.

———. *Curiosity at the Centre of One's Life*. Montreal: Thomas More Institute Papers, 1987.

Lawrence, Frederick G., ed. *Lonergan Workshop*. Vol. 2. Atlanta: Scholars Press, 1981.

———. "'*Cor ad Cor Loquitur*': Bernard Lonergan S.J." *Compass: A Jesuit Journal (Special Issue Honouring Bernard Lonergan, S.J. 1904–1984)* (Spring 1985).

———. "Lonergan as Political Theologian." In *Religion in Context: Recent Studies in Lonergan*, edited by Timothy P. Fallon and

Philip Boo Riley, 1–21. Lanham, MD: University Press of America, 1988.

———. "The Fragility of Consciousness: Lonergan and the Postmodern Concern for the Other." In *Communication and Lonergan: Common Ground for Forging the New Age*, edited by Thomas J. Farrell and Paul A. Soukup. Kansas City, MO: Sheed & Ward, 1993.

———. "The Human Good and Christian Conversation." In *Communication and Lonergan: Common Ground for Forging the New Age*, ed. Thomas J. Farrell and Paul A. Soukup. Kansas City MO: Sheed & Ward, 1993.

———. *On Being Catholic*. Unpublished talk, Boston College, 1994.

———. "Lonergan, the Integral Postmodern?" *Method: Journal of Lonergan Studies* 18 (2000): 95–122.

———. "Grace and Friendship: Postmodern Political Theology and God as Conversational." *Gregorianum* 85, no. 4 (2004): 795–820.

———. "The Ethics of Authenticity and the Human Good, in Honour of Michael Vertin, an Authentic Colleague." In *The Importance of Insight: Essays in Honour of Michael Vertin*, edited by Michael Vertin, John J. Liptay, and David S. Liptay, 127–50. Toronto: University of Toronto Press, 2007.

Liddy, Richard M. *Transforming Light: Intellectual Conversion in the Early Lonergan*. Collegeville, MN: The Liturgical Press, 1993.

Louis, Ravi Michael. "Appropriating Human Desiring." Master's thesis, Regis College, Toronto, 2006.

Lyonnet, Stanislas. "St. Paul: Liberty and Law." *The Bridge: A Yearbook of Judaeo-Christian Studies* 4 (1992): 229–51.

Matthews, William A. *Lonergan's Quest: A Study of Desire in the Authoring of Insight*. Toronto: University of Toronto Press, 2005.

McShane, Philip, ed. *Foundations of Theology: Papers from the International Lonergan Congress, 1970*. Dublin: Gill and MacMillan, 1971.

———. *Language, Truth and Meaning*. Notre Dame, IN: University of Notre Dame Press, 1972.

————. *Music That Is Soundless: An Introduction to God for the Graduate*. Washington, DC: University of America Press, 1977.

Miller, Jerome A. *In the Throe of Wonder: Intimations of the Sacred in a Post-Modern World*. Albany: State University of New York Press, 1992.

Mooney, Hilary A. *The Liberation of Consciousness*. Frankfurt am Main: Verlag Josef Knecht, 1992.

Moore, Sebastian, OSB. *The Fire and the Rose Are One*. London: Darton, Longman & Todd, 1980.

————. *The Inner Loneliness*. New York: Crossroad Publishing Company, 1982.

————. *The Crucified Christ Is No Stranger*. HarperSanFrancisco, 1983.

————. "For Bernard Lonergan." *Compass: A Jesuit Journal* (Spring 1985).

————. *Let This Mind Be in You: The Quest for Identity from Oedipus to Christ*. New York: Harper and Row, Publishers, Inc., 1986.

————. *Jesus, the Liberator of Desire*. New York: Crossroad Publishing Company, 1989.

————. *The Contagion of Jesus: Doing Theology as If It Mattered*. Edited by Stephen McCarthy. London: Darton, Longman & Todd, 2007.

Mueller, Philip J. "Lonergan's Theory of Religious Experience." *Église et Théologie* 7 (1976): 235–51.

Price, James. "Typologies and the Cross-Cultural Analysis of Mysticism: A Critique." In *Religion and Culture: Essays in Honor of Bernard Lonergan, S.J.*, edited by Timothy P. Fallon and Philip Boo Riley, 181–90. Albany: State University of New York Press, 1987.

Progoff, Ira. *At a Journal Workshop: The Basic Text and Guide for Using the Intensive Journal Process*. New York: Dialogue House, 1975.

Quesnell, Quentin. "Grace." In *The New Dictionary of Theology*, edited by Joseph A. Komonchak et al., 442–51. Dublin: Gill and Macmillan, 1987.

————. "On Not Neglecting the Self in the Structure of Theological Revolutions." In *Religion and Culture: Essays in*

Honor of Bernard Lonergan, S.J., edited by Timothy P. Fallon and Philip Boo Riley, 125–33. Albany: State University of New York Press, 1987.

Rende, Michael L. *Lonergan on Conversion: The Development of a Notion*. Lanham, MD: University Press of America, 1991.

Roy, Louis, OP. *Le Sentiment de Transcendance, Expérience de Dieu?* Paris: Les Éditions du Cerf, 2000.

———. *Transcendent Experiences: Phenomenology and Critique*. Toronto: University of Toronto Press, 2001.

Shute, Michael. *Lonergan's Discovery of the Science of Economics*. Toronto: University of Toronto Press, 2010.

Smith, Marc. "Religious Experience and Bernard Lonergan." *Philosophy Today* 23 (1979): 359–66.

Stebbins, J.M. *The Divine Initiative: Grace, World-Order, and Human Freedom in the Early Writings of Bernard Lonergan*. Toronto: University of Toronto Press, 1995.

Tekippe, Terry J. *Bernard Lonergan's Insight: A Comprehensive Commentary*. Lanham, MD: University of Maryland Press, 2003.

Tekippe, Terry J., and Louis Roy, OP. "Lonergan and the Fourth Level of Intentionality." *American Catholic Philosophical Quarterly* 70 (1996): 225–42.

Vertin, Michael, ed. *Appropriating the Lonergan Idea*. Washington, DC: Catholic University of America Press, 1989.

Wade, Alan. "The Theologian as Authentic Subject: Lonergan and the Centrality of Method." PhD dissertation, MCD University of Divinity, Melbourne, 2012.

Williams, Kathleen M. "Lonergan and the Transforming Immanence of the Transcendent: Towards a Theology of Grace as the Dynamic State of Being-In-Love with God." PhD dissertation, Melbourne College of Divinity, 1998.

RELATED WORKS

Allport, Gordon. *The Individual and His Religion: A Psychological Interpretation*. New York: Macmillan, 1950.

Balthasar, Hans Urs Von. *The Glory of the Lord: A Theological Aesthetics*. Vol 1 of *Seeing the Form*. Translated by Erasmo

Leiva-Merikakis. Edited by Joseph Fessio and John Riches. London: T&T Clark Limited, 1982.

Batson, C. Daniel and W. Larry Ventis, eds. *The Religious Experience: A Social-Psychological Perspective*. New York: Oxford University Press, 1982.

Benz, Ernst. "On Understanding Non-Christian Religions." In *The History of Religions: Essays in Methodology*, edited by M. Eliade and J. Kitagawa, 115–31. Chicago: Chicago University Press, 1959.

Bowater, Margaret. *Dreams and Visions: Language of the Spirit*. Auckland: Tandem Press, 1997.

Bracken, Joseph A. "God's Will or God's Desires for Us: A Change in Worldview?" *Theological Studies* 71 (2010).

Bullitt-Jones, Margaret. *Holy Hunger: A Memoir of Desire*. New York: Alfred A. Knopf, 1999.

Carr, Anne E. *Transforming Grace: Christian Tradition and Women's Experience*. San Francisco: Harper and Row, 1988.
———. "Spirituality." In *Women's Spirituality*, edited by Joann Wolski Conn. Eugene, OR: Wipf & Stock, 2005.

De Lubac, Henri. *Surnaturel: Études Historiques*. Paris: Aubier, 1946.

Devine, George. *New Dimensions in Religious Experience*. Staten Island, NY: Alba House, 1971.

Dinesen, Isak. *Babette's Feast and Other Anecdotes of Destiny*. New York: Vintage Books, 1988.

Duffy, S. J. *The Dynamics of Grace. Perspectives in Theological Anthropology*. Collegeville, MN: The Liturgical Press, 1993.

Edwards, Denis. *Human Experience of God*. New York: Paulist Press, 1983.

Ferreira, M. Jamie. "Newman and William James on Religious Experience: The Theory and the Concrete." *Heythrop Journal* 29 (1988): 44–57.

Frings, Manfred. *Max Scheler*. Pittsburgh: Duquesne University Press, 1965.

Grolnick, Simon. *The Work and Play of Winnicott*. New Jersey: Jason Aronson, 1990.

Haight, Roger. "Liturgy as Community Consciousness of Grace." In *The Awakening Church: 25 Years of Liturgical Renewal*, edited by Lawrence J. Madden, 26–45. Collegeville, MN: Liturgical Press, 1992.

———. "Grace." In *The New Dictionary of Catholic Spirituality*, edited by Michael Downey. Collegeville, MN: The Liturgical Press, 1993.

Hardy, Alister. *The Spiritual Nature of Man: A Study of Contemporary Religious Experience*. Oxford: Clarendon Press, 1979.

Haughey, John C. *Housing Heaven's Fire: The Challenge of Holiness*. Chicago: Loyola Press, 2002.

Haughton, R. *On Trying to Be Human*. London: Geoffrey Chapman, 1966.

———. *The Transformation of Man: A Study of Conversion and Community*. Springfield, IL: Templegate, 1967.

———. *The Passionate God*. London: Darton, Longman & Todd, 1981.

Hay, David. *Exploring Inner Space: Scientists and Religious Experience*. Middlesex: Penguin Books, 1982.

———. *Religious Experience Today: Studying the Facts*. London: Mowbray, 1990.

Hayes, Victor C., ed. *Religious Experience in World Religions*. South Australia: A.A.S.R. Publications, 1980.

Heiler, Friedrich. "The History of Religions as a Preparation for the Co-operation of Religions." In *The History of Religions: Essays in Methodology*, edited by Mircea Eliade and Joseph M. Kitagawa, 132–60. Chicago: The University of Chicago Press, 1959.

Hildebrand, Dietrich von. *Christian Ethics*. New York: David McKay, 1953.

Ignatius of Loyola. *Manresa: Or the Spiritual Exercises of St. Ignatius*. London: Burns, Oates & Washbourne, 2015. (Undated edition.)

James, William. *The Varieties of Religious Experience*. Cambridge, MA: Harvard University Press, 1985.

Johnston, William. *The Inner Eye of Love: Mysticism and Religion*. London: Collins, 1978.

———. *Arise, My Love: Mysticism for a New Era*. Maryknoll, NY: Orbis Books, 2000.

———. *The Mysticism of* The Cloud of Unknowing. New York: Fordham University Press, 2000.

Martin, James Alfred, Jr. "Religious Experience." In *The Encyclopedia of Religion*, edited by Mircea Eliade et al., 12:323–30. New York: Macmillan Publishing Co., 1987.

Maslow, Abraham. *Religions, Values and Peak Experiences*. New York: Viking Press, 1970.

Newman, John Henry. *An Essay in Aid of a Grammar of Assent*. London: Longmans, Green & Co., 1930.

O'Murchú, Diarmuid. *The Transformation of Desire: How Desire Became Corrupted—and How We Can Reclaim It*. Maryknoll, NY: Orbis Books, 2007.

Ormerod, N. *Grace & Disgrace. A Theology of Self-Esteem, Society and History*. Sydney: E. J. Dwyer, 1992.

Otto, Rudolf. *Das Heilige: Über das Irrationale in der Idee des Göttlichen und sein Verhältnis zum Rationalen*. 11th ed. Stuttgart/Gotha: Verlag Friedrich Andreas Perthes A.-G., 1923.

———. *The Idea of the Holy*. London: Oxford, 1923.

———. *Mysticism East and West: A Comparative Analysis of the Nature of Mysticism*. London: Macmillan and Co., 1932.

Poulain, A. *Des Grâces d'Oraison: Traité de Théologie Mystique*. Paris: Gabriel Beauchesne et Cie, 1909.

———. *The Graces of Interior Prayer: A Treatise on Mystical Theology*. Translated from the 6th ed. by Leonora L. Yorke Smith. London: Routledge & Kegan Paul Ltd., 1950.

Proudfoot, Wayne. *Religious Experience*. Berkeley: University of California Press, 1985.

Rahner, Karl. *Sendung und Gnade : Beiträge zur Pastoraltheologie*. Innsbruck: Tyrolia, 1959.

———. "Concerning the Relationship between Nature and Grace." *Theological Investigations* 1 (1961).

———. "Nature and Grace." *Theological Investigations* 4 (1966).

———. "Reflections on the Experience of Grace." *Theological Investigations* 3 (1967).

———. *The Trinity*. Translated by Joseph Donceel. London: Burns & Oates, 1970.

Rousseau, Jean Jacques. *Emile: Or, on Education*. Translated by Alan Bloom. New York: Basic Books, 1979.

Sheldrake, Philip. *Spirituality and History*. London: SPCK, 1991.

————. *Befriending Our Desires*. London: Darton, Longman & Todd, 1994.

————. *Spirituality and Theology: Christian Living and the Doctrine of God*. London: Darton, Longman and Todd, 1998.

Stewart, John Alexander. *Plato's Doctrine of Ideas*. Oxford: Oxford University Press, 1909.

Underhill, Evelyn. *Mysticism: A Study in the Nature and Development of Man's Spiritual Consciousness*. London: Methuen, 1911.

Winnicott, Donald Woods. *Playing and Reality*. London: Tavistock, 1971.

Yandell, Keith E. *The Epistemology of Religious Experience*. Cambridge: Cambridge University Press, 1993.

Yungblut, John R. *Discovering God Within*. Philadelphia, PA: The Westminster Press, 1979.